9/2012

P9-AFZ-849

HIV/AIDS and the security sector in Africa

HIV/AIDS and the Security Sector in Africa

Edited by Obijiofor Aginam and Martin R. Rupiya

United Nations University Press

TOKYO · NEW YORK · PARIS

© United Nations University, 2012

The views expressed in this publication are those of the authors and do not necessarily reflect the views of the United Nations University.

United Nations University Press
United Nations University, 53-70, Jingumae 5-chome,
Shibuya-ku, Tokyo 150-8925, Japan
Tel: +81-3-5467-1212   Fax: +81-3-3406-7345
E-mail: sales@unu.edu   general enquiries: press@unu.edu
http://www.unu.edu

United Nations University Office at the United Nations, New York
2 United Nations Plaza, Room DC2-2062, New York, NY 10017, USA
Tel: +1-212-963-6387   Fax: +1-212-371-9454
E-mail: unuony@unu.edu

United Nations University Press is the publishing division of the United Nations University.

Cover design by Andrew Corbett

Printed in the United States of America for the Americas and Asia
Printed in the United Kingdom for Europe, Africa and the Middle East

ISBN 978-92-808-1209-1

Library of Congress Cataloging-in-Publication Data

HIV/AIDS and the security sector in Africa / edited by Obijiofor Aginam and
  Martin R. Rupiya.
    p. cm.
  Includes bibliographical references and index.
  ISBN 978-9280812091 (pbk.)
    1. HIV infections — Africa, Sub-Saharan. 2. Security sector — Africa,
  Sub-Saharan. 3. Soldiers — Health and hygiene — Africa, Sub-Saharan.
  4. Police — Health and hygiene — Africa, Sub-Saharan. 5. Africa, Sub-Saharan —
  Armed Forces. I. Aginam, Obijiofor, 1969– II. Rupiya, Martin Revai.
  RA643.86.A357H543   2012
  362.196979200967 — dc23   2011047937

Endorsements

"The book is without doubt a major contribution to the study of HIV/AIDS and the security sector in Africa. Typically, HIV/AIDS infection rate among the military is more than twice that among the civilian population. The difference is often greater in times of conflict. This bears unique and powerful implications for development and security in Africa. The essays in the book simultaneously take stock, enrich our understanding of the problem and recommend ways of addressing the problem. This is an essential collection for all those engaged in the fight against HIV/AIDS in Africa and elsewhere in the world."

Muna Ndulo, Professor of Law, Cornell University Law School and Director, Cornell University's Institute for African Development

"The sub-Saharan African region has been the epicentre of HIV/AIDS since the mid to late 80s. Although the pandemic has begun to show signs of abating, nonetheless, it still blights the sub-Saharan region more than any other region. Understanding the impact of the pandemic on not just individuals, but also on the region's socio-economic sectors continues to be an essential information base for developing and implementing systemic remedial responses. Without doubt, *HIV/AIDS and the Security Sector in Africa*, which is edited by Obijiofor Aginam and Martin Rupiya, fills an important gap in our understanding of the impact of the epidemic in a neglected sector – the security sector. The book is a systematic study of the impact of HIV/AIDS on the military, peacekeeping forces, the police and correctional services. Its contribution lies in not only comprehensively mapping the impact of the pandemic, but also in meticulously defining the gaps as well as challenges, and advancing possible remedies at both national sub-regional and regional levels using a multidisciplinary approach. The book, which is forward looking, is a most welcome contribution. It should be essential reading for those wishing to acquaint themselves with a multidisciplinary approach to understanding the intersection between HIV/AIDS and the region's security sector. The contributors to *HIV/AIDS and the Security Sector in Africa* display an enormous range of expertise and insights across a whole range of fields, including epidemiology, public health, economics, security needs, policy, law and human rights."

Charles Ngwena, Professor, Director of LLM Programme on Reproductive and Sexual Rights, Faculty of Law, University of the Free State, South Africa

Contents

Figures

Tables

Contributors

Obijiofor Aginam is Academic Officer and Head of Section for International Cooperation and Development in the United Nations University's Institute for Sustainability and Peace, Tokyo, Japan. He is also an Adjunct Research Professor of Law at Carleton University, Ottawa, Canada.

Olajide O. Akanji teaches Political Science at the University of Ibadan, Ibadan, Nigeria.

Ayodele Akenroye is currently a Doctoral Candidate in Law, McGill University, Montreal, Canada. At the time of contributing to this book, he was a Human Rights Officer with the Manitoba Human Rights Commission in Canada.

Charles Bakahumura is a commissioned military officer in the rank of a Brigadier, and Chief of Personnel and Administration of the Uganda People's Defence Forces.

Charles M. Banda is a Police Officer (Trainer) in the rank of Chief Inspector with the Zambia Police Service, at the Zambia Police Training College, Lusaka, Zambia.

Gwinyayi Albert Dzinesa is Senior Researcher at the Institute for Security Studies (ISS), Pretoria, South Africa.

Polycarp Ngufor Forkum is Commissioner of Police in the Human Rights Training Unit, National Advanced Police School, Cameroon.

Nathi Gumede is Executive Director, Conciliation, Mediation and Arbitration Commission, Mbabane, Swaziland.

Gerald Gwinji is currently Permanent Secretary, Ministry of Health, Harare, Zimbabwe. At the time of contributing to this book, he was a serving Military Officer in the rank of Brigadier-General in the Zimbabwe Defence Forces.

Lindy Heinecken is Associate Professor in the Department of Sociology and Social Anthropology, Stellenbosch University, South Africa.

Tayou André Lucien is Director General of Prisons, Cameroon.

Getrude P. S. Mutasa is a Brigadier and Head of Social Affairs in the Zimbabwe Defence Forces.

Babafemi Odunsi is Senior Lecturer in Law, Obafemi Awolowo University, Ile-Ife, Nigeria.

Olubowale Josiah Opeyemi is in the Institute of African Studies, University of Ibadan, Ibadan, Nigeria.

Andrea Ottina has recently volunteered as a facilitator and trainer for the Pan African Centre for Peace, Monrovia, Liberia. At the time of his contribution to this book, he was a research intern in the United Nations University's Institute for Sustainability and Peace, Tokyo, Japan.

Martin R. Rupiya is currently the Executive Director, African Public Policy and Research Institute, Pretoria, South Africa. At the time of his contribution to this book, he was the manager of the Military and HIV/AIDS (MilAIDS) project and Senior Researcher in the Defence Sector Programme at the Institute for Security Studies, Pretoria, South Africa.

Lawson F. Simapuka is a physician and commissioned military officer in the rank of a Colonel in the Zambia Defence Force.

Johanna Stratton is currently Foreign Policy Officer in the Department of Foreign Affairs and Trade, Government of Australia. At the time of contributing to this book, she was Academic Programme Associate in the Peace and Governance programme, United Nations University, Tokyo, Japan.

Acknowledgements

This book – originally conceived as the "HIV/AIDS in the Military (MilAIDS)" research project under the Defence Sector Programme of the Institute for Security Studies (ISS) – was generously funded by The Rockefeller Brothers Fund. Following a conference on the theme "Trends, Impacts and Policy Development on HIV/AIDS and African Armed Forces" held in Johannesburg, South Africa, 2–5 December 2007, and the subsequent publication of the conference proceedings by the ISS, the United Nations University (UNU) and the ISS decided to further collaborate to broaden the theme of the project, invite more contributors and publish a policy-oriented peer-reviewed volume. This book is the product of this collaborative initiative. We would like to thank The Rockefeller Brothers Fund for its initial funding and all the research interns, programme associates and administrative assistants at both UNU and ISS who, at various times, worked with us to produce this volume. In particular, we would like to thank Johanna Stratton, Andrea Ottina, Greg Lowden (UNU) and Nadia Ahmadou (ISS) for their excellent research and administrative assistance. We are grateful to the United Nations University Press for their editorial support.

Obijiofor Aginam, Tokyo, Japan
Martin R. Rupiya, Pretoria, South Africa

Introduction

Obijiofor Aginam and Martin R. Rupiya

Focusing on selected African countries and sub-regional organizations, this book explores the policy dynamics of HIV/AIDS and the security sector. The volume examines the impacts of the epidemic on the security sector in specific countries, the policies that seek to address these impacts, and the challenges that HIV/AIDS poses to bodies such as peacekeeping missions and the military, together with the police and prison services. Accordingly, some of the chapters extend the scope of the analysis by addressing thematic issues such as HIV, gender and related socioeconomic and cultural challenges.

In their introductory overview, which draws the necessary linkages between the chapters in this volume, Aginam, Rupiya, Stratton and Ottina, re-visiting the age-old historical linkages between infectious diseases and (state) security, argue that the securitization of HIV/AIDS raises serious challenges for the security sector in Africa, and these challenges require effective policy responses. These policies, often national and in some instances sub-regional, must be assessed to evaluate their gaps, limits and potentials as relevant and effective interventions to address the impact of the epidemic on the military and related security sectors in Africa.

The book develops across four sections covering different thematic areas. Part I, "HIV/AIDS and the military: National and sub-regional perspectives", comprises 6 chapters that focus on sub-regional policy perspectives from the Economic Community of West African States (ECOWAS) and the Southern African Development Community, and perspectives on national HIV/AIDS policies in the security sectors of Nigeria, Uganda, South Africa and Swaziland.

In Chapter 2, Lindy Heinecken analyses the potential impact of HIV/AIDS on the South African National Defence Force' (SANDF) based on recent publications, empirical findings from other sectors in society, and anecdotal evidence gathered from meetings with SANDF military personnel. The author demonstrates how HIV/AIDS affects the recruitment process of the military, and consequently undermines deployment and operational effectiveness. As the SANDF grapples with ways to prevent the epidemic from infecting and killing its service members, it also tallies the extra costs in terms of recruitment, training and preparing operationally ready forces. Heinecken highlights the difficult policy challenges that the epidemic poses to the SANDF, including meeting the demands of expensive HIV/AIDS treatments and dealing with the human rights implications of such policies.

In Chapter 3, Charles Bakahumura highlights the challenges faced by the Ugandan military in dealing with the threat of HIV/AIDS within its ranks. Situating the problem of HIV/AIDS in Uganda within the broader context of security, he argues that the challenges posed by such non-military threats as poverty, infectious diseases and environmental degradation must be addressed. The author examines the measures that should be taken by the military to mitigate the impact of HIV/AIDS on the Ugandan military forces, including pragmatic recommendations for supporting the victims of the epidemic and policy prescriptions to prevent its further spread within the force.

Ayodele Akenroye's Chapter 4 explores the linkages between HIV/AIDS and national security, focusing on the regional policy framework of ECOWAS. The majority of the countries in the West African sub-region share similar demographic and health indicators: high mortality and fertility rates and similar levels of HIV infection rates. Because the sub-region has witnessed violent conflicts in the past two decades, especially in Sierra Leone and Liberia, the chapter attempts to outline the regional policy framework aimed at tackling the impact of HIV/AIDS on security in the sub-region. Acknowledging the gaps and deficiencies of these sub-regional policies, especially in the context of their implementation in Ghana and Nigeria, the chapter concludes by recommending comprehensive measures and policies aimed at repositioning military institutions to respond much more effectively to the HIV/AIDS crisis.

Human rights and HIV testing within national policy frameworks are the focus of Chapter 5 by Babafemi Odunsi. Providing an insightful analysis of the HIV/AIDS military policy elaborated by public officials for the Nigerian Armed Forces, the author delves into the widely debated topic of the collision between human rights standards and compulsory

HIV testing for military personnel. Accordingly, through a process mediated by the Human Rights Impact Assessment guidelines, this chapter is committed to demonstrating that national policies on HIV/AIDS in the Nigerian forces do not violate human rights, medical confidentiality or privacy standards. Odunsi argues that it remains vital to achieve effective goals that the military leadership refrains from adopting hard-line or coercive tactics in dealing with public health issues. This is important because it fosters collaboration between military and medical personnel through mutual trust and the safety of guaranteed care.

The formidable challenges posed by HIV/AIDS to the regeneration of the armed forces are the focus of Chapter 6 by Gerald Gwinji. The chapter argues that HIV/AIDS-based mortality rates have caused noticeable demographic changes in high-prevalence settings such as southern Africa. The chronic morbidity resulting from HIV/AIDS has negative effects on the available pool of economically active adults. Accordingly, the epidemic has caused an almost apocalyptic level of devastation that affects every stage of the military life-cycle, and constitutes a major impediment to the growth of armies in sub-Saharan Africa. Costs of recruitment have risen as replacement recruitment becomes more frequent. Institutional memory and skills have become endangered as the duration of active service – as well as individual longevity – is reduced. The military has had to deal with severe challenges in order to maintain its numbers at optimum levels. Developing policy responses to these challenges, Gwinji argues, has been problematic for most military institutions in southern Africa. Some policies that have been put in place are controversial because they arguably encroach on the rights of the individual. One example of such a policy is mandatory testing and the associated debate around the infringement of human rights.

Chapter 7 provides a civil society perspective on the Umbutfo Swaziland Defence Force (USDF) policy responses to HIV/AIDS. Nathi Gumede highlights the institutional framework of a collaborative civil–military approach that concentrates on the protection of human rights. Focusing on HIV/AIDS policy development and implementation towards ensuring a reduced impact of the epidemic within the USDF, the author assesses the importance of leadership, capacity-building efforts for policy implementation, and approaches of mainstreaming, collaboration, standardization and the processes of monitoring and evaluation – policies that support the four programmatic areas of prevention, treatment, care and support, and impact mitigation.

Part II, "HIV/AIDS and peacekeeping in Africa", comprises four chapters that focus thematically on the challenges posed by HIV/AIDS to peacekeeping in Africa. In Chapter 8, Gwinyayi Albert Dzinesa explores six African states – the Democratic Republic of the Congo, Liberia,

Sudan, Côte d'Ivoire, Ethiopia and Eritrea – that have recently hosted or are currently hosting UN peace operations. The author notes that incidents of sexual exploitation and abuse that facilitate HIV transmission have been alleged or reported in the majority of these operations. Sexual exploitation and abuse have been attributed to what the author calls "the hyper-masculine military culture" that is embedded in peacekeeping operations. This culture has an impact on peacekeepers' knowledge, attitudes, behaviour/beliefs and practices in relation to HIV transmission and prevention. Dzinesa examines the nexus between culture and HIV/ AIDS in African peacekeeping operations, draws a causal link between the hyper-masculine culture among peacekeeping forces and high-risk sexual behaviour, and discusses the impacts of these factors on HIV prevention and transmission. He argues that a cultural paradigm shift is needed in order to reduce sexual exploitation by peacekeepers. This paradigm shift should be a UN-led effort to empower local communities with the knowledge to handle incidents of sexual abuse and HIV, thus turning them from passive victims into assertive agents.

In Chapter 9, Olajide O. Akanji examines international policy responses through interventions in the HIV/AIDS crisis by the African Union and the United Nations. As a way forward, the author offers some policy recommendations that both organizations could harness to further strengthen their efforts in combating the epidemic. Situating the HIV/ AIDS crisis within the broader public health and development agendas, the author highlights the lack of data on the epidemic's impact and effects on peacekeeping operations and peacekeepers, and argues for the international community to increase its political will and to wage a war on HIV/AIDS in the same way that the United States has led a war on terrorism.

Lawson F. Simapuka's analysis of HIV/AIDS and the peacekeeping experience of the Zambia Defence Force is the focus of Chapter 10. Simapuka argues that, because peacekeepers from diverse cultural backgrounds and from high- and low-prevalence regions are deployed in host countries with varying HIV prevalence, this implies different interpretations of risk and poses numerous challenges to the achievement of consistent and effective HIV prevention. In most peacekeeping missions/ environments, both host communities and peacekeepers are at risk of contracting HIV. The author therefore argues that denying deployment to HIV-positive peacekeepers is discriminatory because host communities are equally able to transmit HIV infection to the peacekeepers. The solution, according to Simapuka, is for all peacekeepers to receive education and training on HIV/AIDS and sexually transmitted infections and to be sensitized to eliminate sexual exploitation and abuse. Predeployment HIV training is the responsibility of the troop-contributing country but, in an effort to establish minimum standards, the United Nations Department of Peacekeeping Operations has developed a standard generic training module on HIV/AIDS, which member states can use in preparation for deployment.

Chapter 11 focuses on the complex linkages between HIV/AIDS and the intervention by the Nigeria-led ECOWAS Monitoring Group (ECOMOG) in the Sierra Leonean civil war in the early 1990s. In this chapter, Olubowale Josiah Opeyemi argues that ECOMOG military intervention in Sierra Leone, with the mandate to restore peace, resulted in humanitarian crises, especially on the issue of HIV/AIDS. Linking the HIV/AIDS epidemic in Sierra Leone to the conflict and the multinational intervention force, the author advocates a new approach to peacekeeping, especially with regard to data-gathering. The HIV crises during the Sierra Leonean conflict could have been contained at an earlier stage if records had been kept of troop infection and if there were mechanisms to report civilian infection. As a way forward, Opeyemi argues that preparations for future peacekeeping operations in Africa should provide for a humanitarian office that, among other things, would collect information about health and humanitarian issues and share this information with the wider civil society, humanitarian organizations and aid agencies.

Part III, "HIV/AIDS: Perspectives on the police and prisons", comprises four chapters that focus on policing, prisons and HIV/AIDS in Cameroon, Zambia and the southern African region. In Chapter 12, Charles M. Banda highlights the difficult issues of stigma and discrimination in the Zambia Police Service. Banda examines the complex web of pre-existing fears, prejudices, attitudes and misconceptions embedded in the Zambian police force. He discusses the factors that account for the police force's disproportionately high HIV prevalence rates and identifies the dearth of serious statistical research on the impact of HIV on the police force as one serious impediment to the fight against the epidemic. Banda recommends robust and pragmatic leadership as the key to ensuring accelerated and sustained action on HIV/AIDS, as well as a new conceptual framework for improving analysis of the risk factors that lead to HIV infection.

In Chapter 13, Polycarp Ngufor Forkum discusses the policy response by the police to HIV/AIDS in Cameroon, primarily in the context of HIV prevention strategies for the uniformed forces. He situates his discussion within the national AIDS control framework in Cameroon. Statistics show that those in uniform are most affected by the disease, with a 16.4 per cent HIV prevalence rate among police recruits in 2003–2005. Although Cameroon is regarded as a relatively successful example in the regional effort to combat AIDS, particularly with the steady increase in the attainment of free anti-retroviral treatment since 2007, Forkum notes that data collection for monitoring and evaluation, the application of human rights principles and laws, and the management of funds and accountability still present difficult challenges.

In Chapter 14, Martin Rupiya's study of HIV/AIDS and prisons in southern Africa underscores the policy failure in combating the epidemic in the prison service sector. Among the 47 sub-Saharan states in which the pandemic has hit hardest, 5 countries from the southern region represent the highest prison population category. In these countries, serious overcrowding and the established prison culture (power relations, exploitation and other internal dynamics) are cited as serious contributory factors to the spread of HIV/AIDS in the prisons. For southern Africa, a region that is the epicentre of the pandemic, Rupiya recommends the development of a template of related policy questions around HIV/AIDS, the prison community and the larger society with a view to combining these with the mainstream HIV/AIDS research agenda to produce more comprehensive policy responses.

Exploring the policy responses to HIV/AIDS in the Cameroonian prison service in Chapter 15, Tayou André Lucien identifies the dearth of official data and research as a serious impediment to addressing the prevalence of HIV in Cameroonian prisons. Without thorough investigative studies on the prison service, Lucien argues that it will be difficult to stem the high rate of HIV infection inside the prisons by developing and implementing effective prevention strategies to control the epidemic.

Part IV, "HIV/AIDS: Gender and other emerging issues", comprises two chapters that explore gender and other related issues in relation to the impact of the epidemic on the security sector. Focusing on gender and HIV/AIDS in the Zimbabwe Defence Forces (ZDF) in Chapter 16, Getrude P. S. Mutasa deploys her field-based research to evaluate how HIV/AIDS programmes have responded to the needs of two important categories of women: female serving members of the ZDF and the spouses of male serving members of the ZDF. She reveals a number of important gender-related and gender-biased phenomena that drive the high risk of HIV transmission to spouses. She explores the debate surrounding the disclosure of HIV status to spouses in light of the apparent conflict between confidentiality and human rights issues. Mutasa's policy recommendations relate to prevention, education and the empowerment of women, including the need to adopt a gender-sensitive approach in addressing the challenges of HIV/AIDS.

Lastly, in Chapter 17, Obijiofor Aginam discusses the increasing use of rape and the wilful transmission of HIV as weapons of war in some of the African conflicts. Focusing on the historical linkages between disease and security, Aginam explains how vulnerable women who are victims of rape and the wilful transmission of HIV by combatants have been neglected in the reconstruction of post-conflict societies. The chapter argues that if, in most Disarmament, Demobilization and Reintegration (DDR) programmes, cash payments are often made to ex-combatants to demobilize and disarm, there is no reason why similar payments should not be made to rape victims infected with HIV in order to, among other things, pay for their anti-retroviral treatment.

This edited volume provides a range of policy perspectives on how the security sector in Africa has responded, or is currently responding, to the complex and multifaceted challenges of HIV/AIDS. The book is not designed to be a comprehensive academic treatise on this very difficult and complex problem but rather is a collection of concise policy insights focusing on select African countries and sub-regional organizations as they confront the challenges of HIV/AIDS in the military, the police forces and the prison services, together with the challenges posed by the epidemic to peacekeeping missions and other core functions of the security sector. This book offers a hybrid of academic and policy-oriented discourse. The chapters are written by African practitioners, including, in some cases, commissioned officers currently serving in the armed forces of some of the selected countries (Uganda, Zambia, Zimbabwe); medical officers and nurses working in the military; and African policy and academic experts who have spent many years working on the planning, evolution, analysis and day-to-day implementation of HIV/AIDS policies in the security sector. This volume does not provide any magic bullets that comprehensively address the impact of HIV and AIDS on the security sector of African countries. By highlighting the gaps, limits and potentials of existing policies on HIV/AIDS and the security sector, we hope that this book not only makes a modest contribution to understanding the ongoing policy debate on this complex problem but also opens new vistas for further research aimed at a more holistic and comprehensive policy reform.

1

Understanding the dynamics of HIV/AIDS and the security sector in Africa: An overview

Obijiofor Aginam, Martin R. Rupiya, Johanna Stratton and Andrea Ottina

Throughout history, the deadly comrades of war and disease have accounted for a major proportion of human suffering and death. The generals of previous centuries knew that disease was a bigger enemy than the army they would face across the battlefield. (Gro Harlem Brundtland,[1] former Director-General, World Health Organization)

The scale and geographic scope of the HIV/AIDS pandemic has only two parallels in recorded history: the 1918 flu pandemic and the Black Death in the fourteenth century. (Laurie Garrett[2])

HIV/AIDS will soon become the greatest health catastrophe in human history – exacting a death toll greater than two world wars in the 20th century, the influenza epidemic of 1918 or the Black Death of the 14th century.... The connection between infectious diseases and human security has been forcefully validated by recent developments – the HIV/AIDS epidemic, the accelerating spread of contagious diseases ..., epidemics that weaken already fragile states. (Commission on Human Security[3])

In recent years, the "securitization" of the Human Immunodeficiency Virus (HIV) and the Acquired Immunodeficiency Syndrome (AIDS) – the link between HIV/AIDS and security – has been hotly debated in academic and policy literature. This debate, which has been insightfully analysed by scholars of diverse epistemic communities,[4] has also emerged as an important agenda item for the "norm-setting" international organizations.[5] The recent and ongoing securitization of the HIV/AIDS debate is reminiscent of the age-old historical links between disease and security.

HIV/AIDS and the security sector in Africa, Aginam and Rupiya (eds), United Nations University Press, 2012, ISBN 978-92-808-1209-1

As Brundtland, Garrett and the Commission on Human Security observed in the quotes above, throughout recorded history disease-driven microbial forces have devastated armies and weakened the capacity of state institutions to perform core security, together with other essential public health functions. Citing as the most evident example the fourteenth-century bubonic plague that killed a third of Europeans in just one year (1348–1349), several scholars have argued in different historical periods that the destruction of a significant percentage of humanity by disease has led to the collapse of states and empires.[6]

In most of health and security literature, intellectual efforts to "securitize" HIV/AIDS have been the subject of an intense debate. This has occurred as a consequence of the fact that the links between HIV/AIDS and security, and the implications of such linkages for the security sector of nation-states, are not well established. In 2002, Bratt observed that "the health and development aspects of AIDS are well known, but less well known, though just as serious, are its security implications".[7] Similarly, Garrett observed:

> Some academics and political theorists ... dismiss both the importance and validity of discerning links between the pandemic and the security of states. ... [T]here are no "smoking guns" to point to – irrefutable data demonstrating that the presence of the virus in any given society was directly responsible for an event that imperiled the stability, capacity, or viability of the state.[8]

Nonetheless, the disagreement over whether high HIV/AIDS prevalence rates might destabilize a nation-state, according to McInnes, "reveals the difficulty in establishing the causal link between HIV/AIDS and state failure".[9] In addition, the securitization of the HIV/AIDS discourse becomes much more complex in the context of conflicts and the role of peacekeepers in the spread or control of the virus. Yet the correlation between the disease and national security is somehow never trivial. For instance, in conflict situations and civil wars, a plethora of scholars have argued that the securitization of the HIV/AIDS discourse is a useful pragmatic paradigm that captures either new emerging or re-emerging unconventional practices in conflicts. These include but are not limited to the increasing use of HIV as a weapon of war through indiscriminate or mass rape of vulnerable women and girls by combatants, and other forms of misconduct by uniformed personnel.[10] Conversely, another school of thought argues for a more nuanced view of the securitization of HIV and AIDS in order to fully understand all the "important AIDS–security feedback loops".[11] According to this school of thought, this is largely owing to the fact that the AIDS–security links are not supported by solid empirical data and evidence. Taking for granted that these two schools of thought are not easily reconcilable, it remains undeniable that they have both enriched the securitization of the HIV/AIDS debate by providing the rationale for many African countries to initiate policies aimed at addressing the impact of HIV/AIDS on their own security sectors.[12]

Furthermore, the ongoing debate about the role of peacekeepers in the spread or control of HIV, although not settled, confronts the policy dilemma, tensions and complex intersections of public health (that is, the need to control the spread of HIV/AIDS) and human rights (that is, the right of anybody not to be subject to compulsory/mandatory medical testing without her/his consent). The imperatives of the human rights versus public health policy dilemma have compelled many African countries to navigate the Scylla of promoting the basic human right to voluntary medical (including HIV) testing and the Charybdis of public health imperatives that might "rightly or wrongly" compel "mandatory" HIV testing of soldiers without their consent at the time either of recruitment or of deployment abroad for peacekeeping and other missions. Because this policy dilemma often plays out in the dispatch of soldiers by African countries to peacekeeping missions outside their countries mandated by the United Nations (UN), the policy of mandatory/compulsory testing is compelled to comply with the relevant provisions of international human rights treaties as well as the policy recommendations of the United Nations Department of Peacekeeping Operations (DPKO) and the Joint United Nations Programme on HIV/AIDS (UNAIDS), which support voluntary counselling and testing (VCT) for HIV/AIDS.[13]

These policy dilemmas have no easy solution. Consequently, most African countries have now adopted policies either nationally or within sub-regional organizations to fulfil their commitment to tackling the crisis of HIV/AIDS in the security sector. An acknowledgement has to be made here. Detailed analysis of the successes or failures of such national or sub-regional policies is beyond the scope of this book. However, their implications for and impacts on the overall health and security discourse of African countries will certainly play a vital role in the course of the analysis.

Given that the policy dynamics of HIV/AIDS and the security sector – the military, prisons, the police – are inexorably linked to the mortality and morbidity burdens of the epidemic on the general population, the securitization of AIDS in Africa cannot be discussed in isolation. Approximately three decades after the "discovery" of HIV, sub-Saharan Africa regrettably remains the most heavily affected region in the world. The 2010 *UNAIDS Report on the Global AIDS Epidemic* "estimates that there were 33.3 million [31.4 million–35.3 million] people living with HIV at the end of 2009 compared with 26.2 million [24.6 million–27.8 million] in 1999 – a 27% increase".[14] Moreover, UNAIDS states that "[s]ub-

Saharan Africa still bears an inordinate share of the global HIV burden. Although the rate of new HIV infections has decreased, the total number of people living with HIV continues to rise. In 2009, that number reached 22.5 million [20.9 million–24.2 million], 68% of the global total."[15]

One noticeable phenomenon of the prevalence of HIV/AIDS in Africa, as UNAIDS notes, is that "the epidemics ... vary considerably, with southern Africa still the most severely affected".[16] Globally, UNAIDS estimates that "34% of people living with HIV in 2009 resided in the 10 countries in southern Africa; 31% of new HIV infections in the same year occurred in these 10 countries, as did 34% of all AIDS-related deaths. About 40% of all adult women with HIV live in southern Africa".[17] In southern Africa, although South Africa's epidemic remains the largest in the world, with an estimated 5.6 million people living with HIV in 2009, Swaziland has the highest adult HIV prevalence in the world (an estimated 25.5 per cent in 2009).[18]

In most of East Africa, UNAIDS states that the epidemics have either declined or stabilized in Tanzania, Kenya, Uganda and Rwanda since 2000. In West and Central Africa, "[t]he HIV prevalence remains comparatively low, with the adult HIV prevalence estimated at 2% or under in 12 countries in 2009 (Benin, Burkina Faso, the Democratic Republic of the Congo, Gambia, Ghana, Guinea, Liberia, Mali, Mauritania, Niger, Senegal, and Sierra Leone). The prevalence of HIV is highest in Cameroon at 5.3% [4.9%–5.8%], Central African Republic 4.7% [4.2%–5.2%], Côte d'Ivoire 3.4% [3.1%–3.9%], Gabon 5.2% [4.2%–6.2%], and Nigeria 3.6% [3.3%–4.0%]".[19]

Across the continent, "[t]he largest epidemics in sub-Saharan Africa – Ethiopia, Nigeria, South Africa, Zambia, and Zimbabwe – have either stabilized or are showing signs of decline".[20] In terms of new infections, UNAIDS reports that the number of people newly infected with HIV peaked in the mid-1990s, and "there is evidence of declines in incidence in several countries in sub-Saharan Africa. Between 2001 and 2009, the incidence of HIV infection declined by more than 25% in an estimated 22 countries".[21]

Despite the reported decline in the incidence of HIV in several African countries, these countries still face enormous challenges because of the existing HIV and AIDS prevalence rates. Because these prevalence rates potentially have an impact on security and other important sectors of African economies, there is a critical need to develop and implement sustainable policies to address the crisis of the epidemic in relation to the security sector. Most African countries strive to develop and implement such policies to reflect their particular social, economic, political and cultural conditions, either nationally or regionally as members of subregional organizations such as the Economic Community of West African

States and the Southern African Development Community. It is therefore imperative to understand the gaps, limits and potentials of such policies and regulations.

Notes

1. Gro Harlem Brundtland, "Bioterrorism and Military Health Risks" speech delivered at the G20 Health Ministers Forum, World Economic Forum, Davos, Switzerland, 25 January 2003, <http://www.who.int/dg/brundtland/speeches/2003/DAVOS/en/index.html> (accessed 14 November 2011).
2. Laurie Garrett, *HIV and National Security: Where Are the Links?* (New York: Council on Foreign Relations, 2005), p. 9.
3. Commission on Human Security, *Human Security Now: Final Report* (New York: Commission on Human Security, 2003), p. 96.
4. Garrett, *HIV and National Security*; Colin McInnes and Simon Rushton, "HIV, AIDS and Security: Where Are We Now?", *International Affairs*, 86(1), 2010, pp. 22–245; Stefan Elbe, "Should HIV/AIDS Be Securitized? The Ethical Dilemmas of Linking HIV/AIDS and Security", *International Security Quarterly*, 50, 2006, pp. 119–144; Stefan Elbe, "HIV/AIDS and Security", in Alan Collins, ed., *Contemporary Security Studies* (Oxford: Oxford University Press, 2006), pp. 331–345; Alan Whiteside, Alex de Waal and Tsadkan Gebre-Tensae, "AIDS, Security and the Military in Africa: A Sober Appraisal", *African Affairs*, 105, 2006, pp. 201–218; UNAIDS, *AIDS and the Military: UNAIDS Point of View* (Geneva: UNAIDS, 1998); Lindy Heinecken, "Living in Terror: The Looming Security Threat to Southern Africa", *African Security Review*, 10, 2001, pp. 7–17; Andrew Price-Smith, *Pretoria's Shadow: The HIV/AIDS Pandemic and National Security in South Africa* (Washington, DC: Chemical and Biological Arms Control Institute, 2002).
5. See, for instance, UN Security Council Resolution 1308 (2000) on the Responsibility of the Security Council in the Maintenance of International Peace and Security: HIV/AIDS and International Peace-keeping Operations, Adopted on 17 July 2000; "Global Crisis – Global Action", UN General Assembly Declaration of Commitment on HIV/AIDS, Resolution S-26/2 of 27 June 2001.
6. Andrew T. Price-Smith, *The Health of Nations* (Cambridge, MA: MIT Press, 2002); Andrew T. Price-Smith, *Contagion and Chaos: Disease, Ecology, and National Security in the Era of Globalization* (Cambridge, MA: MIT Press, 2009); William H. McNeil, *Plagues and Peoples* (New York: Doubleday, 1976); Hans Zinsser, *Rats, Lice and History* (London: George Routledge, 1937); Mark W. Zacher, "International Cooperation to Monitor Infectious Diseases", in Inge Kaul, Isabelle Grunberg and Marc A. Stern, eds, *Global Public Goods: International Cooperation in the 21st Century* (New York: Oxford University Press, 1999), pp. 266–304; Mark W. Zacher and Tania J. Keefe, *The Politics of Global Health Governance: United by Contagion* (New York: Palgrave Macmillan, 2008); Garrett, *HIV and National Security*.
7. Duane Bratt, "Blue Condoms: The Use of International Peacekeepers in the Fight Against AIDS", *International Peacekeeping*, 9(3), 2002, pp. 67–86, at p. 70.
8. Garrett, *HIV and National Security*, p. 13.
9. Colin McInnes, "HIV/AIDS and Security", *International Affairs*, 82(2), 2006, pp. 315–326.
10. Elbe, "HIV/AIDS and Security"; Stefan Elbe, "HIV/AIDS and the Changing Landscape of War in Africa", *International Security Review*, 27, 2002, pp. 159–177; Anne-Marie de

Brouwer and Sandra Ka Hon Chu, *The Men Who Killed Me: Rwandan Survivors of Sexual Violence* (Vancouver: Douglas & McIntyre, 2009).

11. Whiteside et al., "AIDS, Security and the Military in Africa".

12. See, for example, the Nigerian policy on HIV/AIDS and the Armed Forces, *Armed Forces HIV/AIDS Control Policy Guidelines*, Issued under the Authority of the Honorable Minister of Defence, October 2003.

13. See, generally, UNAIDS, *AIDS and the Military* (Geneva: UNAIDS, 1998). See also UNAIDS, "Fact Sheet: HIV/AIDS and Peacekeeping", ⟨http://data.unaids.org/Topics/Security/fs_peacekeeping_en.pdf⟩ (accessed 31 August 2011).

14. UNAIDS, *Global Report: UNAIDS Report on the Global AIDS Epidemic 2010* (Geneva: UNAIDS, 2010), p. 23.

15. Ibid., p. 25.

16. Ibid., p. 28.

17. Ibid., p. 28.

18. Ibid., p. 28.

19. Ibid., p. 28.

20. Ibid., p. 25.

21. Ibid., p. 28.

Part I

HIV/AIDS and the military: National and sub-regional perspectives

2

HIV/AIDS and the South African National Defence Force: Anecdotal evidence from outside and within

Lindy Heinecken

Introduction

At the 2007 International Department of Defence HIV/AIDS Conference in Pretoria, the then South African Deputy President, Phumzile Mlambo-Ngcuka, expressed the concern that "HIV/AIDS in the armed forces could pose a significant security threat".[1] What she was implying is that every soldier infected with HIV/AIDS erodes the capacity of the military to execute their core security mandate, in much the same way as HIV incapacitates its human host. The impact of HIV/AIDS on the armed forces can be linked to the effect this virus has on the human immune system. As Eberson observed:

> The immune system is like the body's army. It is full of little soldiers that are always looking out for bad guys and then killing them as soon as they are spotted. When someone gets HIV, what happens inside his or her body is that the virus is slowly sneaking up on all the little soldiers in the immune system army and killing them one by one. In this way, the immune system army is getting weaker and weaker all the time. Inside the body the immune system army gets weaker because it has fewer and fewer soldiers to fight the sickness. More and more sicknesses are getting into the body and causing bigger and bigger problems. What HIV does is make the immune system army so weak that just about any other sickness can kill them.[2]

According to the "rules of war" vocabulary, the South African National Defence Force (SANDF) is an "already occupied territory", with

HIV/AIDS and the security sector in Africa, Aginam and Rupiya (eds),
United Nations University Press, 2012, ISBN 978-92-808-1209-1

estimates of 23–25 per cent of soldiers and civilian personnel "injured" by HIV. Several other personnel have already been killed.[3] Shell observed that, "if the epidemic were a war, South African generals would be seated in the tents of ignominy, signing articles of capitulation in every single theatre of the conflict".[4] But, as he says, if only "it was a war", then one could at least attempt to destroy the enemy, surrender or come to some peace agreement. Unfortunately, this enemy is invisible and secretly continues to undermine and erode the operational capabilities of the institutions it affects. Thus, knowledge of how this disease is affecting armed forces is as critical as intelligence is to warfare. As the SANDF grapples with ways to prevent this disease from infecting and killing its soldiers, so it tallies the extra costs in terms of recruitment, training and preparing operationally ready forces and meeting the demands of expensive AIDS treatments, while at the same time ensuring that its policies do not violate the human rights of its members.

This chapter examines the potential impact of HIV/AIDS on the SANDF at various levels. The analysis is based on evidence contained in recent publications, empirical findings from other sectors within South African society, information obtained from personnel statistics, and conversations with SANDF military personnel. This chapter aims to provide some factual base from which to uncover the long-term impact that HIV/AIDS may have on the organizational and operational capacity of the SANDF, which at present is the leading military power in the southern African sub-region.

HIV/AIDS and force procurement

Force procurement refers to the ability to acquire suitable recruits for the armed forces. As with most armed forces, the SANDF selects candidates on the basis of a wide range of criteria, including character traits, educational qualifications and physical, mental and overall health profile. In terms of their medical profile, recruits found medically unfit on psychological and medical grounds are not recruited. In terms of current policy, HIV/AIDS is managed in the same way as any other chronic, progressive and potentially fatal disease. Thus, recruitment restrictions that apply to other comparable diseases apply equally to HIV/AIDS. Although this policy is intended to reduce the incidence of HIV within the ranks upon entry, it not only is highly controversial but may limit the ability to recruit suitable personnel in a shrinking skills market.

At present, recruitment does not pose a major challenge. In fact, the SANDF has an oversupply of applications of which only a small portion (fewer than 3,500 members) were recruited into the voluntary Military

Skills Development System in 2007. Of interest is that only 1,882 members completed their two-year initial contract period. In 2008, only 2,506 reported for duty, of whom 96 per cent were black and 31 per cent were female.[5] Owing to budgetary constraints, this is way short of the 10,000 the SANDF envisaged recruiting every year and will have an impact on the SANDF's ability to rejuvenate its ageing forces and supply sufficient personnel for peacekeeping operations. The question is: What does the long-term future hold, given South Africa's youth health profile? Armed forces aim to recruit precisely the age group at greatest risk of HIV infection – those between the ages of 18 and 26.

The 2006 Statistics South Africa estimates of HIV infection in the age group 15–19 were 3.2 per cent for males and 9.4 per cent for females. This increases dramatically in the age group 20–24, with figures estimated at 6.0 per cent for males and an alarming 23.9 per cent for females. Among females, HIV prevalence was highest in the 25–29 age cohort, with figures peaking for males in the age group 30–34, where for the first time they overtook female infection rates.[6] Similar statistics are cited by the Actuarial Society of South Africa, with projections for the 20–24 age category being slightly higher at 7.2 per cent for males and 26.5 per cent for females, and for the 25–29 age cohort at 21.8 per cent for males and 32.5 per cent for females (Figure 2.1). These estimates concur with the Human Sciences Research Council household prevalence survey conducted in 2006.

Should HIV-free status continue to be a criterion for enlistment, it may affect the SANDF in a number of ways. First, the cohort of suitable young recruits who meet the specified health assessment standards is likely to decline unless there is a notable change in infection rates among the youth in years to come. Second, because women are more affected than men in the younger age cohort, there may be difficulties in meeting gender targets, which at present are around 30 per cent. Third, the results of a survey among educators indicate that black South Africans have a significantly higher HIV prevalence rate than other population groups.[7] As reflected in the recent SANDF intakes, white South Africans are no longer volunteering for military service. For example, in 2006, whites comprised only 6.7 per cent of the forces at the lower ranks, while in 2007 the figures were down to 2.3 per cent for privates (troops).[8] Fourth, the level of education among the youth is likely to decline given the growing cohort of AIDS orphans who may either not have had the opportunity to complete their formal schooling or have had a disrupted education (Figure 2.2).

Although the situation differs from society to society, many armed forces and police tend to draw recruits from the poor and disadvantaged youth.[9] The same applies to the SANDF. Although the SANDF has

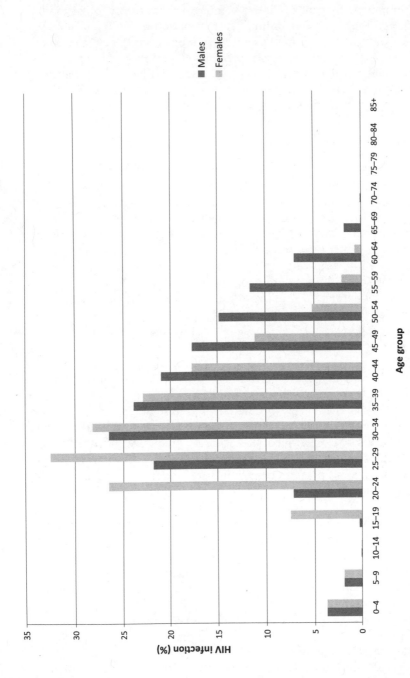

Figure 2.1 Estimated HIV prevalence in South Africa by sex and age, 2006.
Source: R. Dorrington, L. Johnson, D. Bradshaw and T. Daniel, *The Demographic Impact of HIV/AIDS in South Africa: National and Provincial Indicators for 2006* (Cape Town: Centre for Actuarial Research, South African Medical Research Council and Actuarial Society of South Africa, 2006), Figure 5, ⟨http://www.mrc.ac.za/bod/Demographic-ImpactHIVIndicators.pdf⟩ (accessed 29 August 2011).

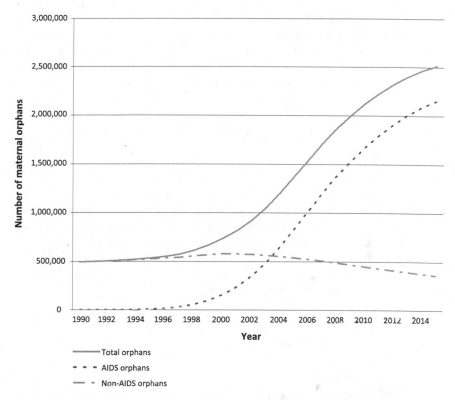

Figure 2.2 Projected number of maternal orphans in South Africa under the age of 18 owing to AIDS and other causes of death, 1990–2015.
Source: Dorrington et al., *The Demographic Impact of HIV/AIDS in South Africa*, Figure 13.

no shortage at present in terms of applicants, it does struggle to recruit members with the necessary mathematical skills for certain specialized posts, and this is likely to worsen. A report by the Joint United Nations Programme on HIV/AIDS (UNAIDS) and the United Nations Children's Fund (UNICEF) on orphan estimates for 2003 indicated that 13 per cent of all children in South Africa under the age of 17 were orphans, of whom 48 per cent were AIDS orphans. It was estimated that, by 2010, orphans would make up 19 per cent of all children. In terms of actual numbers, this amounts to 3.1 million orphans under the age of 18.[10] Invariably orphans suffer from higher levels of malnutrition, lower school enrolment and stigma. They are also exposed to an environment where they are socially, culturally and economically more prone to HIV infection.[11]

Traditionally, the armed forces seek to recruit young adults with a specific character profile: fit young individuals who display leadership skills, are well adapted emotionally, have at least completed secondary school, and have no criminal record. Thus, monitoring how this disease is affecting the youth of South Africa and those volunteering for military service is essential for defence personnel planning. To cite an example, in 2003 in Mozambique, with an infection rate of only 13.6 per cent, more than half of recruits tested HIV-positive.[12]

Where HIV status is used as a criterion for recruitment irrespective of CD4 count or viral load, this may eliminate a potential pool of otherwise suitable candidates. In order to attract and obtain the sorts of skills that are in relatively scarce supply, the SANDF needs to review its current force design and assess which posts should be filled by military personnel with a specific medical classification, which posts can be filled by civilians where HIV status is not a criterion, what functions can be outsourced, and how many reserves need to be trained and maintained to ensure an adequate operational capacity. This becomes critically important should the SANDF lose the case which has been brought to the Pretoria High Court by the AIDS Law Project on behalf of the South African Security Forces Union, which examines whether or not HIV-free status as a criterion for recruitment and deployment is unfair.[13]

HIV/AIDS and force preparation

The impact of HIV on recruitment is negligible compared with the effect it has on human resource management within the Department of Defence (DOD). The military is a highly vulnerable organization because HIV prevalence tends to peak in the 25–44 age group for both sexes, which is the age range when they are most productive and deployable. Furthermore, the military provides exactly the right circumstances for infection to take place. Personnel are generally placed in single-sex barracks (hostels), away from their families for considerable periods of time and on a regular basis. They generally serve in remote locations where recreational activities are limited, alcohol and drug use are common and sex workers are abundant. Added to this, they are often deployed to high-risk environments where exposure to HIV is heightened. This makes the military a highly vulnerable institution and more likely to have employees with high infection rates.

The DOD reported that, during 2006, 34,810 members underwent a comprehensive health assessment – over half of the uniformed component. Of these, 70 per cent were "green status", which implies, among other things, that they were HIV-negative.[14] From this study, one can deduce that HIV prevalence is below 30 per cent among the uniformed component of the SANDF and that the infection rate may well be around the claimed national average of 23–25 per cent for the economically active sector of the population. However, whether the spread of HIV across the different age groups resembles the national average is disputable, because the demographic profile in terms of age, gender and race differs.

On closer scrutiny by age, for example, deaths in the DOD (including civilian) peak in the 30–39 cohorts, declining steadily until retirement. When compared with the national death profile for 2005, an interesting pattern emerges (Figure 2.3). For DOD personnel, death rates are higher in the age bracket 30–39 years but notably lower in the younger (18–24 years) and older (50–64) cohorts. In the younger cohort, this is because the SANDF does not currently recruit anyone who is HIV-positive into the uniformed services. That death rates are notably higher in the 30–39 age group indicates that a substantial number become infected while in

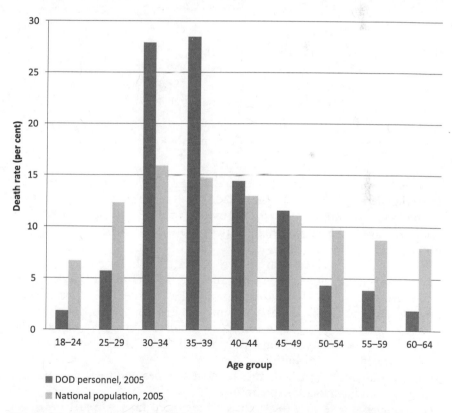

Figure 2.3 Comparison of death rates among Department of Defence personnel and the national population, 2005.
Source: Department of Defence, Personnel Statistics, Statistics South Africa, 2007, p. 9.

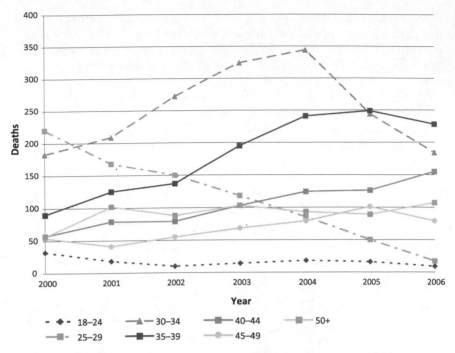

Figure 2.4 Department of Defence death profile by year and age, 2000–2006.
Source: Department of Defence, Personnel Statistics, 2000–2006.

service. However, what appears encouraging is that DOD death statistics
over the period 2000–2006 reveal a decline in death rates in the 25–29
cohort and also, although to a lesser extent, in the 30–34 bracket; rates in
the 35–39 age group show a slight tapering off, but those in the 40–44 age
group picked up (Figure 2.4).

There are many factors that influence these trends, for example the effect of anti-retroviral (ARV) treatments. In 2004, Project PHIDISA was
launched to make ARV treatments available to soldiers, as well as to
provide improved clinical management, psychosocial support and family-
oriented care for HIV-affected military families.[15] This may explain the
general decline in recent years shown by Figure 2.4. Project Masibam-
bisane, which is a prevention campaign designed to raise HIV/AIDS
awareness among SANDF members, their families and their dependants,
has also been having a positive impact.

National statistics for 2005 indicate that more than 90 per cent of all
deaths are from natural causes, although in the age groups 20–24 and 25–
29 there is a higher proportion of deaths owing to non-natural causes.[16]
In older age groups, the percentage of non-natural deaths declines signifi-

cantly. HIV/AIDS as a cause of death is under-reported because the majority of deaths resulting from HIV are misclassified under either tuberculosis or respiratory infection.[17] Most analysts seem to agree that AIDS is responsible for around 47 per cent of all deaths and for a staggering 71 per cent of all deaths in the age category 15–49 years.[18] It can thus be assumed that the number of DOD deaths owing to HIV/AIDS is on a par with, if not higher than, national estimates.

In this analysis, due consideration must be given to demographic variables such as the racial/gender mix of the SANDF. Nationally, women have a higher rate of infection in the 20–24 and 25–29 age groups, and it is only after the age of 35 that male infection rates overtake those for women. Like men, women generally enter the SANDF with an HIV-negative status. By extrapolation, it can be assumed that, because of the lower percentages of women in the SANDF and their negative status upon employment, there will be a difference in HIV infection statistics between the national and Department of Defence profiles.

At present, approximately 19 per cent of uniformed personnel are women. Although only 11 per cent currently serve in the senior ranks of Brigadier General and above, they are well represented in the junior officer ranks of Second Lieutenant and Lieutenant (35 per cent) and Captain (36 per cent), for which the typical age range is 25–29 years. If one compares these rank groups in the armed forces with teachers in the same age group, it is alarming to find that young black female educators (18–24 years old) have a much higher HIV prevalence of 17.4 per cent, compared with 12 per cent among their male counterparts. The difference between the sexes widened substantially for educators aged 25–29, where women had a prevalence of 30.4 per cent, compared with 24.5 per cent among men in the same age group.

The race and age profile of the SANDF also differs from the national profile. There are fewer black South Africans (69.7 per cent) and proportionately more white South Africans (17.7 per cent) in the SANDF than in the general population. Coloured South Africans make up 11.5 per cent of the total human resource composition of the SANDF, and Asian South Africans 1.2 per cent. This ethnic ratio may influence the prevalence rates, because whites tend to be clustered in the upper non-commissioned officer ranks (Staff Sergeant or Warrant Officer) and officer ranks (Major to Colonel) (mostly late thirties to 50 years old). This segment in terms of race and age generally has lower overall HIV prevalence rates.[19] Most SANDF members serve in the ranks of private (20,586 members), of whom only 2.3 per cent are whites. In terms of their level of education, the overwhelming majority have completed high school but are without tertiary education, and almost half of all uniformed members earn below 60,000 South African Rand, or approximately USD 7,500 per annum. As reflected in the educators' survey, both education and income influence HIV prevalence rates.[20] Thus, making assumptions about HIV prevalence based on death statistics is fraught with ambiguity.

As at 2007–2008, the HIV/AIDS epidemic is still largely in the infection stage, with few personnel physically ill or dying from AIDS, so the overall impact on the SANDF is uncertain. The DOD's prevention and ARV programmes may mitigate the impact, but the long-term effect remains disturbing. To date there have been no institutional assessments to determine exactly which sectors are most vulnerable, what the critical posts are and what should be done to avoid future gaps in personnel. Currently gaps are filled either by assigning these duties to another member in the unit (over and above his/her normal duties) or by letting the task stand over until the "sick" member returns or the vacant post is filled. Besides the obvious implications for military leadership and continuity of command, a key consideration is how to provide the required quality and quantity of personnel to meet current deployment commitments.

Besides HIV, the SANDF faces many challenges in ensuring that there are sufficient numbers of adequately trained soldiers. Rising operational commitments, which at the same time have been associated with declining operational budgets, have had a severe impact on force preparation. Because salaries and equipment contracts are excluded from budget cuts, training and maintenance budgets are invariably affected. As Romer-Heitman points out, "for the better part of a decade the SANDF has not been able to train properly, to maintain its equipment properly, or to maintain its infrastructure. Proper unit training is almost impossible, causing operational capability to decline."[21] This is exacerbated by personnel shortages in certain age and skill categories. Clearly this has a spillover effect on future operations, because many of the current members in the junior ranks are either over-age, unfit or ill, and therefore not deployable.[22]

Force employment and deployment

South Africa supports the current United Nations recommendations to deploy only medically fit soldiers, and this includes but is not restricted to HIV-negative status, according to the Department of Peacekeeping Operations (DPKO) guidelines. The argument against deploying HIV-positive soldiers on peacekeeping missions stems from the following:

> First, medical treatment available during peacekeeping missions may not be adequate to meet the special requirements of peacekeepers with HIV. Second,

peacekeepers have to undergo deployment vaccinations and may be exposed to diseases during deployment, both of which pose additional risks to their health. Third, the presence of HIV-positive peacekeepers poses the risk of transmission to medical personnel, fellow peacekeepers and the civilian population.[23]

None of these issues has to do with whether HIV-positive soldiers are physically able to serve in such operations, but concern whether HIV-positive soldiers can be provided with adequate treatment and whether from an organizational perspective it appears opportune to deploy them. With the high HIV prevalence rate within the ranks, the SANDF grapples with the challenge of ensuring sufficient personnel for deployment. The current expectation is that every African Standby Force in the region maintains a brigade of about 3,000 infantry soldiers, as well as 1,258 logistical specialists, signallers, engineers, military police and civilian support staff for rapid deployment in Africa at appropriate notice. In an interview with a Battalion Commander preparing for deployment, it was confirmed that, out of the approximately 18,000-strong SANDF infantry corps, the army struggles to meet requirements to supply current rotations.[24] To have three battalions in the field (which equal one brigade), there need to be at least 3,000 personnel in force preparation, an equal number in combat readiness training, and similar numbers feeding into the system (ideally 9,000–12,000 personnel at various stages).

Another factor affecting the SANDF's ability to sustain an operationally effective force is attrition in the 18–39 age bracket. The rate of attrition in the middle ranks is also extraordinarily high. Acute shortages are already being experienced in critical posts such as airspace control, aircrew, anti-aircraft, artillery, combat navy, engineers and technical posts.[25] Unlike in the business sector, the military cannot readily recruit personnel from the civilian labour market to fill gaps left by "unplanned" attrition owing to death, sickness, medical discharge or resignation. This means that personnel have to be supplied from a variety of units prior to deployment and often there is insufficient time to create formed "cohesive units". Consequently "units are made up by fragments of other units due to health and welfare reasons, resulting in troops working under commanders they do not know and with equipment that is neither theirs nor their responsibility".[26] Clearly this compromises force readiness and performance in the field.

Because the SANDF currently deploys only HIV-negative soldiers, the concern is about how many service members can become infected on deployment. Loneliness, frustration and peer pressure, combined with access to drugs, alcohol and sex workers, induce them to engage in risky behaviours. Their relative anonymity as foreigners also frees them from social norms that guide their judgement when they are with their families or in their own communities and cultures.[27] During 2006, the SANDF had almost 3,500 members deployed in various operations across the African continent, with the largest contingents serving in the Democratic Republic of the Congo (DRC), Burundi, Sudan and the Comoros.[28] Although national HIV rates in these countries are comparatively low, the national prevalence rates in the southern African states supplying troops to these peacekeeping missions exceed 15 per cent.

Most African militaries report that the HIV prevalence within their forces is at least 3–10 per cent higher than the national average. For example, in Kenya in 2005 the national average was 6.4 per cent but the military averaged 9.4 per cent; and in Botswana a 30 per cent national average is contrasted with 40 per cent in the military. In March 2003, the head of the Malawi Defence Force claimed that troop strength was down by more than 40 per cent owing to HIV deaths, with losses most acutely felt in the command-leadership structure. By 2004, according to international observers, "troop strength [in Malawi] had fallen to 50 per cent of the minimum capacity necessary to guarantee state security".[29] Because the United Nations recommends, but does not enforce, mandatory testing of peacekeepers, it is not known how many countries send HIV-positive service members on peace operations or what the actual prevalence rates are within these forces.[30] Even when infection rates are low in the areas where troops are deployed, the risk of infection during such missions increases because peacekeepers may "share" the same pool of sex workers, worsening the situation a over longer period of service.

In the survey conducted among South African teachers, for example, it was shown that frequent nights away from home per week were significantly associated with an HIV-positive status. Those who always slept at home had the lowest HIV prevalence (8.6 per cent), whereas those who stayed away one or two nights per week had a significantly higher HIV prevalence (16.5 per cent), and an even higher prevalence was indicated for those who stayed away from home for longer than six nights or more (27.6 per cent).[31] In comparison, a study by the Civil-Military Alliance in the United States found that peacekeepers returning from Liberia and Sierra Leone had infection rates more than double those of the non-peacekeeping personnel. The risk of HIV infection doubled with each deployment in conflict zones, suggesting a direct link to duty in war zones. Among Nigerian troops deployed to Sierra Leone, HIV prevalence increased from 7 per cent after one year, to 10 per cent after two years, to more than 15 per cent after three years of duty in the operational area.[32]

An often neglected issue is the gendered dimension of military deployments and the impact this may have on HIV transmission. Whereas male soldiers tend to find alternative sexual partners through either consensual relationships or commercial sex workers, women soldiers are more likely to form relationships with soldiers on base.[33] This does not make them less vulnerable to sexual exploitation or HIV infection. Where they face sexual abuse or harassment by their own comrades, few of them actually report it because of the impact it may have on their own careers or their acceptance among male colleagues.[34] In addition, there is concern about their safety while in the field, given that rape is used as a weapon of war. In an interview, a SANDF Battalion Commander commented that the safety of women under his command is "a big issue" and may even at times compromise operations. He cited an example in the DRC of having to take women back to camp because they were threatened by the presence of the Mai Mai, who removed their clothing in front of the female troops and "displayed their wares".[35] His concern seems justified, judging from this report:

> "This thing of rape," said Colonel Edmond Ngarambe [of Rwanda] ... "I can't deny that happens. We are human beings. But it's not just us. The Mai Mai, the government soldiers who are not paid, the Rastas do the same thing. And some people sent by our enemies do it to cause anger against us."[36]

In the DRC, as elsewhere in Africa, "rape has been used to terrorise and punish civilians in Congo who support the 'wrong side'".[37] In addition, SANDF troops themselves have allegedly engaged in rape in the Great Lakes region of the DRC.[38] Such unacceptable sexual behaviour by SANDF soldiers under a peacekeeping mandate has signalled the need to bring greater discipline to troops, coupled with a stronger adherence to the moral code for the military treatment of civilian populations.[39]

In the headquarters of the UN Mission in the DRC in Kinshasa, the SANDF was known to have the worst disciplinary record of the entire mission. Reports suggest that "personnel were allowed to visit brothels and run brothel-like activities in the camp".[40] It may be deduced that, the more professional and disciplined a force, the lower the level of HIV infection. This comes down to good leadership and a sense of responsibility, with the knowledge that there are certain sanctions imposed on sexual misconduct, as well as some serious personal consequences. In this regard, knowing that deployment is not possible if one becomes HIV-positive creates a powerful financial deterrent, owing to the loss of livelihood.

The behaviour of a few soldiers should not be extrapolated to all SANDF peacekeepers, nor should infection rates be ascribed solely to field operations. What remains unknown is behaviour at home. The high divorce rate among military personnel on field operations might suggest that not only soldiers but perhaps also their partners form relationships with others during periods of long separation. Given the high prevalence of HIV within South Africa, infection could occur at home and not necessarily on deployment. In South Africa, there is a lack of research on military families and the impact HIV is having on family relations.

Force sustainment and human rights implications

The extent to which the SANDF is able to sustain its operational effectiveness is a matter not only of human resources but also of finance. At present there are sufficient volunteers to meet the SANDF's recruitment needs. The challenge in these times, when armed forces have downscaled to minimum force strength, is to keep training sufficient numbers of personnel despite insufficient funding. The SANDF does not have a reserve capacity to call upon, nor does it make use of civilian contractors or private military companies to fill personnel gaps or to expand capacity in times of operational need. Thus, the under-utilization of personnel owing to their HIV status has far-reaching implications for force design and how the SANDF balances the mix between uniformed posts, civilians, contractors and reserve forces in the future.

The effect of constantly having to recruit, train and re-train personnel is expected to have a significant impact on the future personnel budget. Various options need to be considered in order to provide an adequate availability of personnel as the HIV epidemic unfolds. An immediate strategy to sustain force readiness is to train members more broadly so as to enable soldiers to perform a wide set of tasks. Multi-skilling allows a degree of flexibility and an ability to fill critical posts more readily from within the ranks. Even so, the greatest challenge lies with having to accommodate large numbers of HIV-positive members who are physically unfit to perform the tasks for which they have been trained. The inability to dismiss personnel on the grounds of their HIV status and the compelling need to continue to use unfit, untrained personnel in support functions when they may lack the necessary training for these posts have the potential to erode operational effectiveness even further. Complicating the placement of HIV-positive officers is the reduction in the number of posts available, as several support positions have been transferred to civilian staff or outsourced. In addition, the majority of the departments are overstaffed with support personnel.

Even though the provision of ARVs may mitigate the effect of skill loss and preserve military command in the short term, the long-term implications are daunting. For instance, HIV-positive members may be deployed internally in borderline duties and in support of the South African Police Service. Recent reports suggest that many HIV-positive soldiers on ARVs "are now running around in the mountains and are now serving in border control units".[41] However, the dilemma is that we know that HIV infection rates are generally higher near border posts. As these members may have become infected while on external deployment and become exposed to other strains in their "new job", the administration of ARVs inevitably becomes more complicated. HIV is a rapidly mutating and adaptable virus and deploying soldiers who have been exposed to various strains raises concerns vis-à-vis the spread of the virus within South Africa's own borders.

The cost of maintaining long-term ARV treatment is another challenge. At present, ARVs are provided to all members and their dependants through the US-funded Project PHIDISA. This five-year programme, which commenced in 2004, provides ARVs at 6 military hospitals, with the intention that it will eventually provide ARV treatment at all 65 military health clinics throughout the organization.[42] The SANDF is heavily reliant on this external foreign funding to provide these treatments. The question is whether this can be sustained and, if not, what the implications are. Because the SANDF cannot provide this service from within its own budget, the government may be pressured to provide more funding to supply ARV treatment to the military. In Zambia, for example, military members argued that they should have priority access to more government funding for ARVs because they are in a high-risk job and because they "contribute to world peace". In Rwanda, high-ranking officers increasingly have access to ARVs that the general population does not have. According to Elbe, "this is part of [a] wider development in Africa, whereby the soldiers of many countries now have greater or better access to health care and AIDS medicines than the civilian population".[43]

Many militaries in the region are committed to providing ARV treatment for their service members. These costs increase where armed forces are compelled by human rights activists to both recruit and deploy HIV-positive soldiers. Amongst these, the AIDS Law Project, acting on behalf of the South African Security Forces Union, filed court papers in the Pretoria High Court challenging the SANDF's "stand that people living with HIV are medically unsuitable and unable to withstand the stress and adverse physical weather conditions" of deployment. The claim is made that there is substantial evidence to show that "HIV-positive people, who are asymptomatic, are able to undertake difficult physical activity with no adverse effects on their health – in fact, regular exercise is beneficial to their health".[44] This claim comes at a time when hundreds of service members have been protesting against alleged discrimination against HIV-positive soldiers going on external deployments and the impact that the Department of Defence policy has on promotion.[45] Whereas nothing is said about members with diabetes being denied similar deployment opportunities, HIV/AIDS as a discriminatory employment practice is highly controversial. According to the AIDS Law Project, the "SANDF violates the right to equality, amongst other rights, by refusing to employ or deploy people within the military on the basis of their HIV status alone, regardless of their actual state of fitness".[46]

The outcome of the AIDS Law Project case has far-reaching implications for the military in terms of financial costs, operational effectiveness and diplomatic relations. Besides the obvious healthcare costs, should exclusion based on HIV status be considered an unfair discriminatory practice in recruitment, the SANDF may have to cope with a higher attrition rate as a result of deaths at a younger age. This will increase training costs and lead to additional losses in the middle ranks even for those with ARV treatment. The deployment of HIV-positive members on peacekeeping operations has other implications in terms of suboptimal healthcare provision, nutrition and compliance while on deployment, which may pose serious risks not only to the individual concerned but also to those reliant on the member in military operations. Although discrimination against HIV-positive members cannot be condoned, serious consideration needs to be given to the stigma associated with this disease versus the implications for morale, discipline and military effectiveness.

Finally, there are the diplomatic implications of deploying HIV-positive soldiers to war-torn areas in Africa, especially for South Africa as the country with one of the highest infection rates in the world. With the litany of sex charges against SANDF peacekeepers, allowing the deployment of HIV-positive soldiers who do not have the internal discipline to control their sexual conduct could brand the SANDF as a vector of HIV. What is at stake are not only the human rights and livelihoods of service members, but also the fact that the potential victims of HIV are innocent civilians, mostly women, whose lives have already been devastated by war, conflict and sexual abuse.

Conclusion

The claim that HIV infection within the armed forces in South Africa is three to five times higher than the national average is a myth that should be dispelled.[47] Nonetheless, it is clear that, based on knowledge of the epidemic in South Africa and among other armed forces in the region, this disease has severe implications for armed forces. As with the human body, HIV/AIDS slowly erodes the institutional capacity of the military at various levels. At the level of recruitment, there will be fewer suitable recruits to serve in the military in South Africa in future. These young recruits will be physically less fit and less well educated, but also almost certainly less disciplined given their disrupted upbringing. The SANDF is strongly advised to monitor how this disease is affecting its recruitment pool not only from a health perspective but also from a sociological one.

At the level of force preparation, there is a need for closer scrutiny of which segments of the military are most affected and in what ways. It is known that the combat branches are most vulnerable, but what are the estimated shortages and how should these be dealt with? Here, some thought needs to go into the future force design to give the SANDF the flexibility to ensure that it has not only enough human resources but the necessary skills. HIV/AIDS and affirmative action policies have been responsible for high attrition rates at the heart of the institution – namely, at the operational level. At present the South African Army is the hardest hit by the HIV epidemic but is coping, and there are promising signs that infection rates may be on the decline. Nonetheless, HIV in South Africa is a long-wave epidemic and astute planning is needed to cope with this pervasive disease.

On force employment, the question of health standards is possibly the most critical issue. Already there is a suggestion of lowering standards in terms of certain health criteria, and this may include HIV-positive status. The deployment of HIV-positive service members has far-reaching implications for the SANDF at the institutional, social, economic and political levels. Whose human rights should weigh more heavily – those of service members who want to serve on external deployment for the "money", or those of innocent civilians who may become infected through soldiers' irresponsible behaviour? The military has a considerable legal arsenal at its disposal to impose good discipline and promote good conduct by its professional military service members. Knowingly infecting others is nothing short of murder. It is, after all, the duty of soldiers to protect lives, not to take the lives of innocent civilians.

In terms of force sustainment, HIV pushes up health costs, diverts resources from line functions and exacerbates existing capacity and skills shortages. ARVs may slow down skills loss, but this is not a long-term solution, especially where the armed forces are reliant on external funding. Projects such as PHIDISA are essential in helping us understand the course of the epidemic, but not the future impact on the military. More open discussion and analysis of recorded data are required to inform decision-making, planning and policy formulation. Without this, we permit this harmful virus to continue on its road of destruction.

Acknowledgements

An earlier version of this chapter was published in *African Security Review*, 18(2), 2009, pp. 60–77. The journal has granted the editors permission to publish this version in this volume.

Notes

1. "Defence Union Takes Offence to HIV Conference Snub", *SABC News*, 2007, ⟨http://www.sabcnews.com/south_africa/general/0,2172,159136,00.html⟩ (accessed 22 February 2011).
2. Miriam Eberson, "AIDS and the Shopfloor – 2002", *SUCCEED* Magazine Special Publication, 2002, p. 3.
3. South African Press Association (SAPA), "SANDF Fighting Different Battle in Form of HIV/AIDS", *Star*, 8 June 2005, p. 6.
4. Robert Shell, "Halfway to the Holocaust: The Economic, Demographic and Social Implications of the AIDS Pandemic to the Year 2010 in the Southern African Region", in *HIV/AIDS: A Threat to the African Renaissance?*, Konrad-Adenauer-Stiftung Occasional Papers, 2000, pp. 7–27, at p. 9.
5. Department of Defence (DOD), *Department of Defence Annual Report FY 2007–2008* (Pretoria: Government Printer, 2008).
6. South Africa (Republic), Statistics South Africa (Stats SA), "South Africa HIV and AIDS Statistics Summary", 2006; for 2008 figures, see ⟨http://www.avert.org/safricastats.htm⟩ (accessed 8 October 2011).
7. Education Labour Relations Council (ELRC), *The Health of Our Educators: A Focus on HIV/AIDS in South African Public Schools*, 2004/5 Survey, Report prepared by the research consortium comprising the Human Sciences Research Council and the Medical Council of South Africa (Cape Town: HSRC Press, 2005), p. 56.
8. DOD, *Department of Defence Annual Report FY 2005–2006* (Pretoria: Department of Defence, 2007).
9. Laurie Garrett, *HIV and National Security: Where Are the Links?* (New York: Council on Foreign Relations, 2005), p. 25.
10. UNAIDS/UNICEF, *Children on the Brink 2004: A Joint Report of New Orphan Estimates and a Framework for Action* (New York: UNICEF, 2004), pp. 26–30, ⟨http://data.unaids.org/publications/External-Documents/unicef_childrenonthebrink2004_en.pdf⟩ (accessed 31 August 2011).
11. Tony Barnett, "A Long-wave Event: HIV/AIDS, Politics, Governance and Security: Sundering the Intergenerational Bond?", *International Affairs*, 82(2), 2006, pp. 297–313, at pp. 299–306.
12. Garrett, *HIV and National Security*, p. 25.
13. SAPA, "SANDF Facing Court Challenge on Approach to HIV", *Star*, 15 May 2007, p. 8.
14. DOD, *Department of Defence Annual Report FY 2005–2006*, p. 163.
15. US Department of State, Diplomatic Mission to South Africa, "Ambassador Frazer and Minister Lekota Sign Agreement to Help Build 'World-Class Medical Research Capability' in the South African Military Health Service", 26 April 2005, ⟨http://southafrica.usembassy.gov/frazer20050426.html⟩ (accessed 31 August 2011).
16. Non-natural causes included events of undetermined intent, accidental injuries, transport accidents, assault, complications of medical and surgical care, intentional self-harm, external causes of morbidity and mortality and legal intervention and operations of war. Stats SA, *Mortality and Causes of Death in South Africa, 2005: Findings from Death Notification* (Pretoria: Statistics South Africa, 2007), ⟨http://www.statssa.gov.za⟩.
17. Stats SA, "South Africa HIV and AIDS Statistics Summary", pp. 16–18, 26.
18. Ibid.
19. Stats SA, *Mortality and Causes of Death in South Africa, 2005*, p. 12.
20. DOD, *Department of Defence Annual Report FY 2005–2006*, p. 13.
21. Helmoed Romer-Heitman, "Is the SANDF Falling Apart?", *Daily News*, 21 August 2005, p. 12.

22. Ibid.
23. US General Accounting Office, *U.N. Peacekeeping: United Nations Faces Challenges in Responding to the Impact of HIV/AIDS on Peacekeeping Operations*, Report to the Chairman, Committee on International Relations, House of Representatives (Washington, DC: United States General Accounting Office, 2001), p. 6.
24. Interview with a Lt Colonel preparing for deployment to the Democratic Republic of the Congo.
25. DOD, *Department of Defence Annual Report FY 2005–2006*, p. 17.
26. Pierre Van Ryneveld, "SANDF Has Become Grim Joke", *Pretoria News*, 8 November 2006, p. 13.
27. Angela De Jong and Delene Visser, "Exploring Sexual Practices of South African Soldiers to Determine Their Vulnerability to the Human Immune-Deficiency Virus", *South African Journal of Industrial Psychology*, 32(1), 2006, pp. 1–11, at p. 1.
28. DOD, *Department of Defence Annual Report FY 2005–2006*, pp. 98–99.
29. Garrett, *HIV and National Security*, p. 27.
30. US General Accounting Office, *U.N. Peacekeeping*, p. 7.
31. ELRC, "The Health of Our Educators", p. 89.
32. Alan Whiteside, Alex de Waal and Tsadkan Gebre-Tensae, "AIDS, Security and the Military in Africa: A Sober Appraisal", *African Affairs*, 105, 2006, p. 206.
33. Centre for Conflict Resolution, *HIV/AIDS and Militaries in Southern Africa*, Report of a Policy Seminar, Windhoek, Namibia, 2006 (Cape Town: CCR, Seminar Report No. 10, 2006), ⟨http://www.ccr.org.za/⟩ (accessed 1 September 2011).
34. Karyn Maughan, "SANDF Peacekeepers Face Litany of Sex Charges", *Pretoria News*, 4 November 2006, p. 1.
35. Interview with a DRC Battalion Commander, Saldanha, September 2007.
36. Chris McGreal, "Brutalised for Being on the 'Wrong Side'", *Mail & Guardian Online*, 19 November 2007, ⟨http://mg.co.za/article/2007-11-19-brutalised-for-being-on-the-wrong-side⟩ (accessed 31 August 2011).
37. Ibid. See also Maria Eriksson Baaz and Maria Stern, *The Complexity of Violence: A Critical Analysis of Sexual Violence in the Democratic Republic of Congo (DRC)* (Uppsala, Sweden: Nordic Africa Institute, 2010).
38. "SANDF Misconduct Will Not Be Tolerated", *SABC News*, 12 November 2007.
39. Garrett, *HIV and National Security*, p. 10.
40. Pierre Van Ryneveld, "SANDF Has Become Grim Joke," *Pretoria News*, 8 November 2006, p. 13.
41. SAPA, "SANDF Fighting Different Battle in Form of HIV/AIDS", p. 6.
42. Irin/Plus News, "SANDF Makes Headway against HIV/AIDS", *Daily Dispatch*, 21 June 2005, p. 12.
43. Stefan Elbe, "Should HIV/AIDS Be Securitized? The Ethical Dilemmas of Linking HIV/AIDS and Security", *International Studies Quarterly*, 5, 2006, pp. 119–144, at p. 130.
44. SAPA, "SANDF Facing Court Challenge on Approach to HIV", p. 8.
45. Canaan Mdletshe, "Soldiers Protest SANDF HIV Policies", *Sowetan*, 19 June 2006, p. 6.
46. Mark Heywood, "Press Release – Mexico Supreme Court Ruling on HIV/AIDS in the Military", AIDS Law Project, ⟨http://www.alp.org.za/modules.php?op+modload&name=News&file=article&sid=350⟩.
47. Whiteside et al., "AIDS, Security and the Military in Africa".

3

Policy, security and outcomes: HIV/AIDS and the Uganda People's Defence Forces

Charles Bakahumura

Introduction

Uganda is one of the sub-Saharan African countries that have grappled with the challenges of HIV/AIDS across multiple sectors of the economy. In the past three decades, following the early HIV/AIDS cases in the 1980s, it gradually became clear to the government of Uganda that HIV/AIDS was not merely a health problem but one that had profound economic, social, political, security and psychological implications.[1] The spread of HIV/AIDS contributed significantly to the rise of poverty levels and the decline in the production of goods and services. It did not take long – within a period of 10 years since the first cases were recorded – for the impact of HIV/AIDS to be felt in many sectors in Uganda. The epidemic implicated human and national security in many complex ways. By the early 1990s, Uganda's HIV prevalence rate was estimated at 20.2 per cent, which was one of the highest in the world.[2] Unless drastic measures were taken, it would not take long for the epidemic to severely undermine national security, stability and prosperity, and reverse Uganda's development gains. This is because HIV/AIDS adversely affected key national institutions such as the military, the police and the civil service, and imposed strains on food security, education, health and other vital sectors.

This chapter demonstrates the challenges faced by the military authorities in dealing with the actual and potential impact of HIV/AIDS in the Uganda People's Defence Force (UPDF). The first section illustrates the

HIV/AIDS and the security sector in Africa, Aginam and Rupiya (eds),
United Nations University Press, 2012, ISBN 978-92-808-1209-1

guidelines laid out in the Ugandan national strategy for combating HIV/ AIDS and how these provisions were correlated with the Ugandan military. Second, the chapter presents the positive outcomes of the measures aimed at mitigating the impact of the virus in the Ugandan army. The chapter then recommends what the military hierarchy need to do in order to support the victims of the epidemic and prevent its further spread across the troops and the wider Ugandan society.

HIV/AIDS and new dimensions to security: An overview

One useful way to explore the problem of HIV/AIDS in Uganda relates to understanding the (human) security implications of the epidemic. Since the end of the Cold War, the concept of security has evolved to encompass non-military threats such as poverty, infectious diseases and environmental degradation.[3] The next generation of Ugandan military leaders need to adjust their mindset from the notion that security is limited to the survival of the state and to inter-state conflicts to thinking more about holistic approaches and linkages between national stability and prosperity. This is because the survival or collapse of the state in most African nations is, among other things, affected by human security, and HIV/AIDS has been identified as, at least, one of the major threats to human security across the continent. Studies have shown that there is a correlation between HIV/AIDS and a range of human security challenges in Africa.[4] In areas hardest hit by this epidemic, the standard of living – including life expectancy at birth – has fallen drastically. This is partly because most of the people who have been affected are aged between 15 and 49[5] – the population group that represents the most active part of the workforce and other critical sectors of society. Uganda's national security is not immune from the continent-wide human security challenges of HIV/AIDS.

The Ugandan military was one of the institutions to be seriously affected by the HIV/AIDS epidemic. The problem was first discovered in 1987 when a large number of troops who travelled to Cuba for military training had to return home after being diagnosed as HIV-positive. Conscious of the security implications of AIDS, the Ugandan government felt that a "non-traditional enemy" had infiltrated the army. Soon, officers and men started dying in significant numbers from AIDS-related illnesses, creating a leadership vacuum at various levels. As a result, an HIV/AIDS control programme was established in the same year in the Ministry of Defence to respond to the special needs of the armed forces.[6]

Uganda's national strategy on HIV/AIDS

In order to understand the military's response to the threat posed by the HIV/AIDS epidemic, it is important to examine the national HIV/AIDS strategy and its impact on the rest of the society. In contrast to the policy of denial and closure by most African countries, in 1987 Uganda and Senegal were the first countries in sub-Saharan Africa openly to declare a clear policy to address the HIV/AIDS epidemic.[7] Because the consequences of HIV/AIDS are multifaceted and have economic, social, health, cultural and psychological implications, the government needed to adopt comprehensive, cross-cutting and multi-sectoral approaches.[8] It therefore developed an approach to control the spread of HIV/AIDS that involved all relevant stakeholders. This approach went beyond taking care of the sick and included raising awareness in the general population by emphasizing sustainable prevention measures. The programme integrated various public agencies, non-governmental organizations (NGOs) and the broader civil society in the fight against HIV/AIDS. Many local and international NGOs, for example, became involved in caring for the large number of orphans who resulted from the epidemic.[9]

The Presidential Office was personally and actively involved in promoting HIV/AIDS public awareness programmes. This campaign emphasized what has been known in international AIDS work as the ABC model: "A" stood for "abstinence", "B" for "be faithful" and "C" for "condom use". Emphasis was put on teaching youth the virtues of abstinence and this resulted in significant behaviour change as far as attitudes towards sex were concerned. The disease carried much stigmatization not only for those who were infected but also for the rest of the family. Special care was taken to provide counselling services for all those who had been affected by the epidemic. Pre-testing counselling was also encouraged and many people publicly testified to their HIV status without fear of stigmatization, ridicule or discrimination. Great efforts have been made to try to educate the general public about changing their attitude towards those who have tested positive for HIV. Both government and civil society organizations played an instrumental role in shaping people's attitudes.

The above-mentioned approach prompted the Ugandan parliament to enact a law in 1992 that established the Uganda AIDS Commission. This Commission was mandated to coordinate multi-sectoral, harmonized approaches involving all the relevant stakeholders.[10] As a result, there was a steady decrease in HIV prevalence over the ensuing 15-year period. The prevalence rate dropped from 20.2 per cent during 1990–1991 to 6.4 per cent during 2004–2005.[11] This is much lower than the rate in most countries in the southern African region. The government, in collaboration with development partners, has been able to secure anti-retroviral drugs (generally known to reduce the viral loads in the blood), thereby prolonging and improving the lives of AIDS patients. In most cases, these drugs are either distributed free of charge or sold at subsidized prices.

Challenges for the military

There are a number of challenges that have put military leaders in a dilemma as they deal with the threat of HIV/AIDS. The biggest challenge has been maintaining an effective force in the face of the epidemic. Many junior and high-ranking officers have become victims of HIV, which has led to the loss of many well-trained and experienced commanders.[12] This undermines the military's capacity and capabilities to perform its core security duties effectively. It takes considerable time and resources to train and develop an officer to the middle and senior levels. Unlike many employment positions in the civilian sphere, where it may be relatively easy to find replacements, this is not the case in the military owing to the particular skills required and the time it takes to develop those skills. Identifying and training commanders to replace those who have become caregivers, fallen sick or died as a result of HIV/AIDS poses a major challenge.

This human resource problem was exacerbated by the need for well-trained and physically fit commanders following the outbreak of the insurgency in the north of Uganda in August 1986. Although scholarly opinions are sharply divided, it has been stated that people in conflict areas may have increased vulnerability to contracting HIV.[13] This was true in Uganda up to the mid-1990s, when the prevalence rates among both civilians and soldiers who were in the conflict zone of northern Uganda increased. As a result of the insistence on testing, prevention and awareness skills within the Ugandan military, prevalence rates soon decreased. In fact, HIV rates are now lower in the military compared with the civilian population in the war-affected areas of northern Uganda.[14] This can be mainly attributed to the strategy adopted by senior military leaders of applying a diversified approach that emphasized effective preventive measures.

In normal circumstances, people who fall sick and are unable to perform military duties are supposed to be discharged and replaced with physically fit people. In Uganda, this has not been the case regarding people living with HIV and AIDS. This is because they will not receive adequate healthcare once they are out of the military. Only those who decide to leave of their own volition are officially released from the army. Apart from the healthcare reason, there is also the danger of being ostracized and stigmatized once they return to the civilian population and are known to be infected. Instead, such personnel are assigned light duties in the military and are allowed access to free medical care, together with their family members.

This humane aspect of the policy has, however, some drawbacks. The retention of such "non-effective personnel" has increased the cost of administration in the military. Nonetheless, this reality runs counter to the spirit of security sector reform prescriptions, which call for a downsized military to handle assessed threats. This policy has also compromised the quality of the military because many of the HIV-positive service people cannot be further trained and deployed. In practice, resources that are intended to develop and improve the capabilities of the military force are instead sometimes diverted to take care of sick personnel. This is a new kind of challenge that senior military leaders are currently facing.

When Uganda started participating in Peace Support Operations (PSOs), the army prescribed mandatory HIV tests. Although the United Nations does not currently require mandatory testing before, during or after deployment,[15] Uganda maintains a policy of screening anybody earmarked for deployment or training abroad. This provision is to ensure that members of the military do not become vectors of this harmful disease in other regions of the world, and also to protect the infected persons from the rigours of active military service. Moreover, there are some countries that feel that troop-contributing states with high HIV/AIDS prevalence rates will increase the risk of infection in the mission areas.

It has to be noted that the Ugandan military leadership is not wholeheartedly in favour of testing all soldiers returning from a PSO. This is a serious flaw that needs to be rectified in order to ascertain the percentage of people who contract the disease while on mission abroad. The practice of subjecting all soldiers to HIV tests before they are deployed outside the country has been interpreted by some individuals as being discriminatory against HIV-positive people. Those who belong to this school of thought argue that medical doctors should establish the viral loads of the persons in question in order to establish whether they will be able to withstand the pressures of work before a decision is made on their fitness for deployment abroad.

Lessons learned

There are a number of measures that senior military leaders should take to mitigate the threat of HIV/AIDS within the military force. First, they should continue to conduct sensitization programmes aimed at spreading awareness of the non-traditional threats to security, such as HIV/AIDS infection, that troops are increasingly facing. High-ranking officials should use every opportunity to communicate a positive message linking abstinence and faithfulness. In addition, the cooperation of religious leaders in instilling moral values within military communities should be encouraged. This would lead to behavioural change for a great number of soldiers.

Meeting groups should be formed inside the barracks with the aim of educating members about preventive measures and family-related issues. It would also be beneficial for the overall policy guidelines to have post-test "clubs" to assist those who tested positive for the virus. These social groups would have the objective of encouraging healthy and safe lifestyles for those who are already infected, and increase awareness about limiting the spread of the disease. Essentially, the anti-AIDS campaign should be one of the core responsibilities of every commander, regardless of his level. Until recently, the response to the HIV/AIDS epidemic in the Ugandan military had mainly been left to the medical department, with limited interdepartmental collaboration. The Chief of Defence Forces of the UPDF, General Aronda Nyakairima, has since instructed that all commanders should get involved in the campaign against AIDS.

Senior military leaders should not discriminate against those who are HIV-positive. Rather, they should treat them with compassion and provide them with the necessary assistance. The practice of screening all soldiers before they are deployed outside the country should be maintained. Proper explanation should be given to all those who test positive as to why they will not be considered for participation in international operations. HIV-positive soldiers who may still be physically and mentally competent should be assigned to light duties, preferably of an administrative nature. Overall, there should be a conscious effort to protect the human rights of all the victims of this disease.

Enforcement of the observance of morals and ethics within the military should be the responsibility of senior leaders. Accordingly, this should include the marital fidelity of all married officers. Senior leaders should lead by example, by being faithful to their spouses and at the same time discouraging promiscuous sexual behaviour. In general, soldiers should be encouraged to enter into monogamous, legal marriages and have stable families. Pre-marriage HIV testing should be encouraged and supported by all military leaders.

There is a need to specifically address HIV/AIDS-related issues within the armed forces, such as by increasing the medical budget to adequately care for and support the infected soldiers and their family members. The procurement of anti-retroviral drugs and counselling services has significantly increased the medical expenses of the Ugandan military. Roughly 80 per cent of patients currently admitted to military hospitals suffer from AIDS-related illness.[16] In the past two decades, more casualties within the ranks of the Ugandan army have resulted from the morbidity and mortality burdens of AIDS-related illnesses than from fighting the war against the Lord's Resistance Army in northern Uganda.[17] An increase in funding is needed if senior leaders are to address this problem in a more comprehensive manner. More counselling services as well as the testing and treatment of a greater number of patients are urgently needed.

There are many people in the Ugandan military who do not know their HIV status. It is most likely that, among these, some might be HIV-positive notwithstanding that they may look healthy. Against this backdrop, all serving military officers and soldiers should be ordered to undergo periodic medical examinations that include testing for HIV. Knowing the accurate percentage of troops who are physically fit for military duties will assist the military authorities in planning and policy development. Such measures will inevitably require additional funding by the government, and this should be reflected in the budget proposals submitted by the Ministry of Defence. The government of Uganda's multi-sectoral approach to tackling the spread of HIV/AIDS has led to behavioural change and reduced the national prevalence rates.[18] This approach should therefore be replicated vigorously within the military. Senior leaders should invite other stakeholders in the fight against AIDS to talk face to face with the soldiers and provide all the support that is needed to tackle this issue.

The United States Agency for International Development has been very supportive as far as the provision of anti-retroviral drugs and condoms to the Ugandan military is concerned. Other international organizations such as UNICEF and Save the Children should be considered important partners, especially in the provision of services such as education and nutrition for HIV-positive children. Considering that HIV/AIDS is a threat that does not respect international borders, every effort should be made to share experiences and strategies with other militaries in the region. Various delegations of military leaders from neighbouring countries have visited Uganda to learn from its experience in controlling the spread of AIDS within the military.[19] National policies should follow this type of thread that encompasses the spirit of regional cooperation in dealing with common security threats. Senior military leaders from Uganda should also reciprocate these visits in order to learn from other countries' experiences. They should always endeavour to attend international meetings, programmes and conferences on HIV/AIDS with a view to acquiring new skills and knowledge on HIV/AIDS control. Finally, there is a need to keep abreast of AIDS research being carried out worldwide on the emerging and re-emerging trends of HIV and AIDS-related illnesses.

Notes

Col. Charles Bakahumura is a serving officer in the Ugandan military in the position of Brigade Commander. The views expressed in this article are not a reflection of the institution he is serving unless otherwise stated. He is grateful to Col. David Muhoozi and Mr Mugerwa Leonard, who proofread the article and provided him with insightful advice.

1. Uganda AIDS Commission, "The Multi-Sectoral Approach to AIDS Control in Uganda", February 1993.
2. Martin Meredith, *The State of Africa: A History of Fifty Years of Independence* (Sydney: Simon & Schuster, 2006), p. 365.
3. Commission on Human Security, *Human Security Now: Protecting and Empowering People* (New York: Commission on Human Security, 2003); Alan Collins, ed., *Contemporary Security Studies* (Oxford: Oxford University Press, 2007); B. Buzan, "New Patterns of Security in the Twenty-First Century", *International Affairs*, 67, 1991, pp. 432–433.
4. See, for example, Kondwani Chirambo, ed., *The Political Cost of AIDS in Africa: Evidence from Six Countries* (Pretoria: IDASA, 2008); Obijiofor Aginam, "HIV/AIDS, Conflicts and Security in Africa", in Muna Ndulo, ed., *Security, Reconstruction, and Reconciliation: When the Wars End* (London: UCL Press, 2007), pp. 26–37; Lt Col. George Gyagenda Kibirango, "A Case for Mandatory HIV Testing for Peacekeepers", unpublished MSc dissertation in Global Security, Cranfield University, 2005, p. 13.
5. Uganda HIV/AIDS Partnership Committee, *Accelerating HIV Prevention: The Road Map towards Universal Access to HIV Prevention in Uganda* (Uganda AIDS Commission, April 2007), p. 1.
6. "Twenty Years of HIV/AIDS in the World: Evolution of the Epidemic and Response in Uganda", Uganda AIDS Commission Secretariat, June 2001.
7. Meredith, *The State of Africa*, p. 366.
8. N. Asingwire and S. Kyomuhendo, "Development of a National Overarching HIV/AIDS Policy for Uganda: A Review of the HIV/AIDS Policy Environment", Makerere University, compiled for Uganda AIDS Commission, January 2003, p. 1.
9. UNICEF Uganda, *Young People: Vulnerability and HIV/AIDS in Uganda, Participatory Analysis and Development of a Conceptual Framework* (Kampala: UNICEF Uganda, 2004).
10. Uganda AIDS Commission, *AIDS in Africa During the Nineties: Uganda, A Review and Analysis of Surveys and Research Studies* (Kampala: Republic of Uganda Ministry of Health, 2003), p. 3.
11. These data were provided by the Uganda HIV/AIDS Sero-Behaviour Survey (UHSBS) cited in Uganda AIDS Commission, "Twenty Years of HIV/AIDS in the World", p. 1.
12. "Ugandan President Says Army Losing Most Officers to AIDS", *The New Vision* (Kampala), 31 January 1999.
13. UN General Assembly Special Session on HIV/AIDS, June 2001, available at ⟨http://www.un.org/ga/aids/coverage/⟩ (accessed 1 September 2011). On this debate, see, generally, Stefan Elbe, *Strategic Implications of HIV/AIDS*, Adelphi Paper 357 (New York: Oxford University Press, 2003); Laurie Garrett, *HIV and National Security: Where Are the Links?* (New York: Council on Foreign Relations, 2005).
14. Stefan Lovgren, "African Army Hastening HIV/AIDS Spread", *JENdA: A Journal of Culture and African Women Studies*, 1(2), 2001, available at ⟨http://www.africaknowledgeproject.org/index.php/jenda/article/view/66⟩ (accessed 1 September 2011).
15. "On the Frontline: A Review of Policies and Programmes to Address HIV/AIDS among Peacekeepers and Uniformed Services", UNAIDS Series: Engaging Uniformed Services

in the Fight Against AIDS, 2003, available at ⟨http://data.unaids.org/publications/IRC-pub05/jc950-frontline_en.pdf⟩ (accessed 1 September 2011). See also, UN Department of Peacekeeping Operations, "HIV Testing for Uniformed Peacemakers", 2004.

16. Interview with Dr James Makumbi, Chief of Medical Services of the Ugandan Military, and former Minister of Health in the Ugandan Government, Kampala, 2008.

17. Interview with Major Dr Stephen Kusasira, Military Officer in Charge of AIDS Control Programme in the Ugandan Military, Kampala, 2008.

18. Tom Barton, *Epidemics and Behaviours: A Review of Changes in Ugandan Sexual Behaviour in the Early 1990s* (Geneva: International Center for Migration and Health, 1997).

19. Such delegations include the Sudan People's Liberation Army as well as delegations from the Kenyan and Tanzanian militaries.

4

The ECOWAS regional framework on HIV/AIDS and the military in West Africa

Ayodele Akenroye

Introduction

It is now widely accepted that HIV/AIDS constitutes one of the greatest developmental challenges facing Africa. Like the other African sub-regions, West Africa is characterized by diversity in terms of language, culture, ethnicity, politics and colonial history. However, within this diversity, the countries in the sub-region share similar health challenges, including high fertility and mortality rates as well as the impact of the mortality and morbidity burdens of HIV/AIDS. These challenges are complicated by poverty and armed conflicts.[1] The impact of armed conflicts on human security and the right to health of the population of West Africa is enormous. Not only do armed conflicts cause deaths and injuries on the battlefield; they also have serious health consequences that follow the displacement of populations, including the breakdown of health and social services and the heightened risk of disease transmission.[2] The widespread violence and instability in conflict situations erode national economic prosperity and diminish the sources of livelihood of the people. Armed conflicts dampen market economies, deflect investments from the social service sector, and decrease employment opportunities by destroying infrastructure and reducing capital.[3]

West Africa has been riddled with conflicts ranging from the protracted civil wars in Sierra Leone and Liberia from the late 1980s to the 1990s, to the civil disorders in Guinea, Côte d'Ivoire and Guinea Bissau. This chapter assesses the regional framework on HIV/AIDS and the military of

HIV/AIDS and the security sector in Africa, Aginam and Rupiya (eds),
United Nations University Press, 2012, ISBN 978-92-808-1209-1

the Economic Community of West African States (ECOWAS). Focusing on Nigeria and Ghana, this chapter explores the challenges faced by ECOWAS member states in the implementation of a regional framework as part of their national policy framework.

The African Union framework on HIV/AIDS: Missing the AIDS and security linkages?

Because ECOWAS is a sub-region within the African Union (AU), it is important to start this discussion with an overview of the AU framework on HIV/AIDS. The AU took a major step towards addressing the impact of HIV/AIDS at the African Summit on HIV/AIDS, Tuberculosis, and Other Related Infectious Diseases, which was held in Abuja, Nigeria, in 2001.[4] The Summit led to the adoption of the Abuja Declaration by the AU member states. With the Abuja Declaration, African leaders declared a state of emergency on the HIV/AIDS epidemic and committed to "place the fight against HIV/AIDS at the forefront and as the highest priority issue in ... national development plans ... for the first quarter of the 21st Century".[5] African leaders also pledged in the Abuja Declaration to "set a target of allocating at least 15% of our annual budget to the improvement of the health sector".[6] Regrettably, African governments have failed to meet the proposed target and have relied on donor support for the advancement of HIV treatment and prevention.

At the AU's annual Conference of Ministers of Finance, Planning and Economic Development in March 2010, a decision was taken to omit budgetary targets – including the Abuja Declaration's 15 per cent target – from the official meeting resolutions, on the grounds that heads of state had made a "colossal mistake" in setting these targets.[7] The absence of concrete targets tends to lead to an unguided effort in reaching goals, and this often results in incoherent decisions with no measurable guidelines. For instance, African governments, on average, allocate 8.7 per cent of their budgets to the health sector.[8] Only six African states had met the 15 per cent allocation to health nine years after signing the Abuja Declaration.[9] In addition, one of the shortcomings of the Abuja Plan of Action is that, although it commits African states to devoting at least 15 per cent of national budgets to the health sector, the initiative did not explicitly address the impact of HIV/AIDS in the continent's security sector. Nonetheless, there have been attempts to mainstream HIV/AIDS initiatives into the activities of the Peace and Security Department of the Commission of the AU.

Although limited in its appraisal of the targets, the Abuja Declaration has established some milestones. There has been an improvement in

HIV/AIDS diagnostics, care, support and prevention, as well as higher coverage of anti-retroviral (ARV) treatments. For instance, in 2002, only 2 per cent of patients in need of ARV drugs were receiving treatment, but the coverage increased to 44 per cent in 2008.[10] HIV prevalence dropped from 5.8 per cent to 5.2 per cent, and the rate of new infections declined by 25 per cent in the same period. Since 2004, the annual number of HIV-related deaths has fallen by 18 per cent.[11]

The Abuja Declaration was reaffirmed by the AU in May 2006, through an African Common Position on HIV/AIDS, which was submitted to the June 2006 United Nations (UN) General Assembly Special Session on HIV/AIDS. The Common Position calls on African leaders to integrate measures to address the HIV/AIDS pandemic with other efforts to fight poverty and food insecurity; treat essential medicines and other basic services as a human right; provide prevention, treatment and care for people affected by conflicts, such as refugees and internally displaced persons; increase the percentage of the continent's health workforce from its global number of 25 per cent; exempt healthcare from the spending ceilings imposed by African finance ministers; and ensure that officials mandated to respond to HIV/AIDS are accountable to parliaments and civil society through parliamentary review of policies and other measures.[12]

Further strategies to address HIV/AIDS were designed in the 2005 Maputo Resolution on Acceleration of HIV Prevention Efforts in the African Region, which was adopted by the World Health Organization (WHO) Regional Committee for Africa. The resolution called on member states to declare 2006 a year for accelerating HIV prevention.[13] In November 2005, the WHO Regional Office for Africa spearheaded an initiative involving the Joint United Nations Programme on HIV/AIDS (UNAIDS), the United Nations Development Programme, the United Nations Educational, Scientific and Cultural Organization, the United Nations Entity for Gender Equality and the Empowerment of Women, the United Nations Population Fund and the United Nations Children's Fund (UNICEF) to support countries in the region to accelerate HIV prevention. The UN agencies signed a declaration and agreed to ensure synergy in implementing a joint regional plan to support acceleration of HIV prevention, including key milestones for 2006 and mechanisms for monitoring implementation.[14]

Further, the AU members signed the "Gaborone Declaration on a Roadmap Towards Universal Access to Prevention, Treatment and Care" in 2005.[15] The Gaborone Summit recommended an integrated AIDS, tuberculosis and malaria healthcare delivery system based on an essential package. Like the Abuja Declaration, the Gaborone Declaration calls for the allocation of at least 15 per cent of the national budget to health.

Another programming effort on HIV/AIDS came in the 2006 "Brazzaville Commitment on Scaling Up Towards Universal Access to HIV and AIDS prevention, treatment, care and support in Africa by 2010". The Brazzaville conference was an African Continental Consultation that resulted in a set of recommendations contained in the Brazzaville Commitment.[16] Participants at the Consultation developed key principles for the expansion of health, social and development programmes and services. They also identified the main obstacles to rapid and sustainable scaling-up of existing national programmes and services. Finally, they made recommendations to overcome the identified obstacles to universal access. The recommended actions to be carried out were grouped into the following areas: financing, human resources and systems, building and strengthening systems, affordable commodities, technology and essential medicines, human rights and gender, and fostering accountability.[17]

None of the aforementioned frameworks specifically considered mitigating the impact of HIV/AIDS in the security sector, including how the epidemic undermines the capabilities of African militaries. In general, AU regional HIV/AIDS programmes and policies have so far unduly confined the epidemic to the public health and development sectors.

ECOWAS sub-regional framework on HIV/AIDS and the military

ECOWAS as a sub-regional organization developed a Plan of Action for 2004–2006 for the control of sexually transmitted infections (STIs) and HIV/AIDS within the armed forces sector. The Plan, nonetheless, lacked a comprehensive approach on how ECOWAS would incorporate HIV/AIDS into the training of the West African Brigade (ECOWASBRIG) of the African Standby Force (ASF) originally scheduled to be established in 2010. Furthermore, the implementation of the Plan of Action faced serious challenges because it was not incorporated into the regional conflict management and strategic plan of the organization. Since 2006, there has been no new sub-regional framework on HIV/AIDS in the West African sub-region. As a sub-regional organization, ECOWAS has failed to address the strategic implications that the epidemic could have for the security sectors of its member states. Existing measures and HIV/AIDS initiatives in terms of prevention, voluntary counselling, testing, care and support have not addressed the actual and potential impact of the epidemic in the military.[18]

The situation appears to be considerably different at the national level, where most West African countries have mobilized all relevant stakeholders to create a multi-sectoral approach against HIV/AIDS. Several countries have established coordinating mechanisms in the form of national AIDS councils/commissions. As discussed below, Ghana and Nigeria, for instance, have adopted National Strategic Frameworks and Plans for HIV/AIDS, which are being implemented. In fact, Côte d'Ivoire has established a Ministry of AIDS tasked with the mandate of strengthening care, prevention and community response to the epidemic.[19] Resources have also been mobilized at each country level for HIV prevention, care and support programmes. In addition, public–private partnerships have been fostered and strengthened between governments, the private sector, faith-based groups, people living with HIV/AIDS and civil society organizations across the countries in the region.

Response to HIV/AIDS in Ghana: An overview

Ghana's first attempt to combat the HIV/AIDS pandemic was characterized by a medical approach in which the disease was viewed as an individual health issue. However, as the disease spread, a public health approach was adopted. This culminated in the formation of a technical committee in 1985 to advise the government. The committee, working with the World Health Organization, was charged with the task of developing a short-term plan for HIV prevention and control.[20] In 1987, the National AIDS/STI Control Programme (NACP) was established within the Disease Control Unit of the Ministry of Health for the prevention, management and control of HIV in the country. Basically, the function of the NACP was the organization of educational campaigns through the mass media, workshops, video shows and other channels to inform the public about how to prevent HIV-related risky behaviours, particularly through the use of condoms.[21]

Condom promotion was a major focus of the advocacy activities of the Ghanaian government. The Ministry of Health, in collaboration with Family Health International, embarked on AIDS prevention, with condom promotion among sex workers as its main goal.[22] This programme was initiated barely a year after the first AIDS case was reported in Ghana. This was followed by HIV antibody testing and blood-screening facilities, which were introduced in 1987.[23] The beginning of the twenty-first century witnessed a major HIV campaign by the government of Ghana and it adopted a multi-sectoral approach to HIV/AIDS programming. The Ghana AIDS/STI Commission (GAC)[24] was established as a supra-ministerial and multi-sectoral body under the leadership of the President to direct and coordinate all HIV/AIDS activities in the country. The GAC was given the mandate to formulate national policies and strategies; to provide high-level advocacy for HIV/AIDS prevention and control; to provide effective leadership in the national planning of programmes; to expand and coordinate the national response; to mobilize, manage and monitor resource allocation and utilization; and to foster linkages and networks among stakeholders.[25]

The GAC published the *Ghana HIV/AIDS Strategic Framework: 2001–2005* to guide the national response. Five key interventions were identified: prevention of new infections; care and support for people living with HIV/AIDS; creation of an enabling environment for the national response; decentralized implementation and institutional arrangements; and research, monitoring and evaluation.[26] Ghana also published the second strategic framework, *Ghana HIV/AIDS Strategic Framework: 2006–2010*, with the goal of reducing new infections among vulnerable groups and the general population; mitigating the impact of the epidemic on the health and socioeconomic systems as well as infected and affected persons; and promoting healthy lifestyles, especially in the area of sexual and reproductive health.[27]

Some achievements were recorded in the increase of available antiretroviral drugs for people living with AIDS in Ghana. For instance, as a result of the accessibility of funds and the efforts by the implementers of some of the policies in place, the care, treatment and support for HIV/AIDS patients were expanded and the number of people accessing these services increased. About 28 per cent of HIV-positive pregnant women and 40 per cent of adults and children with advanced HIV infections received ARV therapy services.[28]

Currently, interventions are being designed to limit the transmission of HIV through heterosexual contacts. Such interventions involve promoting abstinence, faithfulness and reductions in the number of sexual partners, encouraging delays in the onset of sexual activity among adolescents, education for the correct use of and consistent availability of condoms, strengthening programmes for the control of sexually transmitted diseases (STDs), and encouraging voluntary counselling and testing.[29]

Behavioural adjustment is necessary to combat HIV in Ghana. However, existing findings reveal that, although there is high HIV/AIDS awareness amongst the Ghanaian population, this has not translated into behavioural changes because most citizens believe that they are not personally at risk of contracting HIV.[30] This shows the failure of the behavioural adjustment model of HIV/AIDS intervention in this country.

Challenges to the Ghanaian strategies on HIV/AIDS

Although the government of Ghana has designed and implemented a variety of HIV/AIDS policies and strategies,[31] these programmes are confronted by many challenges. Ghana's HIV/AIDS policies and strategies appear to be well designed and robust. However, many of the policies lack implementation clarity, which may have led to disagreements among agencies. For instance, the Ghana HIV/AIDS strategic framework mandates all sector ministries to incorporate HIV/AIDS activities into their programmes and to draw a budget line for such activities. However, as a result of lack of clarity, the definition of roles among the implementing agencies remains largely ambiguous.

Further, there is a thin line of division between the functions performed by the NACP and the GAC and this might lead to a power struggle between the agencies. For instance, the objectives of the NACP are to reduce new infections among the 15–49-year age group, improve service delivery and reduce individual and societal vulnerability, as well as establish a multi-sector and multidisciplinary institutional framework to coordinate programme implementation. However, the GAC, which is seen as the highest policy-making body on HIV/AIDS in Ghana, is mandated to direct and coordinate all activities in the fight against the disease. Apparently, when two bodies are mandated to coordinate the same activity, this may lead to waste of resources and create implementation conflicts between the two bodies.

Although the Ghanaian government has shown strong interest in HIV prevention, the political commitment has remained low. There exists a large gap between government policies on HIV/AIDS and the political commitment to implement these policies. This constitutes a major setback to efforts to lower HIV prevalence. In fact, political commitment to the fight against AIDS has been at a rhetorical level and has reduced the momentum in the allocation of adequate funding to support AIDS control activities. The central government has focused largely on developing policy strategies while ceding funding of activities relating to the policies to external donors.[32]

Response to HIV/AIDS in Nigeria: An overview

The discovery of the Human Immunodeficiency Virus in Nigeria in 1986 led to the creation of a National Expert Advisory Committee on AIDS (NEACA) with the assistance of the WHO.[33] This led to the establishment of nine testing centres in the country. Following the increased infection rate in the country, NEACA recommended the development of a short-term plan to combat the spread of the virus. With the assistance of the World Bank and under the guidance of the NEACA, the Federal Ministry of Health (FMH) implemented the comprehensive Medium-Term Plan for the nation's battle against HIV/AIDS.[34] In 1988, the

National AIDS Control Programme (NACP) replaced NEACA but still under the auspices of the FMH. The programme was expanded in 1991 to include STIs and renamed the National AIDS and STDs Control Program (NASCP). This shifted the focus from a multi-sectoral approach to HIV and other STIs to a response oriented to the health sector. The FMH further developed guidelines on key interventions, which included syndromic management of STIs, voluntary counselling and testing (VCT), prevention of mother-to-child transmission of HIV (PMTCT) and the management of HIV/AIDS, including treatment of opportunistic infections, administration of ARV drugs and home-based care.

The advent of civilian rule in 1999 led to a change of approach on the HIV issue from a medical approach to a multi-sectoral approach. Drastic measures were taken to curb the rising HIV prevalence rate, which peaked at 5.8 per cent. The then President of Nigeria – Olusegun Obasanjo – launched a comprehensive programme to tackle HIV. He placed high priority on HIV prevention, as well as on treatment, care and support for HIV/AIDS patients. The NASCP was replaced with a broader AIDS control programme, comprising the Presidential Committee on AIDS and the multi-sectoral National Action Committee on AIDS (NACA) to coordinate HIV/AIDS programmes at the federal level. At the state and local level, coordination was undertaken by the State Action Committee on AIDS (SACA) and the Local Government Action Committee on AIDS (LACA), respectively.[35]

The NACA developed the first multi-sectoral medium-term plan of action, the HIV/AIDS Emergency Action Plan (HEAP). NACA was charged with responsibility for executing and implementing HEAP. HEAP has three main components: to create an enabling environment through the removal of sociocultural, informational and systemic barriers to community-based responses; to promote prevention; and to provide care and support intervention directly.[36] The implementation of HEAP led to increased HIV-related activities in the country, with networks formed for civil society organizations, people living with HIV/AIDS and HIV/AIDS researchers. Nigeria was also able to attract funding from the World Bank, the United States Agency for International Development, the UK's Department for International Development, the Bill & Melinda Gates Foundation and the Ford Foundation. Several AIDS projects were implemented all around the country.[37]

Despite progress toward achieving HEAP goals, there remained huge gaps in HIV prevention, treatment and care services at community levels. This led to demands for a more wide-ranging response. Some of the criticisms of HEAP were that states were not effectively mobilized to action, coordination was weak at the centre and access to services such as PMTCT and ARV treatments was limited.[38] In 2004, the National HIV/

AIDS Strategic Framework (NSF) 2005–2009 was developed.[39] This replaced the HEAP. The goal of the NSF was to reduce the HIV incidence and prevalence rate by 25 per cent and to provide equitable prevention, care and treatment, and support while mitigating the impact of HIV among women, children and other vulnerable groups and the general public by 2009.[40] However, the NSF is not the only policy document on HIV/AIDS in Nigeria. Other documents include the National Policy on HIV/AIDS, the National Health Policy and Strategy, the National Reproductive Health Policy, the National Youth Development Policy on Women, the National Policy on Population for Sustainable Development, the National Policy on HIV/AIDS in the Workplace, and the National Curriculum on Sexuality Education. Other action plans include the National Health Sector Strategic Plan and the National Behaviour Change Communication Strategy.

An interesting aspect of these policy documents is the process that led to their adoption. The plans were critically accessed at different stages by various stakeholders, including 10 key ministries at different levels of government (health, education, defence, internal affairs, information, women and youth, labour, agriculture and rural development, police affairs, and culture and tourism); the organized private sector; non-governmental organizations; community-based organizations; donor agencies; the academic community; faith-based organizations; and women and youth organizations.[41] The involvement of many organizations in the formulation of these documents gave them the multi-sectoral approach necessary for effective HIV/AIDS programming in Nigeria and it is laudable.

However, one major weakness of these policies is the lack of effective communication of the policies from the federal level to the lower tiers of government, which are expected to implement the policies.[42] For instance, few of the SACAs and LACAs that are charged with translating the multi-sectoral approach to HIV prevention and impact mitigation into reality on the ground are engaged in such transformation activities.[43] In addition, a dominant feature of these policies is the total reliance on external donor agencies and their implementing partners to fund the plans.

Challenges to the Nigerian response on HIV/AIDS

Despite the proliferation of policy documents on HIV/AIDS in Nigeria, there are still some shortcomings that undermine the national response to the AIDS epidemic. First, there is no adequate HIV testing programming. In 2007, only 3 per cent of health facilities had testing and counselling services[44] and only 11.7 per cent of women and men aged 15–49 had undergone HIV testing and were aware of the result.[45] It has been suggested that some health facilities in Nigeria do not follow international standards about confidentiality and ethics.[46] In one particular study, over half of people living with HIV reported that they did not know they were being tested for the virus and around one in seven healthcare professionals admitted to never receiving informed consent for HIV tests.[47]

Furthermore, sex is still viewed as a private subject in Nigeria and attempts to provide sex education to teenagers have been hindered by cultural and religious barriers.[48] In 2009, only 23 per cent of schools were providing HIV education based on life skills, and just 25 per cent of men and women between the ages of 15 and 24 correctly identified ways to prevent the sexual transmission of HIV and rejected major misconceptions about HIV transmission.[49] In some regions of Nigeria, girls marry relatively young, often to much older men. In north-western Nigeria, around half of girls are married by the age of 15 and four out of five girls are married by the time they are 18.[50] Studies have found that those who are married at a younger age have less knowledge than unmarried women about HIV and AIDS and are more likely to believe they are at low risk of becoming infected with HIV.[51] HIV and AIDS education initiatives need to focus on young married women, especially as these women are less likely than other women to have access to health information.[52]

Nigeria's programme to prevent the transmission of HIV from mother to child (PMTCT) started in July 2002.[53] Despite "considerable efforts" to strengthen PMTCT interventions, by 2007 only 5.3 per cent of HIV-positive women were receiving ARV drugs to reduce the risk of mother-to-child transmission. This figure had risen to almost 19 per cent by 2010 but still remains far short of universal access targets.[54]

Nigeria instituted the national AIDS treatment programme in 2002 geared towards expanding access to ARV drugs.[55] The programme aimed to supply 10,000 adults and 5,000 children with ARV drugs within one year. An initial US$3.5 million worth of ARV drugs were to be imported from India and delivered at a subsidized monthly cost of US$7 per person.[56] The programme was described as "Africa's largest antiretroviral treatment programme".[57] However, in 2004, the programme suffered a major setback because too many patients were being recruited without enough supply of drugs to administer. This resulted in an expanding waiting list and a shortage of drugs owing to the high demand. The patients who had already started treatment then had to wait for up to three months for more drugs, which could not only reverse the progress the drugs had already made but also increase the risk of HIV becoming resistant to the ARV drugs. Eventually, another US$3.8 million worth of drugs were ordered and the programme resumed.[58] ARV drugs were being administered in only 25 treatment centres across the country, which was a far from adequate attempt at helping the estimated 550,000 people requiring ARV therapy. As a result, in 2006 Nigeria opened 41 new AIDS treatment centres and started handing out free ARV drugs to those who needed them.[59] Nonetheless, the resources needed to provide sufficient treatment and care for those living with HIV in Nigeria are seriously lacking. A study of healthcare providers found many had not received sufficient training on HIV prevention and treatment and many of the health facilities had a shortage of medication, equipment and materials.[60]

The NSF for 2005–2009 set a target of providing ARV drugs to 80 per cent of adults and children with advanced HIV infection and to 80 per cent of HIV-positive pregnant women by 2010.[61] However, only 34 per cent of people with advanced HIV infection were receiving ARV drugs in 2010.[62] In the revised framework (2010–2015), the date for achieving the treatment goals was pushed back to 2015.[63]

Linking national strategies on HIV/AIDS to the militaries of West Africa

As the discussions on Nigeria and Ghana have shown, most West African states have developed national strategics on HIV/AIDS and these strategies have led to the creation of national commissions on HIV/AIDS in most of the countries. However, these various national policies are focused on public health and socioeconomic sectors. They are often delinked from programmes on HIV/AIDS and the military.

Sierra Leone's efforts to tackle HIV/AIDS as a security-related issue led to the adoption of an HIV/AIDS policy that seeks to protect military personnel from being dismissed from service because of their HIV status.[64] The policy makes an urgent call for ARV drugs to be made available free of charge to military personnel through grants from the World Bank and the Global Fund to Fight AIDS, Tuberculosis and Malaria.[65] The Sierra Leonean military programme on HIV/AIDS involves education activities such as the integration of HIV/AIDS activities into the military training curriculum, sensitizing trainers to the importance of HIV/AIDS and regular workshops with battalion commanders; training soldiers' wives, female soldiers and the leaders of women's groups – "mammy queens" – to act as peer educators and counsellors; training counsellors in each brigade and battalion; establishing VCT centres in each brigade; establishing a programme to improve knowledge about reproductive health; the distribution of condoms; and the provision of ARV drugs to soldiers living with HIV/AIDS and their families.[66] Annual concerts are performed to raise awareness about HIV and about how military personnel can protect themselves and their families from the disease.[67] In addition, short audio-visual dramas have been recorded for distribution to all brigades, battalions and garrisons.[68]

In Ghana, the military established a Technical Committee on AIDS, which was mandated with implementing HIV/AIDS activities and setting up an effective mechanism for HIV/AIDS surveillance.[69] The Ghanaian army first responded to the HIV/AIDS pandemic in 1989 with the establishment of the Ghana Armed Forces AIDS Control Programme mandated to design HIV/AIDS programmes to reduce the spread of STIs and HIV/AIDS within its ranks. During this period, a policy was formulated to promote the health of troops and their families, as well as to address HIV/AIDS. The policy provides for awareness-raising and advocacy within the military command; ongoing HIV/AIDS education, including incorporating an HIV/AIDS component into the training curriculums for young recruits and ongoing awareness-raising among in-service personnel, as well as refresher and upgrade courses; the provision of VCT facilities for both troops and their families; and the training and deployment of STI/HIV/AIDS counsellors and peer educators.[70]

The policy precludes HIV-positive potential recruits from joining the Ghana Armed Forces, and in-service personnel are tested prior to deployment. Those found to be HIV-positive are not allowed on peacekeeping missions or other local deployments, but are allowed to remain within the Ghana Armed Forces and to continue to work for as long as they are able to.[71] The soldiers and their families are guaranteed access to full medical facilities and treatment for opportunistic infections, as well as to ARV drugs. The policy also stipulates that all Ghanaian troops going on overseas courses must be HIV-negative.[72] However, this policy negates the VCT principle advanced by the United Nations Department of Peacekeeping Operations. It is also a breach of the principles of human rights provisions that no one shall be subjected to medical test without her/his consent. This is a contentious issue because physical fitness is an essential feature of military service and HIV/AIDS without treatment erodes the physical fitness that military personnel are expected to possess. It is a well-known fact that a large number of people in West Africa do not have access to the much-needed ARV drugs. No doubt it is essential for countries to respect human rights provisions, but employing men and women into the armed forces without screening for HIV/AIDS will also undermine the very essence of the military service, which is military fitness. This cannot be guaranteed in the new recruits without medical screening for HIV antibodies. Moreover, the West African militaries will face huge financial strains when all HIV-positive personnel have been reassigned from combat duties to administrative duties. This dilemma calls for serious deliberation.

Conclusion

This chapter has examined the existing strategies on HIV/AIDS in the public sector and the linkages between these national strategies and the security sector in West Africa. The chapter has argued for the need to link national AIDS policies and programmes to the security sectors of ECOWAS member states. HIV/AIDS initiatives in West Africa are uncoordinated across the region. Efforts to control the epidemic in the sub-region could benefit from a well-coordinated integration process. Integration provides a platform to harness the region's huge capital, human, material and scientific resources to improve the lives of people in the region. Whereas various sectors such as transport, commerce, telecommunications and finance have benefited greatly from integration efforts in the sub-region, linking HIV/AIDS control programmes to the security sector through an ECOWAS-driven policy framework has been ineffective. Regional integration facilitates mobility of services and resource flows and the free movement of people across the region. Integration further provides an opportunity for promoting synergies and the harmonization of policies within the region. It offers opportunities to synchronize health and security concerns.

Because of the serious human security concerns raised by HIV/AIDS during the civil wars in Sierra Leone and Liberia involving the ECOWAS intervention force, it is important that West African countries pursue a regional framework on HIV/AIDS. Among other things, this should address security-related issues in the fight against the epidemic. Troops being deployed on peacekeeping missions should be educated about the risks of contracting and spreading the disease. Although most West African states have adopted HIV/AIDS policies for their militaries, these various national military policies should link together in a regional context.

Notes

1. United States Agency for International Development (USAID) West Africa, "West African Health Context", ⟨http://www.usaid.gov/westafrica/health/index.htm⟩ (accessed 5 September 2011).
2. C. J. K. Murray et al., "Armed Conflict as a Public Health Problem", *British Medical Journal* 324, 2002, p. 347.

3. David R. Meddings, Douglas W. Bettcher and Roya Ghafele, "Violence and Human Security: Policy Linkages", in Lincoln Chen, Jennifer Leaning and Vasant Narasimhan, eds, *Global Health Challenges for Human Security* (Cambridge, MA: Harvard University Press, 2003), p. 164.
4. African Summit on HIV/AIDS, Tuberculosis, and Other Related Infectious Diseases, Abuja, Nigeria, 24–27 April 2001; ⟨http://www.un.org/ga/aids/pdf/abuja_declaration.pdf⟩ (accessed 5 September 2011).
5. Ibid.
6. Ibid.
7. Geoffrey Njora, "African Finance Ministers Dismiss Development Declarations", *Pambazuka News*, 22 April 2010, ⟨http://www.pambazuka.org/en/category/comment/63894⟩ (accessed 5 September 2011).
8. "Summit to Focus on Maternal and Child Health", *AU Monitor*, 15 May 2010, ⟨http://www.pambazuka.org/aumonitor/comments/2699/⟩ (accessed 5 September 2011).
9. Ibid.
10. Center for Global Health Policy, "WHO Regional Director for Africa Discusses Abuja Declarations", *Science Speaks: HIV & TB News*, 8 May 2010, ⟨http://sciencespeaks.wordpress.com/2010/05/08/who-regional-director-for-africa-discusses-abuja-declarations/⟩ (accessed 5 September 2011).
11. Ibid.
12. African Union, "An African Common Position for the UN General Assembly Special Session (UNGASS) on AIDS, New York, June 2006", Sp/Assembly/ATM/3 (I) Rev.2, ⟨http://www.africa-union.org/root/au/conferences/past/2006/may/summit/doc/en/UNGASS_Common_Position.pdf⟩ (accessed 5 September 2011).
13. Resolution AFR/RC55/R6, "Acceleration of HIV Prevention Efforts in the African Region", 25 August 2005, Maputo, Mozambique.
14. WHO Regional Office for Africa, "HIV Prevention in the African Region, WHO/AFRO Draft"; see also ⟨http://www.afro.who.int/en/clusters-a-programmes/dpc/acquired-immune-deficiency-syndrome/features/2433-turning-resources-into-results.html⟩ (accessed 8 October 2011).
15. 2nd Ordinary Session of the Conference of African Ministers of Health (CAMH2), Gaborone, Botswana, 10–14 October 2005, "Gaborone Declaration on a Roadmap Towards Universal Access to Prevention, Treatment and Care", ⟨http://www.chr.up.ac.za/undp/regional/docs/audeclaration7.pdf⟩ (accessed 1 September 2011).
16. UNAIDS, "Brazzaville Commitment on Scaling Up Towards Universal Access to HIV and AIDS prevention, treatment, care and support in Africa by 2010", 8 March 2006, ⟨http://data.unaids.org/pub/BaseDocument/2006/20060317_ua_brazzaville_en.pdf⟩ (accessed 1 September 2011).
17. Ibid.
18. Centre for Conflict Resolution, *HIV/AIDS and Militaries in Africa* (Cape Town, South Africa), ⟨http://www.ccr.org.za/images/stories/Vol_28_hivaids_militaries.pdf⟩ (accessed 5 September 2011).
19. WHO, "HIV/AIDS Vaccine Country Profile: Côte d'Ivoire", July 2005, ⟨http://www.who.int/vaccine_research/diseases/hiv/aavp/CotedIvoire.pdf⟩ (accessed 5 September 2011).
20. Priscilla A. Akwara, Gabriel B. Fosu, Pav Govindasamy, Silvia Alayón and Ani Hyslop, *An In-Depth Analysis of HIV Prevalence in Ghana: Further Analysis of Demographic and Health Surveys Data* (Calverton, MD: ORC Macro, 2005), p. 10.
21. Ibid.
22. Ibid.
23. Ibid.
24. Ibid.

25. Ibid.
26. Ghana AIDS Commission, *Ghana HIV/AIDS Strategic Framework: 2001–2005* (Accra: Ghana AIDS Commission, 2001).
27. Ghana AIDS Commission, *Ghana HIV/AIDS Strategic Framework: 2006–2010* (Accra: Ghana AIDS Commission, 2006).
28. Ghana AIDS Commission, *Ghana's Progress Report on the United Nations General Assembly Special Session (UNGASS) Declaration of Commitment on HIV/AIDS: Reporting Period January 2008–December 2009*, 2010, ⟨http://data.unaids.org/pub/Report/2010/ghana_2010_country_progress_report_en.pdf⟩ (accessed 5 September 2011).
29. Ministry of Health Disease Control Unit, *HIV/AIDS in Ghana: Background, Projections, Impacts, Interventions, and Policy*, 2001, ⟨http://www.policyproject.com/pubs/countryreports/GHA_AIM3rdEd.pdf⟩ (accessed 5 September 2011).
30. Ibid. See also Akwara et al., *An In-Depth Analysis of HIV Prevalence in Ghana*.
31. The Government of Ghana, through institutions such as the GAC, the National Development Planning Commission (NDPC), Ministries, Departments and Agencies, in collaboration with civil society including the private sector, UN agencies, multilateral and bilateral development partners, developed a number of policies, guidelines, strategic frameworks, Acts and related legal instruments to create an enabling environment to fight the HIV/AIDS epidemic in Ghana. Significant among these were: "Guidelines for Management of Opportunistic Infections and Other Related HIV Diseases", Ministry of Health, October 2008; "Guidelines for Antiretroviral Therapy", Ministry of Health, September 2008; "National Guidelines for Prevention of Mother to Child Transmission of HIV", Ministry of Health, September 2008; "National Guidelines for the Development and the Implementation of HIV Counselling and Testing", Ministry of Health, September 2008; "Guidelines for Management of Sexually Transmitted Infections", Ministry of Health, September 2008; "National Policy Guidelines on Orphans and Other Children Made Vulnerable by HIV/AIDS", GAC, January 2005; "Early Childhood Care and Development Policy", Ministry of Women and Children's Affairs; "National Social Protection Strategy", 2007; "National Gender and Children's Policy", Ministry of Women and Children's Affairs (MOWAC); "National Domestic Violence Policy", MOWAC, 2008; "HIV/TB Workplace Policy for the Revenue Agencies of Ghana", December 2007; "HIV/TB Workplace Policy for Serious Fraud Office of Ghana", November 2007; "HIV/TB Workplace Policy", Ministry of Justice, December 2008; "Growth and Poverty Reduction Strategy (GPRS II) (2006–2009)", NDPC, November 2005.
32. See J. N. Fobil and I. N. Soyiri, "An Assessment of Government Policy Response to HIV/AIDS in Ghana", *Journal of Social Aspects of HIV/AIDS* 3(2), 2006, p. 464.
33. National Agency for the Control of AIDS, *United Nations General Assembly Special Session (UNGASS) Country Progress Report: Nigeria. Reporting Period: January 2008–December 2009*, March 2010, ⟨http://data.unaids.org/pub/Report/2010/nigeria_2010_country_progress_report_en.pdf⟩ (accessed 5 September 2011).
34. Ibid.
35. Ibid.
36. Federal Ministry of Health of Nigeria, *HIV/AIDS Emergency Action Plan* (Abuja: Federal Ministry of Health, 2001).
37. National Agency for the Control of AIDS, *Country Progress Report: Nigeria*.
38. O. Odutolu et al., "The National Response to HIV/AIDS", in O. Adeyi et al., eds, *AIDS in Nigeria: A Nation on the Threshold* (Cambridge, MA: Harvard Center for Population and Development Studies, 2006), p. 249.
39. See National Action Committee on AIDS, *HIV/AIDS Strategic Framework 2005–2009* (Abuja: National Action Committee on AIDS, 2005).
40. Ibid.

41. See ActionAid Nigeria, *Mapping Civil Society's Involvement in HIV/AIDS Programmes in Nigeria* (Abuja: ActionAid, 2001).
42. See, generally, E. Ahanihu, *Closing Ranks: An Account of Nigeria's Response to HIV/ AIDS, 1986–2003* (Ibadan: Spectrum Books, 2005); ActionAid Nigeria, *Mapping Civil Society's Involvement in HIV/AIDS Programmes in Nigeria*; National Action Committee on AIDS, *National HIV/AIDS Behavior Change Communication Strategy (2004– 2008)* (Abuja: National Action Committee on AIDS, 2004).
43. Ahanihu, *Closing Ranks*, p. 250.
44. WHO, UNAIDS and UNICEF, *Towards Universal Access: Scaling up Priority HIV/ AIDS Interventions in the Health Sector. Progress Report 2008*, ⟨http://www.who.int/hiv/ pub/towards_universal_access_report_2008.pdf⟩ (accessed 5 September 2011).
45. National Agency for the Control of AIDS, *Country Progress Report: Nigeria*.
46. Physicians for Human Rights, "Nigeria: Access to Health Care for People Living with HIV and AIDS," 15 August 2006, ⟨http://physiciansforhumanrights.org/library/reports/ index.jsp?page=5⟩ (accessed 5 September 2011).
47. Ibid.
48. Odutolu et al., "The National Response to HIV/AIDS", p. 249.
49. National Agency for the Control of AIDS, *Country Progress Report: Nigeria*.
50. Annabel S. Erulkar and Mairo Bello, "The Experience of Married Adolescent Girls in Northern Nigeria", The Population Council, Inc., 2007, ⟨http://www.popcouncil.org/pdfs/ Nigeria_MarriedAdol.pdf⟩ (accessed 5 September 2011).
51. Ibid.
52. Ibid.
53. National Agency for the Control of AIDS, "National HIV/AIDS Response Review 2005–09", Abuja, Nigeria, 2010.
54. National Agency for the Control of AIDS, *Country Progress Report: Nigeria*.
55. See ABANTU for Development, *Empowering Youth through Comprehensive Reproductive Health Programmes* (London/Accra: ABANTU for Development, 2004); Action-Aid Nigeria, *Mapping Civil Society's Involvement in HIV/AIDS Programmes in Nigeria*.
56. National Agency for the Control of AIDS, *Country Progress Report: Nigeria*.
57. See, generally, O. Falobi and O. Akanni, eds, *Slow Progress: An Analysis of Implementation of Policies and Action on HIV/AIDS Care and Treatment in Nigeria* (Lagos: Journalists Against AIDS, 2004).
58. AVERT, "HIV and AIDS in Nigeria", ⟨http://www.avert.org/aids-nigeria.htm⟩ (accessed 5 September 2011).
59. "Nigeria Opens 41 New AIDS Treatment Centres", *Reuters NewMedia*, 14 March 2006, ⟨http://www.aegis.com/news/re/2006/RE060316.html⟩ (accessed 5 September 2011).
60. Physicians for Human Rights, "Nigeria: Access to Health Care for People Living with HIV and AIDS".
61. WHO, UNAIDS and UNICEF, *Towards Universal Access*.
62. National Agency for the Control of AIDS, "National HIV/AIDS Response Review 2005–09".
63. National Agency for the Control of AIDS, *National HIV/AIDS Strategic Framework (NSF) 2010–15* (Abuja, Nigeria: National Agency for the Control of AIDS, 2009), available at ⟨http://www.ilo.org/aids/legislation/lang--en/docName--WCMS_146388/index. htm⟩ (accessed 5 September 2011).
64. Dr James Samba, "HIV Prevention and Mitigation: The Republic of Sierra Leone Armed Forces", presentation at the "HIV/AIDS, Militaries and Peacekeeping in North and West Africa" seminar, Cairo, Egypt, 8 and 9 September 2007, cited in Centre for Conflict Resolution, *HIV/AIDS and Militaries in Africa*.
65. Ibid.

66. Ibid.
67. Ibid.
68. Ibid.
69. Dr Jane Ansah, "HIV/AIDS and Militaries in West Africa: The Ghanaian Experience", presentation at the "HIV/AIDS, Militaries and Peacekeeping in North and West Africa" seminar, Cairo, Egypt, 8 and 9 September 2007, cited in Centre for Conflict Resolution, *HIV/AIDS and Militaries in Africa*.
70. Ibid.
71. Ibid.
72. Ibid.

5

HIV and the military: A Human Rights Impact Assessment of Nigeria's Armed Forces HIV/AIDS Control Policy Guidelines

Babafemi Odunsi

Introduction

Conflicts and deployments of armies across the world have several conse-quences, which would often include vulnerability to disease. The interplay between armies, conflicts and the spread of disease is particularly impor-tant in the context of the global HIV/AIDS crisis. HIV/AIDS can con-siderably diminish the capacity of militaries to perform the core functions of defending the territories of their states effectively or to participate in international peacekeeping and related military operations.

Nigeria has been a major contributor to international peacekeeping and other military operations in Africa and elsewhere. Accordingly, in ad-dition to their traditional role of defending the Nigerian territory from external aggression,[1] the Armed Forces of the Federal Republic of Ni-geria participate actively in peacekeeping and related international mili-tary operations.[2] With respect to peacekeeping missions mandated by the United Nations, the United Nations relies on member nations to contrib-ute troops whenever the Security Council so requests.[3] If the militaries of member states that contribute troops to the United Nations have been depleted or rendered ineffective by HIV/AIDS, they will not be able to participate in peacekeeping operations. The Nigerian Armed Forces, a key participant in UN peacekeeping operations and regional security ac-tivities, alluded to this in the following words:

> HIV/AIDS is expected to impact on various social and economic sectors of the country, if it is allowed to spread unchecked. In the military it will have untold

HIV/AIDS and the security sector in Africa, Aginam and Rupiya (eds),
United Nations University Press, 2012, ISBN 978-92-808-1209-1

consequences for the military readiness and the country's ability to defend itself *or take on assignments that are necessary to maintain world peace.*[4]

As was the case during the civil conflicts in Liberia and Sierra Leone, the Nigerian military, in collaboration with neighbouring West African countries, nowadays plays an important role in maintaining regional peace and stability. Deployment of the military for internal and external assignments requires fit and strong personnel. These assignments involve deploying young sexually active soldiers away from home for long periods of time, and often to a country with very high HIV prevalence rates where several local women may be compelled to offer themselves to the soldiers as a means of ameliorating the hardships of war and others resort to "commercial sex work" to survive. Because of these risk factors, it remains imperative to analyse and assess the effectiveness of the Nigerian military HIV/AIDS policy. The success or failure of this policy, however, largely depends on a proper understanding of the underlying factors that make the military prone to HIV. Because military HIV/AIDS policies across Africa raise serious human rights issues, this chapter seeks to subject Nigeria's military HIV/AIDS control policy to a Human Rights Impact Assessment analysis.

Overview of the Nigerian military

The Nigerian Armed Forces consist of three arms: the Army, the Navy and the Air Force.[5] The Nigerian military started with the formation of "Glover's Hausas" or the Hausa militia in 1862 by Lieutenant (RN) John Glover, then British Administrator of Lagos Colony.[6] Nigerian military law evolved from British military law and tradition. In fact, the force went through various transformations under British control. On 1 April 1958, the British Army Council transferred control of the Nigerian military to the Government of Nigeria.[7] British officers were still members of the Nigerian Army until 1964, four years after Nigeria's independence.[8] Until 1994, the three different arms were regulated by different statutes.[9] The three arms are currently regulated by the consolidated Armed Forces Act, which came into effect on 6 July 1994.

Historical overview of HIV/AIDS control in the Nigerian military

The Nigerian military has adopted various control measures since the first HIV/AIDS case was diagnosed in 1986. The military opened the first

HIV/AIDS screening centre in the country, and inaugurated an expert committee on AIDS in 1988.[10] Between 1990 and 1991, the Armed Forces Blood Transfusion and AIDS Control Committee was established and the military launched a programme entitled "War against AIDS within the Armed Forces".[11] In 1993, military policy-makers adopted the Armed Forces Programme on AIDS Control (AFPAC), which has been "responsible for planning and implementing various programs aimed at controlling the HIV/AIDS scourge within the [Nigerian] armed forces".[12] Over time, AFPAC has been training and educating military personnel on HIV/AIDS control through seminars, workshops and other means. Between 1994 and 1999, AFPAC formulated and adopted various policy guidelines, setting out its methodology in controlling the disease.[13]

The Nigerian Armed Forces have also benefited from the country-wide national AIDS programme during different periods. In 2000, for instance, the Nigerian government inaugurated the Presidential Committee on AIDS and the National Action Committee on AIDS as part of the institutional framework to control HIV/AIDS. Accordingly, the Nigerian Armed Forces and the Ministry of Defence officials were also members of these committees.[14] In the same year, the committees formulated a three-year HIV/AIDS Emergency Action Plan. This plan consisted of HIV/AIDS control activities and strategies, "which include many targeted at the Armed Forces".[15] At present, the policy for HIV/AIDS control in the Nigerian military is set out in the *Armed Forces HIV/AIDS Control Policy Guidelines*. This policy came into effect in October 2003 "under the authority of the Honorable Minister of Defence".[16]

The Nigerian military HIV/AIDS Control Policy Guidelines

Overview

In their preamble, the Policy Guidelines note that the epidemic poses a potential threat to the security of Nigeria, and that an effective policy to confront it must be based on a multi-sectoral approach.[17] In addition, the Policy Guidelines highlight the goals, principles, objectives, prevention and control strategies, care and support, issues of non-discrimination, and training and programme management for the control of HIV/AIDS in the military. One of the core objectives of the Policy Guidelines is a reduction in the vulnerability of soldiers to the virus. This objective encompasses caring for and supporting those infected with HIV. Further analysis of the salient provisions of the Policy Guidelines is undertaken in the following sections.

Analysis of the policy

HIV/AIDS/STI education and provision of protective devices

The policy is aimed at fostering education about HIV/AIDS preventive measures. This has to be complemented with the provision of the necessary protective devices and materials. HIV/AIDS education starts on enlistment into the military and continues throughout the career of soldiers. Innovatively, the policy provides that HIV/AIDS prevention education is not limited to military personnel but extends to spouses. Educating spouses should serve as an additional impetus in the control efforts. The spouses will be enlightened as to how to protect themselves. Similarly, they can use the knowledge acquired to encourage appropriate behaviour on the part of their spouse in the military.

Voluntary testing, consent and confidentiality

Testing military personnel for HIV can be performed only with their full informed consent.[18] The policy guarantees full confidentiality for medical records and health information on soldiers. Medical information on military personnel can be released only to those who "need to know" and such people equally have a duty to maintain confidentiality.[19] Section 35(1) of the Nigerian Constitution guarantees citizens the right to personal liberty. Deprivation of liberty is not limited to physical restraints, detention or confinement at a particular place. Involuntary testing necessarily entails the compulsory taking of blood samples. By providing for voluntary testing, the policy respects the basic human rights of military personnel. In this regard, the Nigerian Constitution also guarantees the right to privacy.[20] In healthcare settings, the right to privacy is manifested in the right of a patient to medical confidentiality.[21] However, the principle of confidentiality generally does not apply between the military doctor and the soldier patient.[22] Therefore, information obtained in such a relationship does not enjoy any confidentiality and could even constitute evidence in a disciplinary action against the soldier.

The inclusion of privacy provisions in the Nigerian military HIV/AIDS policy conforms to the practice in most countries where it is generally accepted that the protection of the rights of patients is a more effective HIV/AIDS control measure than the violation of such rights. When soldiers come for testing, those who test positive can be encouraged to inform their sexual partners about their condition or to take measures not to infect others. An absence of confidentiality would very likely discourage soldiers from undergoing voluntary tests. Consequently, several infected individuals may remain undetected.

One aspect of concern in the privacy provisions, however, is that the policy does not stipulate the use to which "those who need to know" can put the medical reports of infected soldiers. The Nigerian military, as an employer requiring medical examination to guide its decision, undoubtedly is a party who "needs to know". Doubt or fear over what use the military authority can make of medical information may still discourage some soldiers from going for HIV testing. Therefore, the confidentiality provision in the military HIV/AIDS policy may not have the desired effect of encouraging voluntary testing. It is recommended that there should be a clear-cut assurance that the result of any voluntary test would not be used for any disciplinary purposes against soldiers.

Mandatory HIV testing for foreign missions

Serving personnel assigned to foreign courses or postings are required to undergo HIV screening as part of their medical examination process. However, testing positive does not automatically disqualify a soldier from such posting. Those who test positive can still be eligible, subject to their physical fitness as determined by further medical examination, the nature of the activities to be undertaken and, in the case of foreign operations, the laws of the recipient countries concerning HIV infection. Whatever the case, HIV-positive personnel would receive counselling. Whether HIV-positive or not, all personnel chosen for foreign assignments must, prior to departure, undergo training and education on HIV prevention. This training is repeated on return from such missions.

The policy position on the eligibility of HIV-positive personnel for foreign missions is laudable. It is another indication that soldiers living with HIV would not suffer unwarranted discrimination because of their HIV-positive status. Further, with the condition of fitness being a determinant of eligibility for foreign deployment, infected soldiers would be encouraged to maintain a healthy lifestyle in order to reduce the likelihood of full-blown AIDS.

Mandatory testing at the point of enlistment – exclusion of HIV-positive applicants

At the point of enlistment, the medical examination of applicants for military service includes mandatory HIV screening. Those who test positive will be disqualified.[23] The disqualification is summary and without any reference to the health or ability of such applicants to perform military duties. The basic implication of this provision is that people living with HIV/AIDS cannot serve in the Nigerian Armed Forces, simply because of their HIV status. This raises a question of discrimination against HIV-positive applicants for military service. Because this is a serious human rights issue, it is compelling that the Nigerian military reassess its policy of disqualifying applicants for military recruitment solely on grounds of being HIV-positive. In essence, rather than summary disqualification, the

Nigerian military should consider the health condition and fitness of an applicant vis-à-vis likely duties and the extent to which the applicant constitutes a *real* risk to others in the course of military employment. Summary disqualification as contained in the policy amounts to unfair discrimination.

Care and support for infected military personnel

The Policy Guidelines recommend continuous care and counselling for military personnel infected with HIV as well as their families.[24] Anti-retroviral drugs, post-HIV exposure prophylaxis, drugs to manage opportunistic infections and adequate nutritional support are some of the measures included in the provisions. There is to be equality in access to care and treatment. In some countries, the rights of HIV-positive military personnel to healthcare and non-discrimination have received legal recognition. The Nigerian policy on access to healthcare and non-discrimination is therefore progressive and innovative.

A Human Rights Impact Assessment of the Nigerian military HIV/AIDS policy

The policy document, by its nature, can be considered a public health policy, with members of the Nigerian military as the targeted population. Accordingly, public health policies need to strike a balance between the desired public health goals and the human rights of the targeted population. This approach would engender a better chance of success than where human rights are summarily sacrificed in the interest of public health.[25] In this regard, Human Rights Impact Assessment has evolved as a device for ensuring that public health policies constitute beneficial health strategies without unduly restricting human rights.[26]

To assess how the Nigerian military HIV/AIDS policy reconciles the tension between human rights and public health, I adopt a "seven-step" impact assessment methodology.[27] Step 1 of the assessment is to *find the facts*. In most policy-designing processes, it is important to gather the facts and relevant data through consultation with various interest groups in order to determine clearly the nature of the health problem that the policy seeks to address. In HIV/AIDS control policy, the mode of transmission in a particular society is a crucial factor.

Closely related to the first step is Step 2, which is to *determine if the public health policy is compelling*. In determining the compelling nature of the health policy, policy-makers must display sufficient understanding of and state clearly the specific health goals that the policy is to achieve. These specific and definite goals should take cognizance of the factors responsible for the spread HIV/AIDS among the targeted population. The expression of an indefinite goal may indicate an indeterminate focus on the part of the policy-makers.

Based on its content, the Nigerian military HIV/AIDS policy demonstrably satisfies the requirements of Steps 1 and 2. With respect to the mode of transmission, it identifies risky heterosexual behaviours by military personnel as the principal cause of HIV/AIDS in the Nigerian military.[28] Studies on HIV/AIDS in the Armed Forces corroborate the position of the policy-makers on the epidemiology of HIV/AIDS in the Nigerian military. The policy states that "[t]he goal of the Armed Forces Policy on HIV/AIDS is to reduce the spread and transmission of HIV within the military to the point where it is no longer of public health concern nor a threat to the security of the country through its impact on the Armed Forces".[29] On the surface, it may appear that the policy does not meet the Step 2 requirement of definiteness. However, a deeper look at the relevant provisions highlights the central goal, which is to effect change in the sexual behaviour of soldiers in order to curtail the spread of HIV in the Nigerian military. In line with this, the policy places a premium on HIV/AIDS prevention education, emphasizing the beneficial effect of education that motivates behavioural change.[30] The foregoing analysis shows that behavioural change is a definite goal of the military HIV/AIDS policy and establishes the policy's compliance with Step 2.

Step 3 of the Human Rights Impact Assessment criteria requires that officials evaluate how effectively the policy will achieve the public health purpose.[31] This criterion simply requires that prescribed or adopted control measures have the chance of attaining the desired objective. In the context of HIV/AIDS in the Nigerian military, this connotes that the measures should be the best means of achieving behavioural change in military personnel and curtailing the spread of HIV/AIDS. The military policy satisfies Step 3. In fact, subject to effective implementation, the Nigerian military HIV/AIDS policy has the prospect of attaining concrete aims and objectives. First, safeguarding the human rights of personnel and caring for infected people should encourage military personnel to be open about their status instead of being secretive. This would offer the opportunity for them to be cared for and encourage them to avoid infecting others. Furthermore, education and training on HIV/AIDS prevention should aid the efforts to change high-risk sexual behaviours by military personnel.

Step 4 is to determine whether the public health policy is well targeted and aimed at the appropriate population.[32] Demonstrably, the Nigerian military HIV/AIDS policy meets this requirement. The threat the disease poses to Nigeria's security necessitates that coherent efforts be made to control the disease in the military. The following extract from the policy touches on this point:

> In June 2001, the United Nations General Assembly adopted the Declaration of Commitment on HIV/AIDS, whereby Member States committed themselves to developing and/or strengthening national programs targeting the uniformed services to address HIV/AIDS awareness, prevention, care and treatment. This HIV/AIDS Control Policy Guidelines for the Nigerian Armed Forces represents the commitment and determination of the leadership to stem the tide of this epidemic and mitigate its impact on its personnel.[33]

Step 5 of the Human Rights Impact Assessment requires that policy-makers, in adopting a policy, examine it for possible human rights burdens. This means that there should be a pragmatic balance between public health interests and human rights protection in the drive to control HIV/AIDS. Although it is true that public health demands may justify some restriction of human rights in some cases, this should occur only when it is unavoidable. Broadly speaking, any infraction of human rights should be minimal. Accordingly, the Nigerian military HIV/AIDS policy embraces the protection of the human rights of soldiers along with controlling the spread of HIV/AIDS.[34] The policy thus by and large complies with Step 5 of the Human Rights Impact Assessment.

Step 6 requires policy-makers to reflect on whether the policy to be implemented is, in terms of encroachment on human rights, the least restrictive of the various options for achieving the public health objective. Related to this, Step 7 states that, if a policy that restricts human rights is the most viable option in HIV/AIDS control, it should be formulated in such a way that it will still be fair to those whose rights are affected. There is some correlation between Steps 5, 6 and 7. Taken together, Steps 5, 6 and 7 require the policy-maker to strike a proper balance between the public health benefits of a policy and encroachment on human rights.[35] In other words, human rights must not be unduly violated on the grounds of controlling HIV/AIDS.

Conclusion: Is a rights-based policy a feasible means of controlling HIV/AIDS in the military?

From the foregoing analysis, it has emerged that the Nigerian military HIV/AIDS policy does not unduly restrict the human rights of the military personnel to which it applies. Similarly, the policy does not rely on coercive measures to achieve its purpose. In other words, it qualifies as a public health policy that does not restrict human rights. Based on the "seven-step" Human Rights Impact Assessment analysis, this section suggests that the policy embraces a human rights approach in the control of HIV/AIDS. The makers and implementers of the Nigerian military policy on HIV/AIDS have recognized the importance of human rights protection in the war against HIV/AIDS. The provisions are therefore in reasonable conformity with globally prescribed guidelines for reconciling public health imperatives and respect for human rights.[36]

The importance of adapting HIV/AIDS control measures to mesh with human rights principles cannot be overemphasized. It is generally acknowledged that efforts to control the epidemic are more likely to succeed when they promote and safeguard human rights. The military, notwithstanding the predisposition to use coercion and force to control personnel, remains a vital component of the larger society. As such, the military's HIV/AIDS control measures should not take a route radically different from that of the larger society in the war against AIDS. The military is a state institution and should be mindful of the commitments of its country to human rights protection at both domestic and international levels.

The imposition of draconian military orders and concomitant punishments for engaging in risky sexual behaviours might create a flawed impression that the military is headed in the right policy direction in the war against HIV/AIDS. However, in the long run, such measures are likely to prove unproductive and ineffective in the control of HIV/AIDS. Coercion and sanctions, the major tools for the command and control of military personnel, may not be equally practicable means of controlling the spread of HIV/AIDS. The Nigerian military, apparently recognizing this fact, has avoided a hard-line strategy by adopting a policy that acknowledges a rights-based approach. It is remarkable that this has remained the official policy of the Nigerian military since 2003. Notwithstanding the limitations of this policy, it is commendable that it strives to tackle the complex tensions between public health and human rights.

Acknowledgements

This chapter is adapted from my graduate work as MacArthur Fellow, University of Toronto, Canada. See S. B. Odunsi, "Global Security, Human Rights, Public Health and Military Policies in HIV/AIDS: Nigeria as a Case Study", LL.M thesis, Faculty of Law, University of Toronto, 2005.

Notes

1. *Constitution of the Federal Republic of Nigeria 1999* [hereafter "Nigerian Constitution"], Section 217(1) and (2).

2. US Department of State, "Background Note on Nigeria", section on "Defence", ⟨http://www.state.gov/r/pa/ei/bgn/2836.htm⟩ (accessed 23 September 2011).
3. Charter of the United Nations, Articles 43–45.
4. *Armed Forces HIV/AIDS Control Policy Guidelines*, Issued under the Authority of Hon. Minister of Defence, October 2003, p. 7, Clause 5.
5. Nigerian Constitution, Section 217; Armed Forces Act 1994, Section 1.
6. For a history of the Nigerian military, see O. Achike, *Groundwork of Military Law and Military Rule in Nigeria* (Enugu, Nigeria: Fourth Dimension, 1978), pp. 6–27.
7. Ibid., p. 26.
8. Ibid.
9. Air Force Act, Cap. 15, Laws of the Federation of Nigeria 1990; Nigerian Army Act, Cap. 294, Laws of the Federation of Nigeria 1990; and Navy Act, Cap. 288, Laws of the Federation of Nigeria 1990.
10. *Armed Forces HIV/AIDS Control Policy Guidelines*, p. 9.
11. Ibid.
12. Ibid., pp. 9–10.
13. Ibid., p. 10.
14. Ibid., pp. 10–11.
15. Ibid., p. 11.
16. Ibid., front cover.
17. Ibid., p. 4.
18. Ibid., p. 16.
19. Ibid., pp. 16–17.
20. Section 37 of the Nigerian Constitution 1999 provides that "the privacy of citizens, their homes, correspondence, telephone conversations and telegraphic communications is hereby guaranteed".
21. For a detailed discussion of privacy and medical confidentiality, see J. K. Mason, G. T. Laurie and M. Aziz, *Mason and McCall Smith's Law and Medical Ethics*, 7th edn (Oxford: Oxford University Press, 2006), pp. 253–295.
22. D. W. Webber, *AIDS and the Law*, 3rd edn (New York: Wiley Law Publications, 1997), p. 149.
23. *Armed Forces HIV/AIDS Control Policy Guidelines*, p. 16.
24. Ibid., pp. 21–22.
25. S. Spencer, "AIDS: Some Civil Liberty Implications", in P. Byrne, ed., *Ethics and Law in Health Care and Research* (Chichester: John Wiley, 1990), pp. 105–106. See also Lawrence O. Gostin and Zitta Lazzarini, *Human Rights and Public Health in the AIDS Pandemic* (New York: Oxford University Press, 1997), p. 69.
26. Gostin and Lazzarini, *Human Rights and Public Health in the AIDS Pandemic*, p. 57.
27. Ibid., pp. 57–58.
28. *Armed Forces HIV/AIDS Control Policy Guidelines*, p. 6, Clauses 2 and 3.
29. Ibid., p. 13.
30. Ibid., pp. 15–16.
31. Gostin and Lazzarini, *Human Rights and Public Health in the AIDS Pandemic*, p. 59.
32. Ibid., p. 62.
33. *Armed Forces HIV/AIDS Control Policy Guidelines*, "Foreword".
34. Ibid., p. 16, Clauses 5–8, and p. 22.
35. Gostin and Lazzarini, *Human Rights and Public Health in the AIDS Pandemic*, pp. 65–67.
36. Office of the United Nations High Commissioner for Human Rights and the Joint United Nations Programme on HIV/AIDS, *HIV/AIDS and Human Rights: International Guidelines* (New York and Geneva: United Nations, 1998).

6

Challenges to the regeneration of the armed forces: HIV/AIDS and its impact on the military life-cycle

Gerald Gwinji

Introduction

In order to survive and grow, an organization has to continuously replenish the resources that support its functions. Perhaps the most important of these are human resources because they are capable of unlocking the true value of an organization. From the beginnings of recorded history, there have always been challenges in terms of adequately and efficiently staffing armies. Historically, disease has been a major determinant of the rate at which armies grew, moved and conquered.[1]

The great improvements in public health during the twentieth century provided benefits to the military industry by ensuring the availability of a large pool of healthy service members and recruits. The survival of newborn infants was reasonably assured, populations grew and longevity improved as the common causes of morbidity and mortality, particularly in young children, were controlled or even eradicated – as in the case of smallpox.[2]

Over the past 30 years, however, certain infectious conditions that were previously deemed under control began to reappear. Even more horrifying was the emergence of previously unseen diseases, among them the infection caused by the Human Immunodeficiency Virus (HIV), a permanent, invariably progressive and fatal condition, together with its deadly complication, the Acquired Immunodeficiency Syndrome (AIDS).

HIV/AIDS has caused an almost apocalyptic level of devastation in terms of lives lost.[3] Sub-Saharan Africa, with less than 8 per cent of the

HIV/AIDS and the security sector in Africa, Aginam and Rupiya (eds),
United Nations University Press, 2012, ISBN 978-92-808-1209-1

global population, accounts for an estimated two-thirds of AIDS cases in the world.[4] Accordingly, it is from this high-prevalence population that the armed forces have to recruit and staff their functions. Until recent times, Botswana, Swaziland and Zimbabwe have had national HIV prevalence rates that exceed 30 per cent of the total population.[5] The prevalence rate of HIV/AIDS in their respective military populations is estimated to be much higher.[6] The Joint United Nations Programme on HIV/AIDS (UNAIDS) has also given similar estimates about the militaries.[7]

This chapter makes an in-depth analysis of the predicaments that have faced southern African militaries as they seek to continuously and adequately meet their human resource needs in the face of the HIV/AIDS pandemic. I examine the social, political, economic and security environment of this phenomenon and discuss the impact of HIV/AIDS on the military life-cycle. In addition, I look at the controversies and dilemmas surrounding the response of southern African armed forces to the epidemic in terms of both policy and practice. Their provisions cover a variety of issues, such as HIV testing at recruitment, the correlation between HIV status and intense physical training, retention, re-mustering and advancement. I probe policies and practices by presenting the social evidence from which they originated.

HIV/AIDS in southern Africa: A region under siege

When AIDS, initially described as Gay-Related Immune Deficiency Syndrome, was identified in the United States in 1980–1981, no one knew that it would be recognized as a "global health problem of paramount importance".[8] Six years later, it became evident that the disease had spread across the African continent, especially within the sub-Saharan region. Countries in eastern, central and southern Africa witnessed contagious pandemics.

In an increasingly globalized world, the disease then spread to other continents and countries across the world. Statistical data on the matter are alarming. In 2006, approximately 40 million people globally were living with HIV and 70 per cent of these were in sub-Saharan Africa. In that year alone, an estimated 4.1 million new HIV infections erupted worldwide, along with about 2.8 million deaths owing to HIV/AIDS, again with the majority (80 per cent) occurring in sub-Saharan Africa.[9] Prevalence rates are high and still rising in some countries, although they are stabilizing or beginning to fall in areas of the Southern African Development Community (SADC) region. High adult prevalence rates are evident in Swaziland (33.4 per cent), Botswana (30.0 per cent) and

Lesotho (24.0 per cent). On the east side of this region, Mozambique is experiencing a dynamic contagion, with rates currently at 16.1 per cent but rapidly rising. Here, HIV is spreading even faster in provinces that are linked to major transport highways connecting Mozambique to Malawi, Zimbabwe and South Africa.[10]

In terms of age, the infection in the sub-Saharan region has affected mostly those aged between 15 and 49, consequently altering the demographic structure of its population. Life expectancies have fallen from a previous 65–70 years to a sobering 37–40 years in most of the SADC region, and HIV/AIDS has had a negative impact on human resources in all sectors of the economy.

A study by Quattek in 2000 quantified the impact of HIV/AIDS in South Africa as follows: for every 100 workers, 23.2 were HIV-positive in the agricultural sector, 23.5 in the transport sector, 24.5 in the general government sector, and 23.9 in the construction sector.[11] Clearly, there has been serious erosion of the human resource base in this part of the world, with consequences for various sectors of the economy. Armed forces have not been spared the brunt of this epidemic and the condition of officers is estimated to be worse than that of the general community in terms of the prevalence of HIV, the burden of AIDS consequences and the resulting attrition.

HIV/AIDS in southern African militaries

Army personnel are at relatively high risk of acquiring and transmitting infections because of their age group, the circumstances in which they operate and their behavioural patterns.[12] Most officers are young, sexually active males, who are deployed for lengthy periods away from home, subject to peer pressure, prone to risk-taking and often exposed to opportunities for casual sex, including intercourse with sex workers.[13]

The prevalence of HIV/AIDS in the armed forces of southern African countries has been the subject of conjecture from different parties, including United Nations agencies and non-governmental organizations.[14] Information and data on rates of HIV infection within military populations are uneven and marred by inconsistencies, mainly because the figures are estimates and do not involve the direct cooperation of the officers themselves.[15] Nonetheless, it is highly unlikely that official figures on this issue will be presented to the public by military leaderships. Attempts to compel armed forces to disclose HIV/AIDS statistics have been made through "estimates" published by civil society organizations. These have been met with a "no comment approach" because such information is considered to be security sensitive.

HIV/AIDS prevalence rates of approximately 40–80 per cent have been estimated for various militaries in sub-Saharan Africa. In 1999, for instance, UNAIDS provided the following rates for sub-Saharan African militaries compared with those for the general population: Zimbabwe: 55.0 per cent versus 25.6 per cent; Zambia: 60.0 per cent versus 19.95 per cent; Botswana: 33.0 per cent versus 35.8 per cent. What then are the true representative rates of HIV/AIDS infection in the military? Although the statistics quoted here are speculative, it does appear on the ground that the epidemic has affected the armed forces more severely than the general population. However, these data do suggest that rates within military populations are at least equal to those of civilian populations and, in many cases, are higher than the average national HIV/AIDS prevalence rates.

Armies and military personnel are in constant need of renewing and regenerating resources, especially human ones, in order to assure state survival and territorial integrity. The efficiency and capability of sub-Saharan states' militaries are primarily determined by their substantial strength. Given the impact of HIV/AIDS on the general population as well as on the existing military human base, it is necessary to critically examine the process that involves the armed forces in strengthening their own capacities. To fulfil this analysis, it is therefore necessary to observe the military life-cycle and to determine how HIV/AIDS has affected procedures such as recruitment, development and retention.

The military life-cycle

The military life-cycle begins with recruitment, which is generally followed by military-specific training. Upon completion of training, a period of useful employment will follow during which the initial investment in forming personnel is repaid to the institution. This return is usually maximized by ensuring that officers on service are appropriately maintained. The maintenance period generally overlaps with the first three stages, and perhaps also with the fifth stage, and is intricately interwoven with these. The final stage is discharge but, depending on the policy of the particular military, this does not necessarily imply the end of the institution's responsibility for the discharged individual.

Recruitment

Recruitment involves the ability of the military institution to attract suitable personnel from the general population and incorporate them into the organizational structure. A high level of attention is placed on this process in order to obtain a fair balance between quality and quantity in terms of the individuals recruited.[16] The challenge here for the sub-Saharan African militaries is twofold. On the one hand, recruitment is conducted across a population with an already high HIV prevalence rate, as will be examined below. On the other hand, the widely adopted practice of testing candidates and excluding HIV-positive ones from service has stirred controversy. Social and medical scientists, as well as legal and human rights activists, condemn the practice for various reasons. This issue will be considered later in a separate section.

Recruiters of sub-Saharan armies generally target the demographic group of males aged 18–25. This is a sub-group of those who are most vulnerable to HIV infection in the general population, specifically males aged between 15 and 40. With adult prevalence rates of 20–30 per cent, this means that one-third to one-fifth of all potential recruits could be infected. As a result, given the existing policies of exclusion of HIV-positive candidates, it is necessary to screen a large number of candidates to achieve the target recruitment quantity.

Broadly speaking, recruitment has recently become a more costly and resource-intensive process. For instance, in Zimbabwe between the late 1980s and the early 1990s, 1,300–1,500 candidates were invited for screening in order to potentially obtain 1,000 recruits. The extra number of invitations (300–500 individuals) served as a buffer for non-attendance and for those who did not pass the medical test or meet the general administration qualifying parameters such as age, education and the availability of relevant personal documents. Since the mid-1990s, in contrast, 3,000–3,500 candidates had to be invited and screened in order to reach the same potential number of recruits. This was because testing positive for HIV antibodies became the predominant reason for exclusion from the army. In terms of budgetary costs, compared with 1,500 HIV tests per 1,000 men recruited in 1989, 3,500 HIV tests were needed for the same number of recruits in 1999.

Another consequence of recruiting from a population with high HIV prevalence concerns the quality of personnel, as measured by education levels and motivation for joining the armed forces. The negative socio-economic effects of HIV/AIDS on communities are enormous. Among other consequences, disruption of education or withdrawal from school remain a major concern. This occurs because parents and children's guardians often fall seriously ill, consequently losing their employment or dying from AIDS.[17] The young adults join the pool of potential recruits and bring with them their relatively low educational base, which affects the overall quality of the military. In addition, a young recruit's motivation to join the military may be a mere survival tactic instead of a genuine commitment, with reported cases of individuals lying about their age.

This situation means that the criterion of bringing true value to the armed forces is not met.

Nevertheless, the widely practised policies of testing for HIV and the exclusion of HIV-positive candidates may also limit the military's ability to recruit suitable personnel in a shrinking skills market. Furthermore, suitable candidates may be deterred from a military career for fear of taking an HIV test, thus depriving the military of potentially good-quality personnel. Failure to provide the right quality and quantity of personnel has a bearing on the effectiveness of the security offered. The social implications of HIV testing policies are more appropriately discussed in a later section.

Sadly, in the absence of treatment, infection by HIV inevitably results in death through AIDS and related complications. The loss of a soldier means a reduction in the military strength of the country, and this loss in turn triggers further recruitment for replacement purposes. Equally, HIV/AIDS has increased the baseline mortality rates in southern African militaries, which has inflated the recruitment rates, therefore significantly increasing the military budget.

Training

Training in the use of force is concerned with imparting the relevant technical and professional skills to new recruits. It also involves developing and maintaining the acquired competencies amongst active service members. With the spread of HIV across the military's rank and file, the loss of experienced infantry trainers has affected the quality of the overall training regime. It is also debatable whether strenuous training, characterized by intense physical effort, food deprivation and other stresses, may inadvertently speed up the transition to AIDS among otherwise stable HIV-positive soldiers.

Period of useful employment

During this phase, the military institution deploys the personnel who have previously been recruited and trained. Individual and collective skills are harnessed to develop a cohesive, homogeneous fighting force. If any component of the whole system presents weaknesses then the overall effectiveness is reduced. Regrettably, the age group most vulnerable to HIV infection almost exactly overlaps with the age group required for active military duty.[18] Add to this the high-risk environment in which this demographic group operates, and there exist favourable conditions for high HIV prevalence.[19] Based on this scenario, there are several implications for the armed forces.

First of all, a high prevalence of HIV translates into major burdens related to the disease, given that HIV/AIDS is incurable. Such burdens mean a reduction in effective strength and, ultimately, reduced combat effectiveness. This is not an ideal situation for any army in the world. Consequently, as argued by De Waal in a study on this topic, the security imperatives mean that military leaderships are likely to make every effort to try to replace and retrain staff.[20] This requires substantial resources. De Waal posits that the potential scale of the epidemic renders it difficult for militaries to maintain optimal levels of operational effectiveness, particularly in resource-limited settings.[21] Most militaries in sub-Saharan Africa face this reality of both high recruitment and expenditure rates. This rapid turnover is not ideal for institutional experience and is likely to leave strategic gaps, with junior leaders falling ill and needing to be replaced from other units, affecting discipline, morale and cohesion. Needless to say, the effectiveness of an organization in this setting is substantially reduced.[22]

The second effect of high HIV/AIDS prevalence in the armed forces is the direct negative impact on resources intended for a wide variety of activities. As more funding is redirected towards HIV/AIDS prevention, treatment and mitigation efforts, other military activities become subject to budget cuts and under-funding. Recruitment procedures too are affected by such shortages. Inadequate funding of recruitment can result in two situations. On the one hand, a failure to recruit can occur, with a subsequent deterioration in the capacity of the overall armed forces. On the other hand, the quality of the human resources recruited is reduced as the usually stringent and comprehensive screening and validation processes are pared back or removed.[23] In summary, in one way or another, numbers may certainly be achieved but quality will be compromised.

Maintenance

Force maintenance or sustainment refers to the ability of armed forces to clothe, feed, equip and support soldiers during their time of service. Such support also includes health assistance. HIV/AIDS is responsible for increasing both morbidity and mortality rates, both of which reduce the actual strength and force capability. Despite this heavier burden, the military must still carry out its mandated duties while also supporting the sick service members. Regrettably, mortality is an easier task to deal with because it requires only the use of resources for further recruiting. Treating illness, in contrast, involves double-tasking and the spread of duties for the army apparatus. In most sub-Saharan armies, 75–80 per cent of hospital beds are currently occupied by HIV/AIDS patients, whose duties still have to be performed by someone else. HIV now represents the heaviest burden on military health budgets. This means that large portions of the total defence budget are directed towards combating HIV/AIDS, thus impairing the use of resources in other areas such as training and equipment.

Armed forces' responses to HIV/AIDS

Considering that national armies constitute the primary tool for safeguarding territorial integrity, HIV/AIDS poses a real challenge because of its devastating impact.[24] HIV/AIDS prevention programmes are thus of paramount importance and should be implemented within well-thought-out and unambiguous policy frameworks. HIV/AIDS is a relatively recent phenomenon, and tackling this issue represents uncharted waters for policy-makers. As experience grows and lessons are learned, policy positions are consequently modified. Controversies, however, still plague HIV/AIDS policy-making. In general terms, the policy debate and the discourses generated within military leaderships worldwide seem to contradict the basic principles of individual human rights. In this regard, here I discuss the major areas of concern.

Testing for HIV in the military

Among the many areas covered by military policies on HIV/AIDS, controversy has arisen around testing and the implications of a positive test result. A closer look at testing is perhaps necessary to put the issues into their proper perspective. The procedure of testing in the context of HIV/AIDS takes at least four forms and is continuing to evolve.

The first type is mandatory testing. This implies that the person has not consented to undertake the test, regardless of whether they had previously been informed. UNAIDS does not support mandatory testing of individuals for HIV in public health policies.[25] Conversely, the agency does support mandatory HIV testing of all blood that is destined for transfusion or for the manufacture of blood products.[26] In addition, it supports mandatory HIV testing of organs, fluids or body parts destined for transfer to other individuals.

Secondly, there is voluntary counselling and testing. This implies that the process is client initiated and is based on the willingness of a person to find out about his or her HIV status. According to UNAIDS, this approach remains critical to the effectiveness of HIV prevention,[27] although authorities often question the applicability and the efficacy of such measures.[28]

A third form is diagnostic HIV testing, which, according to UNAIDS, is initiated whenever a person shows signs or symptoms that are consistent with HIV-related disease or full-blown AIDS. It is aimed at facilitating clinical diagnosis and management.

A fourth form of testing for HIV is referred to as the routine offer of HIV testing by healthcare providers, also called provider-initiated testing. This form of testing was strengthened by the advent of anti-retroviral (ARV) treatment, because clinics had the possibility of offering post-testing care. UNAIDS recommends that, in the realm of public health, provider-initiated testing should be offered in clinics for sexually transmitted diseases, in antenatal clinics that are equipped to carry out ARV prevention of mother-to-child transmission of HIV, and within clinical or community-based settings where HIV is prevalent and ARV drugs are also available.[29]

These four approaches are not mutually exclusive and have different roles in a hypothetical comprehensive HIV/AIDS programme. Nonetheless, they are all applicable in the military setting at different stages of the life-cycle of a soldier.

Recruitment testing: Which approach?

The biggest criticism voiced by civil society organizations is the exclusion of HIV-positive recruits from joining the military.[30] This practice underlines the division between developed and developing countries.[31] A closer look at this practice shows that the justification for its adoption has evolved over time. This is not because the military has taken a "justify-by-any-means" approach to the issue, but rather because knowledge about HIV/AIDS has increased over the past two decades in both the public and the military domains.

The testing method initially adopted was mandatory, becoming more informed over time. In the days when the "new" disease was spreading, the available knowledge suggested that it was infectious and inevitably led to death. There was no coherent guiding policy at local, regional or international levels, and practitioners tried to deal with HIV within the context of already existing health policies. At that time, military institutions had long-established policies of mandatory and strict medical screening of recruits. These typically covered a wide range of diseases and natural anatomical or physiological defects, including but not limited to hypertension, diabetes, asthma, short stature, flat feet and poor eyesight. Anyone who suffered from these conditions faced automatic exclusion. Communities did not question such practices; they were to some extent socially accepted. In the early phases of the epidemic, testing for HIV was treated in exactly the same way as other conditions. It was only when various medico-ethical, economic, legal and human rights issues emerged around HIV that informed consent became the accepted practice.

Examination of military policies shows that southern African militaries officially adopted the concept of informed consent in their HIV/AIDS policies over time.[32] Potential recruits had the option to decline if they were not willing to undergo the test. What may require evaluation is the consistency and the extent to which this concept of informed consent is applied. In summary, military institutions applied existing policies and practices during the early days of the spread of HIV but these have since evolved along with the increasingly sophisticated understanding of HIV/AIDS.

Recruitment testing: Exclusion of the HIV sero-positive

Another area of controversy concerns the exclusion of potential recruits on the grounds of their positive HIV status, irrespective of the stage of disease progression.[33] The rationale provided in the early days of the epidemic centred on reducing incidence rates within the ranks. That decision was based on information that has since been superseded by new data on HIV. Evidence that has subsequently emerged suggests that an exclusionary policy is not an effective public health intervention, particularly in high-prevalence settings.[34] It is also argued that more people acquire HIV after recruitment than would have otherwise been brought in by recruiting from a pool of men from the high-risk target group aged 18–49.

In addition, agreement exists on the fact that a one-off test does not necessarily exclude those who are infected, because insufficient antibodies may have been generated in order to test positive.[35] One-off testing during recruitment is therefore inconclusive on its own, and further evaluation is required at a later stage.[36]

The military's justification for a policy of excluding HIV-positive recruits now appears ill informed, and certain experiences in the military have also raised concern. One aspect that needs to be considered is the rapid progression from a physically fit, HIV-positive recruit to a symptomatic AIDS one during the first two to three months of initial training. This occurs widely in scarcely resourced settings.[37]

In most sub-Saharan African militaries, training may be physically intensive and psychologically demanding. Intense physical activity, coupled with periods of relative deprivation of food, water and sleep, as well as exposure to adverse environments, is known to accelerate progression to AIDS or to worsen the AIDS status.[38] It is arguable that the exclusion of an HIV-positive recruit constitutes a pre-emptive measure against premature deterioration. It is noteworthy that this issue has been the subject of an intense policy debate. Calling for urgent research into this issue,

Kingma and Yeager have observed that the conclusions often drawn about the links between intensive physical activity in the military and acceleration of AIDS are currently based mostly on casual observation and anecdotal evidence, on small samples and on an absence of reliable data on stages of infection or CD4 cell counts.[39]

Some military authorities, particularly from the most advanced armies, have argued that their troops are subject to a wide variety of vaccines, some for exotic diseases to which they may be exposed during a tour of duty.[40] Some of these vaccines are composed of weakened and live pathogens that still have the potential to cause disease in a person with defective immune responses. Such a complication is taken as an additional justification by the United States Department of Defense for excluding HIV-positive recruits.[41]

Global understanding of HIV/AIDS is evolving rapidly. As evidence is gathered and new experiences are gained, it is important that policy and programmes should adapt correspondingly. In earlier times, policy-makers treated HIV as a permanent infection inevitably progressing to incapacity and death along a more or less variable time line. At this stage, it seemed unreasonable to employ infected troops. More recently, ARV treatment has to a certain extent converted HIV into a manageable chronic condition, with some infected individuals living for long periods and enjoying a productive life under stable conditions. Further positive developments in this area, providing guarantees of longevity and fitness, may allow militaries to gradually loosen their recruitment criteria, especially for personnel not involved in infantry operations.

HIV testing during active service

Controversy has arisen over the implications of a positive testing process during active service in stages such as deployment, posting, advancement and promotion.

It is common practice in most sub-Saharan African militaries to deploy HIV-positive personnel who are physically fit in most internal operations.[42] Deployment of such personnel to international missions, however, is limited by the requirements of the host country or the international organizing body, most notably the United Nations. Although the United Nations does not prescribe mandatory testing prior to deployment for peacekeeping missions, in practice the Department of Peacekeeping Operations (DPKO) recommends that countries should not send infected individuals on peacekeeping missions by acknowledging that fitness to perform and a negative HIV status should be determining factors.[43] For the administrator on the ground, this means that the DPKO will not recruit, deploy or retain HIV-positive individuals, implying a double standard in relation to national policy. The DPKO rationalizes its chosen strategy as a public health intervention: "the intention is to conduct quality assessments, to protect the host population, to protect other peace-keepers and the individual being deployed, and to stop the spread of the HIV virus."[44]

Military leaderships in southern Africa have accepted the above prescription, but not without problems.[45] Generally, when a country is asked to provide forces, such as for a UN mission, the administration nominates eligible officers and publishes a list of names, thereby informing the nominees of the intended task and their potential requirements. Following this stage, the nominees convene for administrative and health screening. Successful applicants are notified through a final publication followed by specific administrative instructions. Often, rejection from this selection process has been interpreted socially as indicating a positive HIV sero-status, therefore giving rise to stigmatization issues. Counselling services are deemed crucial during this phase. The Zimbabwean experience shows that personnel tend to ignore internal counselling services and opt for privately organized ones. Owing to confidentiality protocols, it is difficult to monitor the efficacy of these services.

Another problem that arose initially but has since been contained is the validity of test results. It has been reported that a considerable number of soldiers in the region sent "surrogates" to take HIV tests on their behalf. This was done in order to surmount the selection process and to be assigned to a post in a host country. Fortunately, tighter monitoring has curtailed this problem.[46]

HIV sero-positivity and advancement and promotion within the military

With respect to the advancement and promotion of HIV-positive personnel, the general practice in southern Africa has been non-discrimination. Policies guiding assessment for suitability in the military currently exist, and personnel whose suitability is questioned, regardless of the use of ARV treatment, are assessed accordingly.

Other challenges facing the military in dealing with HIV/AIDS

Sensitivities about military data

Given the highly sensitive nature of the work carried out at times by military institutions, certain activities and data are unfortunately not available for public consumption and scrutiny. Researchers and policy-makers outside of the military have noted just how difficult it is to access internal information that may be crucial for planning and decision-making.

Resources needed for HIV/AIDS

HIV/AIDS programmes require substantial resources and these can often exceed the budget allocated to the majority of armed forces in southern Africa. Direct access to donor funding has also proved difficult, which can be explained as resulting from two conditions. On the one hand, there is a mistaken perception, shared by foreign donor agencies, that African military agencies are already over-funded. On the other hand, funding institutions employ a carrot-and-stick approach, requiring data disclosure as a condition of resource allocation. These obstacles have created a situation in which potentially effective programmes have never got past the paper proposal stage.

Policy implementation

Policy and programme guidelines are only as good as the support that goes into their implementation. The political will to address HIV/AIDS within the military is unmistakable, as evidenced by various declarations by local government leaders over the past decade.[47] The SADC, through its military health services, is also committed to the effort of combating HIV/AIDS.[48] The greatest challenge is still to find adequate resources in order to fund these projects.

Nonetheless, the implementation of policies can be beset with obstacles. For instance, despite agreement on mainstreaming HIV/AIDS into all the training programmes of the Zimbabwe Defence Forces, trainers perceive this as disrupting routines and as an inconvenience to the already scarce time dedicated to training. As a result, less time than is needed is allocated to this form of educational activity. Needless to say, an important opportunity to empower young recruits is lost because of disagreements between the different departments of an organization.

Conclusion

HIV/AIDS-based mortality rates have caused noticeable demographic changes in high-prevalence settings such as southern Africa. In addition, the chronic morbidity resulting from HIV/AIDS has negative effects on the available pool of economically active adults. This has brought challenges to those organizations that are human resource intensive, such as the armed forces. The costs of recruitment have risen as replacement recruitment becomes more frequent. Institutional memory and skills have become endangered as the duration of active service – as well as individual longevity – is reduced. The military has had to deal with severe challenges in order to maintain its numbers at optimum levels. Developing policy to guide the response to these challenges has itself been problematic for most military institutions in southern Africa. Some policies that have been implemented are controversial because it is argued that they impinge on the rights of individuals. Evidence used for the policy-making process has been subject to scrutiny. Armed forces constantly face policy dilemmas in properly addressing HIV/AIDS issues, which calls for continued debate both within the organizations themselves and with the public. Civil society and the military mutually benefit by engaging constructively. The armed forces present a unique opportunity to learn about issues surrounding HIV/AIDS because they constitute a large, demographically varied but stable sub-set of the general population.

Notes

1. B. S. Kakkilaya, "History of Malaria during Wars", 2006, ⟨http:/www.malariasite.com/malaria/history_wars.htm⟩ (accessed 6 September 2011).
2. J. Chin, ed., *Control of Communicable Diseases Manual, 17th Edition* (Washington, DC: American Public Health Association, 2000).
3. E. Kalipeni, S. Craddock, J. R. Oppong and J. Ghosh, eds, *HIV & AIDS in Africa: Beyond Epidemiology* (Malden, MA, and Oxford: Blackwell, 2004).
4. Ibid.
5. Joint United Nations Programme on HIV/AIDS (UNAIDS), *AIDS Epidemic Update: 2004* (Geneva: UNAIDS, 2004).
6. Kalipeni et al., *HIV & AIDS in Africa*.
7. UNAIDS, *AIDS Epidemic Update: 2004*.
8. H. Mahler, quoted in *Preparatory Documents for the First International Conference on the Global Impact of AIDS*, London, 8–10 March 1986, p. 78.
9. UNAIDS, *AIDS Epidemic Update: Special Report on HIV/AIDS, December 2006* (Geneva: UNAIDS, 2006).
10. UNAIDS, *Report on the Global HIV/AIDS Epidemic: 2002* (Geneva: UNAIDS, 2002).
11. K. Quattek, "The Economic Impact of AIDS in South Africa: A Dark Cloud on the Horizon", in *HIV/AIDS: A Threat to the African Renaissance?* Konrad Adenauer Stiftung Occasional Paper (Johannesburg, 2000).
12. H. Jackson, *Aids in Africa: Continent in Crisis* (Zimbabwe: SafAIDS, 1998).
13. UNAIDS, *On the Frontline: A Review of Policies and Programmes to Address HIV/AIDS among Peacekeepers and Uniformed Services* (Copenhagen: UNAIDS Office on AIDS, Security and Humanitarian Response, 2003).
14. S. J. Kingma, "HIV and the Military: Prevention Education Is the Key to Protection", address at First International Conference of Military and Police Medicine, Yaoundé, Cameroon, 23–24 February 1995.

15. S. J. Kingma, "Civil Military Alliance to Combat HIV/AIDS", presentation to the 2nd Regional Policy Workshop for Eastern and Southern Africa, Malawi, 23–26 April 1996.
16. P. Fourie and M. Schonteich, "Africa's New Security Threat: HIV/AIDS and Human Security in Southern Africa", *African Security Review*, 10(4), 2001, pp. 29–44.
17. L. Heinecken, "Living in Terror: The Looming Security Threat to Southern Africa", *African Security Review*, 10(4), 2001, pp. 6–17.
18. Jackson, *AIDS in Africa*.
19. UNAIDS, *On the Frontline*.
20. A. De Waal and T. Gebre-Tinsae, "HIV/AIDS and Conflict in Africa: A Report Prepared for DFID", February 2003.
21. Ibid.
22. C. Heyman, "Incidence of HIV/AIDS Higher amongst Soldiers", *VOA News*, 12 January 2001.
23. Heinecken, "Living in Terror".
24. J. McDermott, H. Kitchen and A. Friedman-Kein, *Global HIV/AIDS: A Strategy for US Leadership* (Washington, DC: Center for Strategic and International Studies, 1994).
25. UNAIDS Global Reference Group on HIV/AIDS and Human Rights, "UNAIDS/WHO Policy Statement on HIV Testing", June 2004, ⟨http://data.unaids.org/una-docs/hivtestingpolicy_en.pdf⟩ (accessed 6 September 2011).
26. Canadian HIV/AIDS Legal Network and Center for Health and Gender Equity, "Outcomes of the Symposium on HIV Testing and Human Rights, Montreal, 24–25 October 2005", Briefing Paper, Canadian HIV/AIDS Legal Network, November.
27. UNAIDS, "UNAIDS/WHO Policy Statement on HIV Testing".
28. Canadian HIV/AIDS Legal Network and Center for Health and Gender Equity, "Outcomes of the Symposium on HIV Testing and Human Rights".
29. UNAIDS, "UNAIDS/WHO Policy Statement on HIV Testing".
30. R. D. Yeager, C. W. Hendrix and S. J. Kingma, "International Military Human Immunodeficiency Virus/Acquired Immunodeficiency Syndrome Policies and Programmes: Strengths and Limitations in Current Practice", *Military Medicine*, 165(2), 2000, pp. 87–92.
31. R. Yeager, "Military HIV/AIDS Policy in Eastern and Southern Africa: A Seven-Country Comparison", Civil-Military Alliance to Combat HIV and AIDS, Occasional Paper Series No. 1, 1996.
32. Ibid.
33. M. Rupiya, "A Further Perspective on Exclusion of Potential Recruits Who Are Human Immune Virus (HIV)-positive from Enlisting with the Security Sector in Africa", *ISS Today*, 13 June 2007.
34. Canadian HIV/AIDS Legal Network and Center for Health and Gender Equity, "Outcomes of the Symposium on HIV Testing and Human Rights".
35. G. J. Stine, *AIDS Update 2003* (New Jersey: Prentice Hall, 2003).
36. J. G. Barlett and J. E. Gallant, *Medical Management of HIV Infection* (Baltimore, MD: Johns Hopkins University, 2003).
37. Zimbabwe Defence Forces, "HIV/AIDS and Strenuous Training", presentation at the SADC Inter-State Defence and Security Committee Military Health Services Work Group Conference, Harare, 9–13 September 2002.
38. S. M. T. Mudambo Kaka, T. Marufu and A. Tafirenyika, "The Type, Intensity, Frequency and Duration of Exercise Causes Rapid Deterioration in HIV Seropositives (HIV-SP) Leading to Opportunistic Infections and an Early Onset of Full Blown AIDS during Military Training", A Study on the Zimbabwe Defence Forces, 1999.

39. S. J. Kingma and R. D. Yeager, "Military Personnel: On the Move and Vulnerable to HIV/AIDS and Other STIs", in Y. Apostolopoulos and S. Sonmez, eds, *Population Mobility and Infectious Diseases* (New York: Springer, 2007), pp. 98–99.

40. E. A. Feldman, "Testing the Force: HIV and Discrimination in the Australian Military", *AIDS & Public Policy Journal*, 13(2), 1998, pp. 85–90.

41. R. Bazergan, "HIV/AIDS and Peacekeeping", Presentation at the Asia-Pacific Military Medicine Conference XIII, Bangkok, Thailand, 12–16 May 2003.

42. Canadian HIV/AIDS Legal Network and Center for Health and Gender Equity, "Outcomes of the Symposium on HIV Testing and Human Rights".

43. UNAIDS, *On the Frontline*.

44. G. Schnepf, "HIV/AIDS in the US Department of Defense", Presentation at the Asia-Pacific Military Medicine Conference XIII, Bangkok, Thailand, 12–16 May 2003.

45. Yeager, "Military HIV/AIDS Policy in Eastern and Southern Africa".

46. Ibid.

47. For example, SADC, "Maseru Declaration on the Fight Against HIV/AIDS in the SADC Region", Gaborone, 2003.

48. SADC, "Recommendations of the HIV/AIDS Workshop of the SADC Interstate Defence and Security Committee, Military Health Services Work Group", Pretoria, 30–31 January 2003.

7

A civil society perspective on the Umbutfo Swaziland Defence Force policy response to HIV/AIDS

Nathi Gumede

Introduction

This chapter examines the policy response of the Umbutfo Swaziland Defence Force (USDF) towards reducing the impacts of HIV/AIDS within its ranks. Using primarily secondary data and available policy documents, this chapter discusses the relevance of research in the development of an effective USDF HIV/AIDS policy. Further, it assesses the role of leadership in HIV/AIDS policy-making, capacity-building efforts for policy implementation, and the processes and approaches to mainstreaming, collaboration, standardization, monitoring and evaluation. In Swaziland, the major policy decisions have focused on the four programmatic areas of prevention, treatment, care and support, and impact mitigation; other policy interventions have focused on the cross-cutting issues of research, leadership, capacity-building, mainstreaming, collaboration, standardization, monitoring and evaluation. Although the USDF has instigated major policy initiatives to address the impact of HIV/AIDS, this chapter argues that the Force could still learn some lessons from the policies of the other security forces in Swaziland.

Research

The USDF currently maintains a database of critical HIV/AIDS indicators. USDF research work on HIV/AIDS has been carried out in partnership with local and international agencies. One example of such joint

HIV/AIDS and the security sector in Africa, Aginam and Rupiya (eds),
United Nations University Press, 2012, ISBN 978-92-808-1209-1

research projects was conducted by the Family Life Association of Swaziland (FLAS), the Joint United Nations Programme on HIV/AIDS (UNAIDS) and the United Nations Population Fund (UNFPA).[1] Despite these joint research initiatives, there appears to be some disconnect between research and policy. How best could research feed into, and influence, policy? To address this problem, there is a need to understand the most effective ways to translate research into policy; select, train and supervise peer educators; address the prevalent gender and sociocultural factors; and effectively monitor and implement programmes. Although it would appear that HIV/AIDS is a subject that has been over-researched – going by, for instance, the over 9,000 abstracts that were accepted to be presented at the 15th International AIDS Conference in Bangkok, Thailand, in 2004, and the same volume of abstracts for subsequent international AIDS conferences in Toronto, Canada (2006), Mexico City, Mexico (2008), and Vienna, Austria (2010) – in Swaziland there still exist research gaps in USDF HIV/AIDS policy. A confidential report on the Swaziland Uniformed Services Alliance for HIV/AIDS affirmed that, "despite the passage of well over two decades, a striking paucity of data, computer modelling, or empirically based analytical materials exists to guide policymakers in their understanding of the relationship between the epidemic and such clear aspects of security as troop strength and behavior".[2]

According to this report, the exact "HIV prevalence among the services is currently unknown although believed to be at least as high as in the civilian sector".[3] In support of this view, Simelane, Kunene and Magongo observed that "the HIV and AIDS situation in the USDF seems to correlate closely to the situation at the national level".[4] Relating these findings to the 2006 UNAIDS *AIDS Epidemic Update*, the UNAIDS figures could be used as a baseline for research, action and policy on HIV/AIDS among the security forces in Swaziland.[5]

Swaziland has a population of just over 1 million. The population growth rate is 2 per cent; life expectancy is 39 for women and 36 for men. The number of people living with HIV/AIDS is 220,000 and the prevalence rate among adults aged between 15 and 49 is 33 per cent. In its 2007 Report, UNAIDS reported a decline in the prevalence rate among adults to 26 per cent. This decline also applies to the security forces. However, based on the risky environment and behaviour of uniformed forces, the Royal Swaziland Police Service holds the view that "HIV prevalence rates among the [uniformed] services are significantly higher than among the general population".[6] One serious implication of HIV/AIDS, as Laurie Garrett observed, is that the epidemic is affecting the security of states throughout the world, weakening economies, military and police forces, government structures and social structures.[7] Relating this to the uniformed forces in Swaziland, Simelane, Kunene and Magongo argue:

> While financial limitations continued to be prohibitive, the USDF recognised that young productive soldiers occupying critical and skilled operational and supervisory roles are affected by such opportunistic infections as pulmonary tuberculosis, chronic dermatitis, chronic or carposis sarcoma, herpes zoster, chronic diarrhoea, lymphadenopathy, STIs [sexually transmitted infections], etc. . . . and needed to be protected.[8]

The challenges of policy-making

Because policy-making in any organization is a dynamic process that requires constant monitoring to ensure viability and sustainability, HIV/AIDS policies within the USDF should be understood in the context of the alliance of uniformed forces and the broader national security organizations. It should also be analysed in relation to the National Multisectoral HIV and AIDS Policy 2006. This policy aims at providing the framework, direction and general principles for sustainable HIV/AIDS interventions.[9]

In a study of HIV/AIDS in the armed forces of southern African countries including Swaziland, the authors observed that, in the majority of the countries under scrutiny, in the absence of a guiding policy national armies have implemented mandatory HIV testing of recruits.[10] Under these provisions, any person found to be HIV-positive is then denied access to serve in the armed forces. In addition, as part of a broader programme including annual fitness test regimes, security forces have implemented mandatory testing among all ranks. In the same study, Rupiya noted that these practices not only violate individual rights but also go against the employment recommendations of the International Labour Organization.[11]

The issue of human rights violations in the army is intensely debated given the nature of military hierarchy and the fact that most military operations are confidential. The security-related nature of these operations makes it difficult to align them with the provisions of international human rights treaties. For these reasons, USDF HIV/AIDS policies may not easily be amenable to effective human rights scrutiny.

The need for leadership

A committed leadership is essential for an effective and sustainable HIV/AIDS policy. In the USDF, as in most military forces, the highest authority in terms of policies rests with the Commander-in-Chief. In analysing the relationship between political leadership and HIV/AIDS in Uganda, South Africa, Lesotho and Botswana, Wallis observed that the available data do not support a correlation between political commitment and effective HIV/AIDS intervention. According to Wallis:

> Whilst there is no doubt that political leadership in all four states is serious in intent ... the results of that intensity are not conclusive and do not show a reversal ... [but] at best ... a measure of containment.[12]

On leadership and HIV/AIDS, Garrett observed that few leaders of the hardest-hit countries of sub-Saharan Africa embraced the link between HIV and their nation's security until the disease had spread and killed their people for more than two decades.[13] Further, Garrett observed that silence and denial have characterized the response of many African leaders to this catastrophe. Although more African leaders are beginning to speak openly on HIV/AIDS, policies and resources remain inadequate in tackling this crisis.[14] To address these leadership gaps and deficits in Swaziland, there is a need to support capacity-building initiatives within the USDF.

The USDF and capacity-building initiatives

In a 2005 study entitled *Umbutfo Swaziland Defence Force (USDF) Knowledge, Attitudes, Practices and Behaviour (KAPB) Study*, FLAS Research and Evaluation Unit (supported by UNAIDS and UNFPA) found that: (i) knowledge of HIV/AIDS among soldiers varies in scope; (ii) although 99 per cent of soldiers have knowledge of HIV/AIDS and its mode of transmission, their risky behaviour – such as not using condoms – does not reflect full awareness; (iii) about 81 per cent of soldiers generally display non-discriminatory attitudes towards people living with HIV; (iv) about 88 per cent of soldiers are willing to engage in positive practices aimed at HIV and AIDS prevention; and (v) about 73 per cent of soldiers are willing to use voluntary counselling and testing (VCT) services.[15]

As a result of these findings, the study made programmatic recommendations that include appropriate training, targeted HIV and AIDS prevention and care programmes, development of relevant Information, Education and Communication materials, provision of adequate drugs to treat sexually transmitted infections (STIs), and the opening of new VCT centres to be integrated within the sexual and reproductive health services.

To implement these policy recommendations, the USDF is currently engaged in an intensive and nationwide capacity-building initiative, conducting workshops on all four HIV/AIDS programme areas. This capacity-building initiative is part of the wider policy framework of mainstreaming HIV/AIDS.

HIV/AIDS mainstreaming

The national HIV/AIDS policy encourages all stakeholders to mainstream HIV/AIDS into their plans and programmes. The UNAIDS Secretariat observes that mainstreaming HIV/AIDS is a process that enables institutional actors to address the causes and effects of HIV and AIDS in an effective and sustained manner, both through their usual work and within their workplace.[16] The effect of mainstreaming is the achievement of organizational goals. Essential factors for a sustained and effective mainstreaming process include enlisting ongoing leadership commitment, the involvement of all levels on the issue of concern, resource mobilization and the promotion of continuous learning. The Regional AIDS Training Network states that mainstreaming involves research and changing policies, programmes, projects and institutions so that they actively promote the fight against HIV/AIDS.[17] This is done largely through the nomination of focal points and task teams, the mobilization of technical assistance, capacity development, change management and evaluation. The HIV/AIDS mainstreaming efforts of the USDF are currently being carried out in collaboration with the other uniformed forces in the country.

Collaboration between the USDF and other security forces

Collaboration implies transparency, participation and partnership. Though the USDF appears to be isolationist in programme implementation and conservative with information, some efforts have been made to collaborate with other partners in the fight against HIV/AIDS. It is now apparent that the more HIV/AIDS information in the USDF is kept secret, and the more HIV/AIDS initiatives are implemented in secret, the more the disease becomes complex, as do the policies to respond to it. The USDF has initiated collaboration with relevant stakeholders across the entire security sector. This is because the USDF is part of the Swaziland security forces, which also include the Royal Swaziland Police and His Majesty's Correctional Services. These institutions have the mandate to oversee national security. Under the laws of Swaziland, the security forces were established pursuant to Part 2 of the Constitution of the Kingdom of Swaziland Act of 2005, which also created the Civil Service Commission.[18]

National security, in this context, is defined as the protection of the people and the preservation of territorial integrity, national sovereignty, and political, social, economic and defence institutions against direct and indirect threats.[19] Here, the concept of security is broader than the mere safeguarding of territorial integrity, and is holistically situated within the collaboration of all the relevant political, social and economic agencies of the state. The legal status, composition and structure of the security forces are critical questions in considering collaboration among these entities. One school of thought holds that both the USDF and the Royal Swaziland Police operate under civilian control and are responsible for external and internal security.[20] This view is grounded on the fact that both organizations are administered by Government Principal Secretaries. The fact that the Principal Secretary for the Ministry of Defence works alongside the Commander of the Armed Forces gives the USDF a dual administrative structure, which has considerable policy implications for the HIV/AIDS response (see Figure 7.1).

In an attempt to intensify the fight against HIV/AIDS through collaboration among the uniformed personnel, the authorities of the Swaziland security forces, including the Customs and Excise Department and the fire and emergency services, have combined to form a civil–military alliance called the Swaziland Uniformed Services Alliance for HIV/AIDS (SUSAH). Amongst the military personnel working in this body, not all of them are regular officers. SUSAH is largely funded by the National Emergency Response Council for HIV/AIDS (NERCHA). NERCHA's

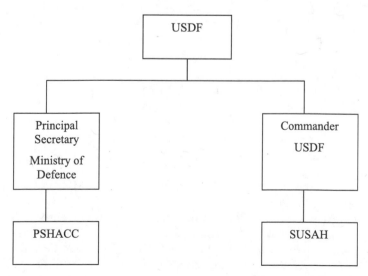

Figure 7.1 Administrative structure of the USDF HIV/AIDS policy response.

statutory mandate includes the development and implementation of national HIV/AIDS policies and strategies in collaboration with all stakeholders and implementing partners, including the USDF. NERCHA divides its interventions into the following sectors: HIV/AIDS prevention; support and care to patients already suffering from HIV/AIDS; and impact mitigation for affected and infected people. The four basic objectives of the national HIV/AIDS policy are: (i) to prevent the transmission of HIV; (ii) to improve the delivery of treatment, care and support to all those infected and affected by HIV/AIDS; (iii) to mitigate the social and economic effects of the epidemic on Swazi society; and (iv) to create an enabling environment for an improved national response to the AIDS epidemic.[21]

In the National Multisectoral Action Plan for HIV/AIDS 2006/7, the NERCHA budget includes funds for programmes by uniformed forces as well as funds for the production and distribution of Information, Education and Communication materials to raise HIV awareness. NERCHA describes the public service as including the uniformed forces – police, army, correctional services, customs, and the fire and emergency services. As a result, the Action Plan for HIV/AIDS provides for the NERCHA budget to support the Public Sector HIV/AIDS Coordinating Committee (PSHACC) in the areas of promotion of collaboration for behaviour change; enhancing Committee coordinating capacity; sector policy development; human rights training; and monitoring of policy implementation.

Other HIV/AIDS funds for the security forces are channelled through the PSHACC HIV/AIDS initiatives. Since its establishment in 2004, the PSHACC has coordinated public sector initiatives and responses to the HIV/AIDS epidemic. The PSHACC has undertaken the following activities:

(i)   training of HIV/AIDS coordinators to manage workplace programmes;
(ii) establishment of ministerial HIV/AIDS committees;
(iii) training of peer counsellors and peer educators;
(iv) organization of workshops for Principal Secretaries and Under-Secretaries on HIV/AIDS workplace programmes;
(v)   assessment of the impact of HIV/AIDS on central ministries of the Swaziland government;
(vi) review of the structure of the public sector HIV/AIDS response, and support for training on HIV/AIDS.[22]

The Ministry of Public Service and Information is currently in the process of initiating the relevant policies for managing the HIV/AIDS epidemic in the civil service. The PSHACC is leading this initiative. Like SUSAH, PSHACC is in line with the international HIV/AIDS guideline of "Three Ones": one coordinating body, one strategic plan and one monitoring and evaluation framework. The HIV/AIDS policy of the security forces is premised on the "Three Ones" insofar as the security forces operate within the agenda of PSHACC and SUSAH.

The major challenge of the PSHACC initiative is the need for the Ministry to negotiate its operating modalities with the Swaziland National Association of Civil Servants, which is the trade union responsible for collective bargaining for civil servants. This may delay the HIV/AIDS response among civil servants who work in the Ministry of Defence. The SUSAH initiative is, however, based on a command structure and is implemented on the basis of directives from those in authority. SUSAH should view its membership of PSHACC as a good basis for its planned participation in the International Civil-Military Alliance to combat HIV and AIDS.[23] It is estimated that the public sector has 22,000 employees, including uniformed forces who number approximately 7,000.[24] SUSAH appears to have been inspired by the regional consultations with uniformed forces from Ghana, Zambia, South Africa, Kenya and Eritrea, and the international alliance models of uniformed forces in Cambodia and Thailand.[25]

There is, however, no formal agreement, memorandum of understanding or constitution that binds SUSAH members together. Such formalized agreement is not likely to materialize in the near future given that, except for the army, all the other forces are perceived to be civilian. SUSAH is critical to the realization of the second National Multisectoral HIV and AIDS Strategic Plan 2006–2008, which seeks to implement the National Multisectoral HIV and AIDS Policy 2006. The plan and policy are premised on a united effort against HIV/AIDS within sectors.

Standardization

Where there is a similarity of baseline information in HIV/ AIDS situations, it is wise not to reinvent the wheel. This does not imply the uncritical adoption of best practice; certainly the critical contextualization and adaptation of initiatives is preferable to unnecessary duplication of tasks. What is needed is standardization of HIV/AIDS policy-making and programming. SUSAH is based on the similarity of the work culture among its members. This similarity resembles that of the Tanzanian forces. According to Lwehabura and Ndyetabura:

> HIV/AIDS within the defence sector, particularly uniformed service personnel, is predominantly transmitted through unsafe sexual behaviour. Uniformed service personnel live and work in a range of environments where the circumstances of their treatment, rank and operational deployment may predispose them to contracting HIV/AIDS.[26]

The policies of the USDF and other members of SUSAH would therefore need continuous attention, including review and dissemination. It is expected that all members of the Alliance will draft and review their policies, implement dissemination activities for their policies, and seek additional funding – in collaboration with UNFPA and other international agencies – to develop a strategic plan.

The earliest USDF policy on HIV/AIDS, which dates back to 1996, envisioned strategies for combating HIV/AIDS in the military. The policy was intended to provide guidelines on the prevention of HIV/AIDS and care and support for infected and affected USDF personnel. The policy focused on the following key objectives:

(i)   increasing the capacity of the USDF to protect its personnel against HIV/AIDS and STIs;

(ii) improving the management of USDF HIV/AIDS programmes and monitoring their implementation and effects;

(iii) safeguarding the human rights of USDF personnel living with HIV/AIDS;

(iv) ensuring that USDF personnel have access to appropriate Information, Education and Communication programmes on HIV/AIDS and STIs; and

(v)   providing comprehensive healthcare and social support for USDF members living with HIV/AIDS.[27]

In the pursuit of collaboration and standardization, SUSAH was initiated by the USDF. The leadership has since been passed on to the police. It is not clear, however, whether the policies of the Alliance will be relevant to the USDF simply because the USDF is not a civilian institution like the other institutions that comprise the alliance.

Conclusions and policy recommendations

There is a need to track HIV/AIDS programmes to determine policy evolution and effective implementation. In the context of the security sector in Swaziland, this involves understanding the impact, gaps and limits of past, existing and evolving policies, and evaluating the lessons learned and new approaches for overcoming barriers in effectively implementing programmes. First, priority should be given to research that addresses ways to effectively influence policy-makers and address cultural factors relating to HIV/AIDS. Second, there is a need for a plan of action for the implementation of recommendations made by researchers together with a sustainability plan by the USDF leadership. The current HIV/AIDS capacity-building initiatives should be improved and supported. Third, the USDF should adopt a more pragmatic and open approach in collaborating with other security forces and local partners in the fight against HIV/AIDS. Equally, USDF HIV/AIDS initiatives should incorporate key human rights principles and considerations, and should be aligned with the standard HIV/AIDS practices and policies of the other security agencies. This will enable the USDF to enhance its policies and programmes and leverage resources for maximum impact. Although the USDF has made some progress in addressing the menace of HIV/AIDS, there are still a number of lessons that it could learn from the experience of the other security forces.

Notes

1. FLAS Research and Evaluation Unit, *Umbutfo Swaziland Defence Force (USDF) Knowledge, Attitudes, Practices and Behaviour (KAPB) Study: Study Findings Report* (FLAS, 2005).
2. Swaziland Uniformed Services Alliance for HIV/AIDS (SUSAH), "Summary of activities", personal communication, 2007, p. 18.
3. Ibid.
4. H. S. Simelane, S. C. Kunene and T. Magongo, "HIV/AIDS in the Umbufto Swaziland Defence Force", in M. Rupiya, ed., *The Enemy Within: Southern African Militaries' Quarter-Century Battle with HIV and AIDS* (Pretoria: Institute for Security Studies, 2006), pp. 65–90, at p. 89.
5. Joint United Nations Programme on HIV/AIDS (UNAIDS), *AIDS Epidemic Update: Special Report on HIV/AIDS: December 2006* (Geneva: UNAIDS, 2006), p. 460.
6. Government of the Kingdom of Swaziland, *The Royal Swaziland Police Service HIV and AIDS Prevention, Care and Impact Mitigation Programme: Strategic Plan 2007–2009* (Mbabane: Government of the Kingdom of Swaziland, 2006), p. 12.
7. L. Garrett, *HIV and National Security: Where Are the Links?* (New York: Council on Foreign Relations, 2005); ⟨http://www.cfr.org/publication/8256/hiv_and_national_security.html⟩ (accessed 7 September 2011).
8. Simelane, Kunene and Magongo, "HIV/AIDS in the Umbufto Swaziland Defence Force", p. 75.
9. Government of the Kingdom of Swaziland, *The National Multisectoral HIV and AIDS Policy* (Mbabane: Government of the Kingdom of Swaziland, 2006), p. iii.
10. Rupiya, *The Enemy Within*, pp. 1–18.
11. Rupiya, "Lessons Learned", in *The Enemy Within*, p. 196.
12. M. Wallis, "Political and Managerial Leadership and the HIV&AIDS Pandemic: Four Cases from Africa", unpublished AAPAM paper, 2007.
13. Garrett, *HIV and National Security*.
14. Human Rights Watch, *World Report 2002* (New York: Human Rights Watch, 2002).
15. FLAS Research and Evaluation Unit, *Umbutfo Swaziland Defence Force (USDF) Knowledge, Attitudes, Practices and Behaviour (KAPB) Study*.
16. UNAIDS Secretariat, "Strategy Note and Action Framework, 2004–2005", in *Multidisciplinary Programme for Integrating HIV/AIDS and Development into Curricula of Selected African Universities Learning Package for Module 5 and 6* (University of Limpopo, SIDA, UNDP, UNOPS, 2005), pp. 40–75.
17. Regional AIDS Training Network, "Module on Gender and HIV&AIDS: An Overview", Nairobi, Kenya, 2005, p. 13.

18. Government of the Kingdom of Swaziland, *The Constitution of the Kingdom of Swaziland Act, 2005*, ⟨http://www.gov.sz/images/stories/Constitution%20of%20%20SD-2005A001.pdf⟩ (accessed 7 September 2011).
19. Garrett, *HIV and National Security*, p. 7.
20. US Department of State, "Swaziland: Country Reports on Human Rights Practices", Bureau of Democracy, Human Rights, and Labor, 2004, ⟨http://www.state.gov/g/drl/rls/hrrpt/2003/27754.htm⟩ (accessed 7 September 2011).
21. Government of the Kingdom of Swaziland, *The National Multisectoral HIV and AIDS Policy*, p. 4.
22. Government of the Kingdom of Swaziland, *The Royal Swaziland Police Service HIV and AIDS Prevention, Care and Impact Mitigation Programme*, p. 12.
23. SUSAH, "Summary of Activities", 2007.
24. Government of the Kingdom of Swaziland, *The Royal Swaziland Police Service HIV and AIDS Prevention, Care and Impact Mitigation Programme*, p. 14.
25. Ibid.
26. J. M. K. Lwehabura and J. K. Ndyetabura, "Implementation of Tanzanian National Policy on HIV/AIDS in Relation to the Defence Sector", in Rupiya, *The Enemy Within*, pp. 125–155, at p. 137 .
27. Simelane, Kunene and Magongo, "HIV/AIDS in the Umbufto Swaziland Defence Force", p. 81.

Part II

HIV/AIDS and peacekeeping in Africa

8

Culture and HIV/AIDS in African peacekeeping operations

Gwinyayi Albert Dzinesa

What I believe has happened in the UN peacekeeping missions is that a hyper-masculine culture prevails there. Even the women who work there act in a traditionally male-gendered manner. (Sarah Martin[1])

The UN is also struggling with aspects of military culture that can contribute to sexual misconduct by peacekeepers ... Soldiers are, of necessity, trained to be aggressive, physically dominant and willing to take risks. It has long been recognized that such battlefield virtues can spill over into relations between troops and local civilian populations – particularly when large numbers of young men are removed from the cultural and legal constraints back home. (Michael Fleshman[2])

Introduction

Many African states, including the Democratic Republic of the Congo (DRC), Liberia, Sudan, Côte d'Ivoire, Ethiopia and Eritrea, have recently hosted United Nations (UN) peace operations. Incidents of sexual exploitation and abuse that facilitate HIV transmission have been allegedly reported in the majority of these operations. These phenomena have been attributed to a hyper-masculine military culture that is embedded in troops involved in peacekeeping. This culture has an impact on individual soldiers' characteristics such as knowledge, attitudes, behaviour/beliefs and practice, thus favouring HIV transmission and hindering prevention. It does not, however, usually operate in isolation from the local socio-economic contexts in conflict and post-conflict societies, which are often characterized by poverty and lack of opportunities for sustainable

HIV/AIDS and the security sector in Africa, Aginam and Rupiya (eds),
United Nations University Press, 2012, ISBN 978-92-808-1209-1

livelihoods. This chapter examines the nexus of culture and HIV/AIDS in peacekeeping. The discussion follows in three main sections. The first section explains a conceptual framework for analysing the links between culture, HIV/AIDS transmission and HIV/AIDS prevention in a peacekeeping environment. It does this by looking at the broader definition of culture as well as military-specific sub-cultures. The second section comprises empirically informed and context-specific analyses of the relationship between culture in its various forms and HIV/AIDS. The discussion here adopts two modes of assessing the connection between culture and HIV/AIDS and examines the context of current operational areas and main troop-contributing countries. The third and concluding section suggests policy interventions to cultural factors in the transmission, prevention and care of HIV/AIDS in peacekeeping.

Conceptualizing culture and HIV/AIDS in a peacekeeping environment: A framework for analysis

Peace operations are generally provided with three main categories of personnel: military, police and civilian.[3] The empirical analysis is here focused on the military component, which represents the most substantial amongst the operations in the African region. Recently, there have been six UN operations in the area, which involve 54,841 uniformed personnel. This section provides a conceptual backdrop of culture and HIV/AIDS in a peacekeeping environment. HIV/AIDS prevention and transmission are located in the broader cultural context in which people's sexual knowledge, attitudes, behaviour/beliefs and practice, as well as sexual health, are embedded. Culture is a crucial determinant of how peacekeepers conduct themselves in an operational environment. Diverse cultural backgrounds and settings influence knowledge, attitudes, behaviour/ beliefs, practice and sexual health in different ways.

Culture, which is probably one of the most difficult terms to define, can indicate a range of accepted and shared intergenerational norms and values. In this chapter's review of the cultural dynamics relating to sexual practice, HIV/AIDS and health in a peacekeeping context, military culture is depicted as a unique way of life that is learned through socialization training such as boot camps. It is broadly shared by its members (for example, saluting), adaptive to changing conditions and symbolic in nature (for example, rank insignia and language jargon make sense only within a military context).[4] It represents the complex capacity of military forces to prepare for and adequately perform in combat situations.

The military culture and the HIV/AIDS nexus have two broad dimensions – transmission and prevention. The transmission dynamic emerges from the characterization of the military culture by its combat, masculine-warrior (CMW) paradigm.[5] Lindsay and Mieschier refer to masculinity as a culturally and historically constructed "cluster of norms, values, and behavioural patterns expressing explicit and implicit expectations of how men should act and represent themselves to others".[6] Cultural constructions of masculinity also legitimize male authority.[7] The stereotypical image of CMW is based on the military institution being primarily composed of men, with its culture, values and norms shaped by men themselves. The hyper-masculine military culture that stresses male physical strength is embedded in peacekeeping operations and is linked to incidents of sexual abuse and exploitation[8] that could facilitate HIV transmission. According to Valenius,

> Peacekeepers' camps are masculine spaces. Men dominate and define the space by their sheer numbers and uniform bodily presence. More precisely, it is not exactly men who characterize the space, but there is a certain type of masculinity that permeates and defines it, the heteromasculinity of 22–24 year old men. It is a type of masculinity with which not everyone, man or woman, can identify, but has to be tolerated in order to cope with their daily reality ... When this kind of masculinity is accepted as the norm, it is easy to slide in the essentialist "boys will be boys" explanation when sexual harassment and other violations of the code of conduct take place.[9]

> One of the problems in addressing sexual exploitation and abuse in UN peacekeeping missions is the hyper-masculine culture and the tradition of silence that has evolved from this culture. The bulk of personnel in peacekeeping missions are men. As of July 2004, women represented 4.4% of civilian police and 1% of military personnel working in peacekeeping operations.[10]

The hyper-masculine military culture has an impact on HIV prevention and transmission in peacekeeping environments. This is because peacekeepers are inclined to the military "macho-image/risk-taking ethos" and behaviour.[11] In a context where death and injury are common, there is a tendency to perceive HIV simply as an additional threat to health/life. The CMW paradigm and the social construction of virile masculinity and invincibility increase risk-taking by peacekeepers. Masculinity is associated with physical strength and bravery, a key coping mechanism whereby peacekeepers deal with harsh and dangerous theatres of operations. It is imbued with a sense of manly physical strength, personal invulnerability and high levels of sexual activity. The CMW paradigm may thus undermine the culture of correct and consistent condom use by peacekeepers in favour of engaging in the more pleasurable but dangerous flesh-to-flesh sexual encounters. This is also linked to beliefs that ejaculating semen inside a woman signifies virile potency. Although the UN Department of Peacekeeping Operations (DPKO) provides condoms, some peacekeepers mentioned "that being in the field meant that they did not have to wear a rubber".[12] Ironically, AIDS symptoms such as distress and a weakened body represent the inverse phenomenon of this idea of masculinity.

Peacekeepers enter and exit different cultures through deployment in diverse missions abroad. They thus fit the popular image of male travellers through their journey, who reminisce about encounters abroad upon debriefing. Peacekeepers are likely to have stories to tell when they return home. In most instances the "interesting" tales about the tour of duty of the hyper-masculine traveller include: the quantity of trophies or scalps, the figure of foreign women with whom they had sexual intercourse, or of whom they had a tattoo, or even how many of these women were impregnated. All of the abovementioned factors fall into the CMW paradigm. The CMW idea, combined with weapon possession and the potential higher financial resources, may facilitate male sexual domination over women and girls and consequently jeopardize health conditions in areas of deployment. As Loconte observed in *The Weekly Standard*:

> Various UN reports and interviews with humanitarian groups suggest that international peacekeeping missions are creating a predatory sex culture among vulnerable refugees – from relief workers who demand sexual favours in exchange for food to UN troops who rape women at gunpoint.[13]

Peacekeepers, because of these abuses, have been characterized as "hypermasculine men, barely able to control their rampant heterosexuality".[14] Instead of being bearers of peace, they become predators of the war-torn citizenry they are supposed to protect. This has the effect of further intimidating and suppressing the rights of indigenous female individuals. The scourges of "sexual exploitation and abuse occur in most communities fragmented by conflict and devastated by war and poverty".[15] Yet the misconduct of a few soldiers can undermine the image of the majority of those peacekeepers who are committed to discipline and to upholding the purpose of their mandate.

Peacekeeping bases attract sex workers and women in poverty and war-stricken regions for two main plausible reasons. First, deployed peacekeepers have "economic power gained from allowances"[16] and represent "a hot commodity" for sex workers.[17] Higate noted that soldiering and prostitution are considered to be the "two oldest professions" and that they "feed off one another and exist in a symbiotic relationship".[18] Peacekeepers become the "demand side" of an act of sexual misconduct. Cultures of poverty provide the "supply side"[19] since the exchange of money for sexual services violates the standards of conduct expected of peacekeepers.

The ready availability of commercial sex opportunities in the vicinity, coupled with the CMW paradigm of peacekeepers, conspires to complicate sexual exploitation. The pre-deployment, induction and in-mission HIV/AIDS education and training may not necessarily result in positive behavioural changes in the field. The "500k" rule in the masculinized military culture – that is, "when you are over 500km from home, sex with someone other than your wife or girlfriend is acceptable"[20] – illustrates this prevailing worldview of a sizeable number of peacekeepers. Peacekeeping environments restrict opportunities for the development of stable sentimental relationships. The "boys will be boys" culture[21] may result in soldiers engaging in sexual misconduct and commercial or consensual peacekeeper-to-peacekeeper sexual intercourse. In these instances, consistent condom use can only be hoped for.

The second plausible reason for the attractiveness of these camps to women may possibly be rooted in the traditional masculinity–security–provider dynamic. In fact, protection is traditionally associated with men and masculinity. In conflict zones where women might have faced threats from the diverse warring factions, the presence of peacekeepers symbolizes protection. In the eyes of insecure women, peacekeeping soldiers are perceived as the sole providers of real security. Accordingly, sexual exploitation evolves into a means of survival. In this context, women stationing close to these secure environments inevitably provide sexual favours to soldiers. Sexual favours are often perceived as an expression of gratitude to the protective male peacekeepers while performing their "men" jobs. These behavioural patterns further integrate into the broader hyper-masculine culture of military bases.

The cultural construction of gender-disempowered women has a negative impact on their control of their own bodies and undermines sexual health. This situation creates a favourable scenario for the spread of HIV. The social prevalence of patriarchy in conflict-ridden operational contexts and institutionalized male dominance correlates to hierarchy, gender, culture and violence.[22] Alex de Waal observed that "[t]he subordinate position of women and girls – politically, socially and in sexual encounters – is ingrained in every aspect of the epidemic".[23] Poverty, coupled with low levels of assertiveness and confidence among women, is an important aspect in the numerous cases of sexual abuse and exploitation committed. Iain Levine, of Human Rights Watch, stated:

[S]o often, when you have a peacekeeping situation with extreme poverty where women and girls with extremely low standing in society, with very limited economic opportunities and a lack of accountability on the part of peacekeepers, we have seen sexual exploitation and abuse as a result.[24]

Broadly speaking, women who live in impoverished and insecure conflict environments are much more likely to lack control over their life and sexual health. Starvation has much more immediate consequences compared with the generally more gradual effect of HIV/AIDS. To aggravate the situation, certain traditional and religious contexts promote "a culture of cover-up, in which babies born to peacekeepers and sex crimes committed by UN staff ... have been kept secret because of a 'fear of shame and embarrassment'".[25] This was the case in conservative and deeply Catholic Timor, where Timorese victims of UN peacekeepers' misconduct were stigmatized by their own communities.

The narrative of women as "helpless victims of poverty and male dominance" may not be universal, and assertive women may be even more vulnerable in relation to demure women. As Caprioli noted: "Although the power and the role of women vary across cultures, women are always unequal in both the economic and the political sphere ... thus making gender equality a useful cross-national variable."[26]

Male-dominated cultures exist where women are socialized to "over-respect" men and to relate to them in a submissive and obedient manner. Women in societies shattered by conflict also typically lack the economic, psychological and social support resources to protect their sexual health. Culture – as a concept within peace operations and in the areas of deployment – is a critical factor in the transmission and prevention of HIV. Peace operations themselves are not monolithic in culture or their understanding of masculinity. Troops may come from areas of low sero-positivity rates but come into contact with peacekeepers from different countries, cultures and masculinities. This may influence behaviour bordering on sexual misconduct during deployment.

The military cultures' HIV prevention dimension can be linked to the customary good order and discipline of soldiers. Well-functioning armies are likely to be those that are highly disciplined in order to facilitate command and control.[27] Peacekeepers also undergo pre-deployment, induction and in-mission training in HIV/AIDS. Some southern African militaries also have policies of mandatory pre-deployment testing. (If, however, the peacekeepers are tested during the "window period" during which those infected will have no antibodies against HIV, it may be difficult to come up with a definitive diagnosis. This means that discipline and consistent condom use are critical.)[28]

The United Nations has a clear zero tolerance policy on sexual exploitation and abuse, and has codes of conduct for peacekeepers. These are clearly outlined in two UN documents: "We Are United Nations Peacekeepers"[29] and "Ten Rules: Code of Personal Conduct for Blue Helmets".[30] These codes of conduct hold peacekeepers accountable for specific standards of behaviour and thus provide a mechanism to regulate their differential power as well as manners. Current UN operations have policies that aim to improve and implement conduct together with discipline.[31] Peacekeepers are given condoms by the DPKO[32] and HIV/AIDS awareness cards by the Joint United Nations Programme on HIV/AIDS (UNAIDS). In an ideal world, the knowledge acquired would result in 100 per cent correct condom usage and would become embedded in the peacekeepers' culture of discipline. Nonetheless, the diversity of cultures among peacekeepers needs to be considered when crafting these intervention strategies. The above factors combined may reduce acts of risky sexual behaviour and misconduct by peacekeepers. Against this backdrop, the culture of "boys will always be boys" may be addressed, theoretically making peacekeepers agents of change so that they become capable of assisting with HIV prevention in areas of deployment. In order to do this, they would need to be sensitive to the social and cultural contexts in deployed areas.[33] As a result of some of the factors mentioned above, sound knowledge, training and possession of condoms do not necessarily result in healthy and responsible sexual behaviour.

Culture and HIV/AIDS in a peacekeeping environment: An empirical and contextual survey

Notwithstanding that current operations are in low HIV-infected areas (see Table 8.1), there is a possibility that non-infected peacekeepers may get infected with HIV when in areas of deployment. The depressed

Table 8.1 Locations of peace operations in Africa and levels of HIV infection as at 2007

Operation	Total uniformed personnel	Percentage of adults (15–49) infected with HIV/AIDS
DRC	18,352	3.2
Liberia	15,318	2–5
Sudan	10,066	1.6
Côte d'Ivoire	9,196	7.1
Ethiopia	1,686	0.9–3.5
Eritrea		2.4
Western Sahara	223	N/A

Sources: Peacekeeping figures as of 30 September 2007 obtained from UN Department of Peacekeeping Operations, ⟨http://www.un.org/Depts/dpko/dpko/⟩ (accessed 7 September 2011); HIV/AIDS infection rates based on data published by UNAIDS in 2007 on "Country Specific Estimates on HIV/AIDS"; see also UNAIDS, *AIDS Epidemic Update* (Geneva: UNAIDS and WHO, December 2007), available at ⟨http://data.unaids.org/pub/epislides/2007/2007_epiupdate_en.pdf⟩ (accessed 27 September 2011).

Table 8.2 Top 10 troop-contributing African countries and levels of HIV infection

Country	No. of peacekeepers	Percentage of adults (15–49) infected with HIV/AIDS
Ghana	2,905	2.3
Nigeria	2,470	3.9
Senegal	1,921	0.9
Ethiopia	1,826	0.9–3.5
Morocco	1,550	0.1
Benin	1,312	1.8
South Africa	1,180	18.8
Kenya	1,089	6.1
Egypt	959	< 0.1
Namibia	654	19.6

Sources: Peacekeeping figures obtained from UN Department of Peacekeeping Operations, "Ranking of Military and Police Contributions to UN Operations", 30 April 2007, ⟨http://www.un.org/Depts/dpko/dpko/contributors/2007/apr07_2.pdf⟩ (accessed 7 September 2011); HIV/AIDS infection rates based on data published by UNAIDS in 2007 on "Country Specific Estimates on HIV/AIDS"; see also UNAIDS, *AIDS Epidemic Update* (Geneva: UNAIDS and WHO, December 2007), available at ⟨http://data.unaids.org/pub/epislides/2007/2007_epiupdate_en.pdf⟩ (accessed 27 September 2011).

socioeconomic conditions in war-torn countries that play host to peace operations create situations of vulnerability.

Despite the absence of statistics on the link between cultures, HIV and peacekeeping, the virus may be spread to local communities by peacekeepers, especially where the cultural dynamics permit. The majority of the major African troop-contributing countries have relatively low infection levels (see Table 8.2). According to HIV prevalence estimates by UNAIDS, the West African sub-region – home to four of the top troop-contributing countries – has consistently had low prevalence rates.[34] Only South Africa and Namibia have exceptionally high levels that may entail a danger of peacekeepers transmitting HIV to the local populations or peacekeepers from other countries. For the latter, modes of transmission may include accidental contact with contaminated blood and other blood products and sharing syringes and other equipment for intravenous drug use in addition to unprotected sexual intercourse. We should, however, take note of the pre-deployment HIV testing by most countries. Notwithstanding this, as mentioned earlier in this chapter, the window period remains a challenge and there is a need to ensure that the genuine negatives maintain that status throughout deployment.

Morocco, for instance, is a low-prevalence country but has a high infection rate among narrow high-risk populations, especially sex workers. By and large in North Africa, the general population is "confined by the Islamic marital and social order".[35] Sexual misconduct may normally not be acceptable in Moroccan culture. However, being deployed in peace operations offers Moroccan peacekeepers an opportunity to enter different cultures and engage in sexual liaisons normally morally unacceptable in their homeland. A Moroccan battalion deployed 732 Blue Helmets under the United Nations Operation in Côte d'Ivoire (UNOCI). Commenting on the rich traditions and customs that the Moroccan Blue Helmets brought to UNOCI, Mohamed Selloum, Commanding Officer in Charge of operations for UNOCI's Moroccan battalion, stated that "the cultural diversity and richness of the Kingdom of Morocco dates back to between 600 and 800 BC. The various regions keep their identities, values and traditions even as they all melt into the Kingdom of Morocco".[36] The involvement of Moroccan peacekeepers in sexual exploitation and abuses jeopardized these "rich traditions and customs".

Notwithstanding UN Security Council Resolution 1325 on "Women, Peace and Security", which aims to ensure equitable representation of men and women at all levels of peace operations, the peacekeepers from African troop-contributing countries are predominantly composed of male soldiers. Consequently, gendered representation of operations will be greatly tipped in favour of male peacekeepers. Against such possible backdrops, the hyper-masculine culture will prevail in the presence of a limited number of female peacekeepers. The difficulty faced by women officers – particularly married ones – who may be willing to pursue UN missions abroad aggravates the gender representation imbalances.[37] Some African countries have policy directives that expressly prohibit women from participating in peace operations abroad. Although this is not necessarily saying that women may be less inclined towards sexual misconduct, war has gendered consequences entailing the need for serious mainstreaming of gender in peace operations and other intervention strategies where sexual violence was used as a tactic of war.[38]

An overview of select missions

Despite the United Nations' "zero contact" and "zero tolerance" policy, incidents of sexual and other abuses and exploitation abound in peace operations.[39] This section briefly isolates – in the absence of comprehensive empirical evidence – the nexus between culture, sexual misconduct and risks of HIV transmission in specific peace operations.

Liberia

The United Nations Mission in Liberia (UNMIL) has dealt over time with allegations of sexual abuse and exploitation. These allegations have been explained mainly in terms of culture, poverty and desperation among the local communities, juxtaposed with the relative "economic power" of peacekeepers. The United Nations Development Programme's 2006 Human Development Report stated that 76 per cent of Liberia's population were living below the poverty line, on less than US$1 per day, and 52 per cent were living in extreme poverty, on less than US$0.50 per day.[40] On sexual abuse and exploitation in Liberia, Esfahani et al. stated that:

> Extreme poverty and desperation are primary reasons why so many people are vulnerable to exploitation; poverty is a driving factor that facilitates the supply side of sexual exploitation. When people are in extreme need, they are likely to do whatever someone asks in order to fulfill that need, especially when they have family members depending on them. In such a state of need and without protection, people are highly vulnerable to sexual exploitation and abuse.[41]

Refugees International observed that "the girls in Liberia are very good at marketing themselves. Some girls are so desperate that they would sleep with a man just to have a bed for the night."[42] The local community was also culpable, with a UN official noting that "people will offer peacekeepers their sister or daughter if it [UNMIL] would get them a job".[43] The spread of sexual abuse is, unsurprisingly, explained as a legacy of the prolonged civil war – during which rape and survival sex were common – and the resultant widespread social trauma that makes people more resigned and desensitized to sexual abuse and exploitation.[44]

The hyper-masculine peacekeepers armed with their differential power allegedly exploit the facilitative local context away from the "culturally and legally" restraining situation back home to engage in abusive sexual liaisons with desperate women. This increases the risk of the spread of HIV. The Moroccan contingent was at the centre of these allegations of engaging in sex with underage girls in Bouake, Côte d'Ivoire. This led the United Nations to confine the whole battalion pending investigations. Refugees International quoted a Liberian man's complaint that "this behaviour would not be acceptable in the home country of these soldiers. Why are these soldiers playing around with our children?"[45] Esfahani et al. interestingly noted that, although peacekeepers have been implicated in Liberia, it is the relatively powerful local males who have been the major perpetrators.[46]

The Democratic Republic of the Congo

MONUC, the United Nations Mission in the Democratic Republic of the Congo, is currently the largest peacekeeping operation in Africa. It functions in a context of violence and devastated infrastructures and other failed social institutions, as a result of longstanding conflicts in the Congo.

Sexual scandals involving peacekeepers initially went unpublicized. This regrettable "wall of silence" was attributed to the masculine culture of UN peacekeeping operations, according to Refugees International.[47] In 2004, Clayton and Bone reported for *The Times* that a widespread sex scandal in the Congo threatened to become "the UN's Abu Ghraib".[48] UN peacekeepers from Morocco based in Kisangani were alleged to have impregnated 82 women and girls.[49] Interviews with UN investigators confirmed regular sexual contact between Congolese girls, some as young as 13, and peacekeepers. A UN report subsequently revealed widespread sexual misconduct. The report isolated 68 cases of alleged rape, prostitution and paedophilia by multinational troops, including those from Morocco, Nepal, Tunisia, Uruguay and South Africa.[50] The peacekeepers used the power imbalances to sexually exploit local women and children, including illiterate orphans, for as small a payment as two eggs or US$5.[51]

These "consensual" acts of sexual misconduct may easily fit the description "rape disguised as prostitution". The UN Under-Secretary-General for Peacekeeping, Jean-Marie Guehenno, alluded to the link between the climate of generalized poverty and the hyper-masculinized and economically viable peacekeepers as follows: "You are in a broken country, with extreme misery, and you insert a force with power, with money. The imbalance between power and money and that extreme misery ... the risk of that imbalance creating an exploitative environment is quite high."[52]

Sexual exploitation and abuse increase the chances of HIV transmission in an environment where UNAIDS reports high levels of prevalence among the 15–24 age group. Morocco charged soldiers who were part of MONUC with criminal offences, and South Africa filed criminal charges against two soldiers for alleged misconduct in the Congo. Regrettably, the lack of local support and social structures for the peacekeepers' victims is saddening. The Congolese reportedly adopted a culture of indifference. Martin noted that "the Congolese themselves don't see this [peacekeepers' preying on desperate girls and women] as a problem; this is a Western thing to get upset about it".[53] However, such misdemeanours by peacekeepers will certainly have a negative impact on the locals' perceptions of UN operations.

Sudan

The United Nations Mission in the Sudan (UNMIS) has also been affected by media reports of abuses perpetrated by UN peacekeepers in the southern part of the country. Consistent with the United Nations' zero tolerance policy towards sexual exploitation and abuse, in January 2007 the Government of Sudan and UNICEF agreed to set up a joint task force to deal with any possible incidents of sexual misconduct.

Critically, this was done with the involvement of UNMIS and the African Union Mission in Sudan (AMIS).

Côte d'Ivoire

UN investigations found that peacekeepers deployed under UNOCI perpetrated sexual misconduct, including exploitation and abuse. The implication of the Moroccan battalion of ONUCI in widespread sexual abuse over a three-year period demonstrates the continuance of sexual- and gender-based exploitation in peacekeeping contexts.

Conclusions and recommendations

This chapter has given a preliminary empirical indication that there is a link between cultures and HIV transmission and prevention in peacekeeping contexts. The hyper-masculine culture of peacekeeping operations influences sexual exploitation and abuse, and in turn facilitates HIV transmission. The first recommendation, given the limited availability of empirical studies, is that this is an important subject area that needs further exploration. A comprehensive methodology and tools sensitive to policy and local sociocultural contexts should be designed to empirically assess the relationship between cultural traditions in their various forms and HIV/AIDS in particular peacekeeping contexts. This should involve both qualitative and quantitative analysis. The UN operations have dedicated conduct and discipline capacities as well as HIV/AIDS focal points that will be critical partners in further empirical research. These two offices should have an elaborate and ongoing data collection, monitoring, evaluating and reporting system that readily provides information on the subject.

Culture in its various forms influences the transmission and prevention of HIV in different and specific social settings. Consideration of culture must be made when mapping appropriate interventions around the nexus between HIV and peacekeeping. In addition, peace missions should be adequately familiar with the indigenous culture. This should be supported by a tradition of respecting the diverse cultures that coalesce in a peacekeeping environment.

Sexual exploitation and abuse thrive in devastated socioeconomic contexts of vulnerability in theatres of operations. Peacekeeping operations need to nurture a culture that permits the assertiveness and confidence of women and girls. Closely related to this is the need for crafting and implementing longer-term post-conflict peacebuilding and reconstruction programmes that raise the socioeconomic status of women in specific cultural contexts. This may address the issue of reliance on commercial sex for survival. It is instructive that AIDS control is a visible component of the planned post-conflict national poverty reduction strategy in the DRC.

The culture of knowledge has two dimensions: on the one hand peacekeepers, on the other local communities. Whereas the peacekeepers are covered by the induction training programmes, public information programmes should be devised by the United Nations to explain to local communities the consequences of sexual exploitation and abuse. The local communities and authorities – devastated by conflict and vulnerabilities – should be clear on the need to report abuse (and how to do this) and how the perpetrator will be disciplined. They may provide information on instances of sexual exploitation and abuse. It becomes critical for local communities to participate in comprehensive, context-specific, culturally appropriate programmes to address sexual exploitation and abuse and HIV. This turns them from passive victims into agents. The codes of conduct should be strictly enforced to hold peacekeepers accountable and address the CMW paradigm.

Notes

1. S. Martin, "'Must Boys Be Boys?': Confronting Sexual Exploitation and Abuse in UN Peacekeeping Operations", The Boston Consortium on Gender, Security and Human Rights, Meeting Notes, 1 February 2006; ⟨http://genderandsecurity.umb.cdu/meeting.htm⟩ (accessed 7 September 2011).
2. M. Fleshman, "Tough UN Line on Peacekeeper Abuses", Africa Renewal, 19(1), 2005, ⟨http://www.un.org/ecosocdev/geninfo/afrec/vol19no1/191peacekeep.htm⟩ (accessed 7 September 2011).
3. Contemporary UN peace operations are in fact peacebuilding operations. The military component is tasked with security and stability creation; the civilian police with ensuring law and order; and the civilian component with the human rights, humanitarian and developmental aspects.
4. See K. O. Dunivin, "Military Culture: Change and Continuity", Armed Forces and Society, 20, 1994, pp. 531–547.
5. Ibid.
6. L. A. Lindsay and S. F. Mieschier, "Introduction: Men and Masculinities in Modern African History", in L. A. Lindsay and S. F. Mieschier, eds, Men and Masculinities in Modern Africa (Portsmouth: Heinemann, 2003), p. 4.
7. T. Sideris, "'You May Have to Change and You Don't Know How!': Contesting What It Means to be a Man in Rural South Africa", in G. Reid and L. Walker, eds, Men Behaving Differently: South African Men Since 1994 (Cape Town: Double Storey Books, 2005), p. 113.
8. Former UN Secretary-General Kofi Annan defined sexual exploitation and abuse as "any actual or attempted abuse of a position of vulnerability, differential power, or trust, for sexual purposes, including, but not limited to, profiting monetarily, socially or politically from the sexual exploitation of another" ("Special Measures for Protection

from Sexual Exploitation and Sexual Abuse", *Secretary-General's Bulletin*, 9 October 2003). Sexual interactions and misconduct include sex with adult commercial sex workers and crimes such as rape and paedophilia.

9. J. Valenius, "A Few Kind Women: Gender Essentialism and Nordic Peacekeeping Operations", *International Peacekeeping*, 14(4), 2007, pp. 510–523 at p. 517.

10. S. Martin, "Must Boys Be Boys? Ending Sexual Exploitation & Abuse in UN Peacekeeping Missions", Refugees International, Washington, DC, October 2005, p. 5, ⟨http://www.refugeesinternational.org/policy/in-depth-report/must-boys-be-boys-ending-sexual-exploitation-abuse-un-peacekeeping-missions⟩ (accessed 7 September 2011).

11. D. Bratt, "Blue Condoms: The Use of International Peacekeepers in the Fight against AIDS", *International Peacekeeping*, 9(3), 2002, pp. 67–86; S. Elbe, *The Strategic Dimensions of HIV/AIDS* (Oxford: Oxford University Press, 2003).

12. Bratt, "Blue Condoms".

13. J. Loconte, "The U.N. Sex Scandal", *The Weekly Standard*, 10(16), 3 January 2005. On abuses and other consequences of UN peacekeeping, see C. Aoi, C. de Coning and R. Thakur, eds, *Unintended Consequences of Peacekeeping Operations* (Tokyo: United Nations University Press, 2007).

14. P. Higate, "Peacekeeping and Gendered Relations", ⟨http://www.operationspaix.net/IMG/pdf/PeaceConflictMonitor_Higate_pk_gender_2003-07_-2.pdf⟩ (accessed 7 September 2011).

15. UN News Centre, "Joint UN-Sudan Government Task Force to Deal with Issue of Sexual Exploitation", 18 January 2007, ⟨http://www.un.org/apps/news/story.asp?NewsID=21274&Cr=sudan&Cr1=%0D%0D⟩ (accessed 7 September 2011).

16. Centre for Conflict Resolution, *HIV/AIDS and Militaries in Southern Africa*, Seminar Report No. 10, 2006, p. 27.

17. Martin, "'Must Boys Be Boys?': Confronting Sexual Exploitation and Abuse in UN Peacekeeping Operations", p. 10.

18. Higate, "Peacekeeping and Gendered Relations".

19. Thoraya Ahmed Obaid, "Joining Forces to Combat Sexual Violence: The Brussels Call to Action", *UN Chronicle*, 33(4), 2006, ⟨http://vlex.com/vid/joining-forces-sexual-violence-brussels-56842162⟩ (accessed 27 September 2011).

20. Bratt, "Blue Condoms", p. 79. On the complex interaction of peacekeepers, sex workers and AIDS in conflict and war situations, see, generally, A. Price-Smith, *The Health of Nations* (Cambridge, MA: MIT Press, 2002); R. L. Ostergard, Jr, "Politics in the Hot Zone: AIDS and National Security in Africa", *Third World Quarterly*, 23(2), 2002, p. 333.

21. Martin, "Must Boys Be Boys? Ending Sexual Exploitation & Abuse in UN Peacekeeping Missions".

22. K. Rajoo, "Sexual Abuse and Exploitation: Power Tools in Peacekeeping Missions", *Conflict Trends*, 4, 2005.

23. A. de Waal, *AIDS and Power: Why There Is No Political Crisis – Yet* (Cape Town: David Philip, 2006), p. 20.

24. Obaid, "Joining Forces to Combat Sexual Violence". According to the UN Department of Peacekeeping Operations (DPKO), between 1 January 2004 and 21 November 2006, investigations had been completed against 319 peacekeeping personnel in all missions, leading to the dismissal of 18 civilians and the repatriation of 17 police and 144 military personnel.

25. "Call to Action: End Sexual Violence in Conflict & Beyond", *PeaceWomen*, 22 August 2006, ⟨http://www.peacewomen.org/publications_enews_issue.php?id=54⟩ (accessed 7 September 2011).

26. M. Caprioli, "Gendered Conflict", *Journal of Peace Research*, 37(1), 2000, p. 52.

27. De Waal, *AIDS and Power*, p. 5.
28. M. Rupiya, ed., *The Enemy Within: Southern African Militaries' Quarter-Century Battle with HIV and AIDS* (Pretoria: Institute for Security Studies, 2006), pp. 14–15.
29. UN DPKO, "We Are United Nations Peacekeepers", ⟨http://www.un.org/en/peacekeeping/documents/un_in.pdf⟩ (accessed 7 September 2011).
30. United Nations Conduct and Discipline Unit, UN Standards of Conduct, "Ten Rules: Code of Personal Conduct For Blue Helmets", ⟨http://cdu.unlb.org/UNStandardsofConduct/TenRulesCodeofPersonalConductForBlueHelmets.aspx⟩ (accessed 7 September 2011).
31. The United Nations, however, has direct jurisdiction only over its own civilian personnel; individual troop-contributing countries are responsible for disciplining any erring soldiers.
32. This poses a dilemma because the code of conduct prohibits fraternization with prostitutes or children under 18, yet the United Nations provides peacekeepers with free condoms for their protection.
33. J. Tobin, "The Challenges and Ethical Dilemmas of a Military Medical Officer Serving with a Peacekeeping Operation in Regard to the Medical Care of the Local Population", *Journal of Medical Ethics*, 31, 2005, pp. 571–574.
34. Data published by UNAIDS in 2007 on "Country Specific Estimates on HIV/AIDS". See also UNAIDS, *AIDS Epidemic Update* (Geneva: UNAIDS and WHO, December 2007), available at ⟨http://data.unaids.org/pub/epislides/2007/2007_epiupdate_en.pdf⟩ (accessed 27 September 2011).
35. J. Iliffe, *The African AIDS Epidemic: A History* (Oxford: James Currey, 2006), p. 56.
36. UNOCI, Public Information Office, July 2005.
37. Martin, "Must Boys Be Boys? Ending Sexual Exploitation & Abuse in UN Peacekeeping Missions".
38. See Valenius, "A Few Kind Women", p. 510.
39. Aoi et al., *Unintended Consequences of Peacekeeping Operations*.
40. UNDP, *Human Development Report 2006. Beyond Scarcity: Power, Poverty and the Global Water Crisis* (New York: Oxford University Press, 2006), available at ⟨http://hdr.undp.org/en/reports/global/hdr2006/⟩ (accessed 27 September 2011).
41. A. Esfahani, S. R. Lee, N. Mechem and A. Van Antwerp, "Countering Sexual Exploitation and Abuse in Liberia", 2 May 2007, p. 20, ⟨http://www.gwu.edu/~oid/Capstone/2007%20Capstone/Countering%20Sexual%20Exploitation-Liberia.pdf⟩ (accessed 7 September 2011).
42. Sarah Martin, "Sexual Exploitation in Liberia: Are the Conditions Ripe for Another Scandal?", Refugees International, 20 April 2004, ⟨http://www.sos-sexisme.org/English/Sexual_Exploitation.htm⟩ (accessed 27 September 2011).
43. Ibid.
44. Esfahani et al., "Countering Sexual Exploitation and Abuse in Liberia".
45. Martin, "Must Boys Be Boys? Ending Sexual Exploitation & Abuse in UN Peacekeeping Missions", p. 5.
46. Esfahani et al., "Countering Sexual Exploitation and Abuse in Liberia".
47. Martin, "Must Boys Be Boys? Ending Sexual Exploitation & Abuse in UN Peacekeeping Missions", p. 5.
48. J. Clayton and J. Bone, "Sex Scandal in Congo Threatens to Engulf UN's Peacekeepers", *The Times*, 23 December 2004, ⟨http://www.timesonline.co.uk/tol/news/world/article405213.ece⟩ (accessed 27 September 2011).
49. "U.N. 'Peacekeepers' Rape Women, Children", *WorldNetDaily*, 24 December 2004, ⟨http://www.worldnetdaily.com/news/article.asp?ARTICLE_ID=42088⟩ (accessed 7 September 2011).

50. C. Lynch, "U.N. Sexual Abuse Alleged in Congo: Peacekeepers Accused in Draft Report", *Washington Post*, 16 December 2004.
51. Rajoo, "Sexual Abuse and Exploitation", p. 19.
52. United Nations Radio Transcript of the Special Programme on "United Nations Sexual Abuse Scandal in the DR Congo", recorded 27 January 2005, ⟨http://www.un.org/av/radio/unandafrica/transcript32.htm⟩ (accessed 7 September 2011).
53. Martin, "'Must Boys Be Boys?': Confronting Sexual Exploitation and Abuse in UN Peacekeeping Operations".

9

The African Union and the HIV/AIDS crisis: Harnessing alternative policy options

Olajide O. Akanji

Introduction

The HIV and AIDS crisis is now largely construed as a (human) security issue. HIV virulence has already reached crisis proportions in many developing regions of the world, and it constitutes a threat to peace, security and development in most of Africa. Africa, more than any other region, bears the major mortality, morbidity and human security burdens of HIV and AIDS. Consecutive global AIDS epidemic updates by the Joint United Nations Programme on HIV/AIDS (UNAIDS) state that sub-Saharan Africa is the worst hit in comparison with other regions of the world. Every aspect of the continent's life is directly affected by the crisis, in particular the economic, social, political, cultural and, more recently, the military and related security sectors. The impact is most visible in the rising numbers of the workforce – including the military – either dying of AIDS or unable to find a job because of society-induced stigmatization of HIV.

In order to tackle this multitude of issues, diverse policy interventions have been introduced by the African Union (AU) and the United Nations (UN). However, the effectiveness of current international policy interventions and the possibility of alternative policies to strengthen the existing ones still remain uncertain. There is already a massive scale-up of HIV prevention, treatment and care, with the aim of coming as close as possible to the goal of universal access to treatment.

Several national and international conferences and workshops resulting in declarations, resolutions and commitments of funds and human

HIV/AIDS and the security sector in Africa, Aginam and Rupiya (eds),
United Nations University Press, 2012, ISBN 978-92-808-1209-1

resources to address the crisis have taken place, and an increasing number of these are currently being designed. Notwithstanding this consistent commitment, the rate at which HIV/AIDS continues to mutate in complexity and outreach seems to surpass existing international efforts to combat the crisis. This is corroborated by existing statistics showing increasing HIV infections and AIDS-related deaths. Over 65 million people in the world have been infected with HIV, more than 25 million people have died, and 15 million children have been orphaned by AIDS. Nonetheless, of the 40 million people currently living with HIV, over 95 per cent of them live in the developing world, with over 70 per cent in sub-Saharan Africa.[1] This chapter examines some of the AU and UN policy interventions in the HIV/AIDS crisis, and suggests innovative policy guidelines that could provide more effective responses to the issue for both organizations.

The HIV/AIDS crisis: Africa and the wider world

Since its discovery in 1981, the Human Immunodeficiency Virus has constituted a major problem for the global community. The disease's tentacles reach across all nations, classes and sexes. Although sub-Saharan Africa remains the epicentre of the epidemic, AIDS has also become a global problem. HIV/AIDS particularly affects women, children and several other vulnerable groups. These include young and elderly people, homosexuals, sex workers, transgender individuals, detainees, migrant labourers, orphans, peacekeepers, refugees, HIV/AIDS outreach workers, civilians in conflict and post-conflict situations, and internally displaced persons.

With its high prevalence rates, Africa has been literally scourged by the virus. For example, between 1981 and 2003, over 20 million people in Africa were believed to have died of AIDS.[2] In 2003 alone, statistics show that almost 5 million people became newly infected with HIV, the greatest number in any one year since the beginning of the epidemic. At the global level, the number of people living with the disease continues to grow: from 35 million in 2001 to 38 million in 2003[3] to 40 million in 2006.[4] Of the 40 million people currently living with HIV worldwide, more than 70 per cent live in sub-Saharan Africa, despite the fact that the region accounts for only 10 per cent of the global population.[5] In 2005 alone, between 2.8 million and 3.9 million people in the region became infected, and 2.4 million adults and children died of AIDS.[6] The 2006 UNAIDS report indicated that almost 25 million people are living with HIV in sub-Saharan Africa.[7] As mentioned, women, children and young people in general are the most affected target groups. For example, up to two generations of people have now been orphaned by HIV/AIDS. In many parts of the continent, parental death and orphanhood resulting from HIV/AIDS have become the pre-eminent cause of single parenthood and child families. According to the United Nations Children's Fund (UNICEF), over 15 million children have lost one or both parents to AIDS.[8] The high prevalence rate of the disease among children is shown by the global report of 2.3 million children living with HIV. As of 2005, around 38,000 children had died of AIDS and approximately 540,000 were newly infected.[9] As of 2003, about 15 million children under the age of 18 were said to have been orphaned by HIV/AIDS, of whom 80 per cent lived in sub-Saharan African.[10]

Compared with men, women are generally more vulnerable. Apart from being highly prone to contract the deadly virus either from their husband, or as a rape victim, or as a victim of any type of sexual and gender-based violence, they equally carry the burden of care should any member of the family get infected or killed by the disease.

There are a number of reasons why Africa, and particularly the sub-Saharan region, has remained the epicentre of the AIDS epidemic. The continent's myriad sociopolitical, economic and cultural problems complicate the HIV crisis. These include but are not limited to poverty, unemployment, armed conflicts, a culture of stigmatization, corrupt public and elected officials, and gender-stereotyped relationships. Consequently every effort, at national, regional and international level, to combat the crisis must take into consideration the eradication – or tangible reduction – of the preponderance of such problems on the ground. This has to some extent informed the current international responses, as will be shown in the following section of this chapter. The current multi-sectoral approach and a comprehensive framework of global partnerships are intended to help individual states in the global community to scale up their national responses to the crisis.

Global and regional responses: The United Nations and the African Union

The United Nations has committed its universal convening power to fight HIV/AIDS through research, human capacity-building, care and other strategies. UN efforts to tackle HIV/AIDS are predominantly channelled through UNAIDS. Needless to say, it is important to remark that almost every activity of the United Nations and related agencies in the area of global economic development since the 1980s has included a concern for HIV. Specifically, UNAIDS is a joint programme of 10 agencies: the United Nations Development Programme (UNDP), the International

Labour Organization (ILO), the United Nations Population Fund, the United Nations Educational, Scientific and Cultural Organization, the World Health Organization (WHO), the World Food Programme, the World Bank, UNICEF and the Office of the United Nations High Commissioner for Refugees (UNHCR).

These organizations, working in partnership and jointly forming UN-AIDS, also individually undertake their own institutional interventions in tackling HIV/AIDS. For instance, UNDP, amongst its other responsibilities, focuses on providing comprehensive support to countries in addressing the development challenges and impact of the AIDS epidemic. It specifically focuses on three strands that are complementary and mutually reinforcing: (i) HIV/AIDS and human development; (ii) governance of the HIV/AIDS response; and (iii) HIV/AIDS, human rights and gender.[11]

At the same time, ILO operates on the assumption that AIDS is a workplace issue because it affects workers and their families, enterprises and the communities that depend on them. At the same time, the workplace is considered to have a role to play in the wider struggle to control the epidemic. Consequently, the agency sets codes of practice on HIV/AIDS in the workplace and campaigns for an end to stigmatization of and discrimination against HIV victims there.[12]

UNICEF, on the other hand, works for the rights of children, their survival and their development. The organization undertakes widespread studies on the impact of the disease on children and considers diverse ways of addressing it. It provides anti-retroviral (ARV) drugs for children and families and supplies emergency treatment to people in humanitarian crises, as well as offering assistance to governments and their partners in the procurement of HIV-related medicines.[13] Generally, UNICEF fights the cause of children affected by AIDS by: (i) preventing mother-to-child transmission of HIV and providing paediatric treatment; (ii) preventing infection among adolescents and young people; and (iii) protecting and supporting children affected by HIV/AIDS.

On its own, UNAIDS has five focus areas: leadership and advocacy; strategic information and technical support; tracking, monitoring and evaluation; civil society engagement; and mobilization of resources. Nonetheless, with its 10 co-sponsors, UNAIDS assists in ensuring better coordination among the partner organizations in the UN system, governments, civil society, donors, the private sector and others in the fight against HIV/AIDS.[14]

Apart from those already mentioned, several other programmes initiated, sponsored, coordinated or assisted by the United Nations are currently aimed at combating the spread. On the policy level, the United Nations and its agencies have passed numerous declarations and resolutions on the HIV and AIDS crisis. Examples include the United Nations Millennium Declaration by the UN General Assembly in 2000, which resolved to halt and reverse the HIV/AIDS scourge by 2015 and to provide assistance to children orphaned by AIDS.[15] In 2001, heads of state and government representatives of 189 UN member states participated in the Special Session of the UN General Assembly on HIV/AIDS. They unanimously adopted the Declaration of Commitment on HIV/AIDS, acknowledging that the AIDS epidemic constitutes a "global emergency and one of the most formidable challenges to human life and dignity".[16] The Declaration highlighted key priorities, including prevention, treatment and care, and funding. It was designed as a blueprint to meet the Millennium Development Goal of halting and beginning to reverse the spread of HIV/AIDS by 2015. In 2000, the UN Security Council held a session that recognized HIV/AIDS as a threat to international peace and security. The Council's Resolution 1308 (2000) has over time become a major policy tool, especially in addressing the impact of HIV/AIDS on UN peacekeeping operations.[17]

With regard to the African Union, the enormous burden the epidemic is placing on African people and governments has necessitated the development of different coping strategies by the regional body. For their own part, AU political leaders have, at different times, shown appreciable concern in the fight against the disease. In historical terms, the declaration of "Health For All" by the WHO Health Assembly in 1977 and the adoption in Alma-Ata in 1978 of the primary healthcare approach as the strategy by which the ultimate objective of Health For All would be attained were perhaps the starting point of intensive collaborative efforts between Africa and the international community in respect of health issues. The sudden emergence of HIV/AIDS on the global health scene in the 1980s further deepened this partnership between Africa and the rest of the world. It was a widespread realization of the devastating effects of the disease on the socioeconomic development of the continent and its people, as well as the peace, security and development of the global community, that triggered this new international partnership.

Since the 1980s the African Union has initiated several interventions. Amongst these, the following examples are relevant to note. In 2001, in the Abuja Declaration on HIV/AIDS, Malaria and Tuberculosis, AU leaders committed themselves to allocate 15 per cent of their national budget to health. Prior to the Abuja Declaration, the African Union had in 1987 issued a "Declaration of Health as a Foundation for Development".[18] This Declaration underlined:

"that Agricultural and other efforts at production (macro or microeconomic) are frustrated by the inadequate health status of many populations in Africa, the vicious cycle of ignorance, poverty and disease persists; poor health is delaying economic 'Take off'" and "that production of healthy people (Health Development) is a developmental imperative – many apparently healthy persons are harboring illnesses, are medically unfit and are living in insalubrious environments".[19]

This recognition of the interface between health and development was a fundamental starting point in getting African states to refocus on the issue of health. Similarly, the African Union Extra-Ordinary Summit on Employment and Poverty Alleviation held in Burkina Faso in 2004 acknowledged the link between health, development and poverty, and adopted a Declaration and Plan of Action to promote a multi-sectoral approach to the reduction of poverty.[20]

In furtherance of the 2001 Abuja Declaration, the Fourth Ordinary Session of the African Union, which took place in Abuja, Nigeria, from 30 to 31 January 2005, reaffirmed the commitment of African heads of state to allocate at least 15 per cent of their annual budget to the improvement of the health sector, to invest increased resources in health and to address obstacles impeding their utilization. Within this context, member states were urged to take the lead in negotiations on trade-related aspects of intellectual property rights (TRIPS) and to implement measures identified to promote access to affordable generic medicines. The Assembly further resolved to take all necessary measures to produce, with the support of the international community, quality generic medicines in Africa.[21] The follow-up session of the AU Commission (the Fifth Ordinary Session of the AU Assembly of Heads of State and Government) in Sirte, Libya, in July 2005 focused on and debated the programme of Accelerated Action for Child Survival, with particular emphasis on the Millennium Development Goals.

An example of a collective effort at tackling the crisis was the Commission's strategic framework of action adopted in Abuja in 2006. The content of the framework was determined by the outcome of the 2005 Commission-initiated continent-wide consultation on the development of a continental framework on human rights and people living with HIV/AIDS. The Abuja Special Summit in 2006 first reviewed the progress made since the 2001 Abuja Declaration on HIV/AIDS, Malaria and Tuberculosis. The Summit adopted the "Abuja Call for Accelerated Action Towards Universal Access to HIV and AIDS, Tuberculosis and Malaria Services in Africa" and "Africa's Common Position to the UN General Assembly Special Session on AIDS (June 2006)" in New York.[22] The African Union Commission's *2004–2007 Strategic Framework* identified health, with a focus on HIV/AIDS, malaria, tuberculosis and polio, and the strengthening of health systems, as one of the 23 priority areas.[23]

The AU Assembly at the 2006 Abuja Summit also resolved to take all necessary measures to produce, with the support of the international community, quality generic medicines in Africa. It also requested that the AU Commission, within the framework of the New Partnership for Africa's Development (NEPAD), lead in the development of a pharmaceutical manufacturing plan for Africa. Specifically, with respect to HIV/AIDS, the AU Commission developed a strategic plan to provide leadership, mobilize resources and promote accountability, amongst several other objectives. It also set up the Secretariat of AIDS Watch Africa (a committee of African heads of state intended to provide political leadership on HIV/AIDS advocacy and resource mobilization). The AU Commission, in collaboration with WHO and UNAIDS, organized a Continental Consultation on Universal Access to HIV/AIDS Prevention, Care, Treatment and Support in March 2006. This culminated in the Brazzaville Commitment, which identified four key areas that must be addressed to ensure universal access. These areas were human resources, public health goods and commodities, sustainable financing and human rights.[24] In addition, African heads of state and government under the umbrella of the African Union have been networking with the Group of Eight Industrialized Countries (G8) for resources and for debt cancellation so that they could have more assets with which to combat the problem of poverty. Records show that many countries on the continent have accessed considerable funding from global health partnerships, private foundations and bilateral and multilateral sources.

In addition, to demonstrate their resolve to fight the scourge, about 85 per cent of African countries have established HIV/AIDS national coordinating bodies, with over half of them chaired by the President, Vice-President or Prime Minister. About 43 per cent have taken the fight more seriously by putting in place sub-national HIV/AIDS coordinating bodies. Progress reports indicate that countries of southern and East Africa are generally more determined and committed: 85 per cent of the countries in the two regions have developed national strategic frameworks on HIV/AIDS and about 40 per cent of them produce annual HIV/AIDS reports.[25] Similarly, the "Three Ones" agreement between national health authorities working in partnership with other bodies is one means that the African continent has been using to promote universal coordination in the fight against HIV/AIDS.[26]

This suggests an impressive continental and international response to the problem of HIV/AIDS in Africa. However, whereas the UN commitment appears commendable, the strategies adopted so far by the African Union are more political statements than effective actions. Many meetings, workshops and conferences, resulting in a series of declarations and plans of actions, have indeed taken place on the continent, but these have not been realized in concrete terms. The missing link – as can be deduced from the tones of the resolutions, declarations and plans of action – is the political will of government leaders to implement the policy contents of these documents. For instance, although the heads of state and government of the African Union committed themselves in the 2001 Abuja Declaration to allocate 15 per cent of their national budget to health, assessment in 2006 on the progress of this commitment revealed that only six countries had either achieved or were close to achieving this target. Overall, 33 per cent of countries had allocated 10 per cent or more of their national resources to health.[27] This is quite a small number to address a grave issue such as HIV/AIDS.

The current approach by the continental body is deficient because it does not provide for adequate monitoring mechanisms. Each member state is left to determine and report officially the extent to which it has complied with the various declarations and plans of action. In the same vein, the absence, to some extent, of tangible mechanisms for enforcing compliance with AU-agreed resolutions and decisions by member states makes these efforts a mere political activity. It is surprising that, in spite of the high prevalence of the disease on the continent, a set of proactive and pragmatic policy options, anchored in the readiness to commit the necessary human and material resources no matter what the cost, is still missing.

Alternative policy options

The statement by the AU heads of state and government at the Special Summit in Abuja in 2006 that "[u]rgent and extraordinary problems require urgent and extraordinary responses"[28] is the guiding maxim for the suggestions made in this section as a way of strengthening and reinforcing existing policy options within both the African Union and the United Nations. First, as already demonstrated, continental and international responses to the HIV/AIDS crisis seem to be widespread and comprehensive. The result on the ground, however, reveals an urgent need for more proactive and pragmatic responses. To this end, I first and foremost call for a global rethink and re-conceptualization of the nature of the HIV/AIDS problem. To all intents and purposes, the nature of the HIV/AIDS epidemic is such that the global community should consider it a global emergency requiring total commitment. Indeed, it would not be out of place to view the HIV/AIDS problem as another global war. But instead of an actual war in which two or more human parties are involved, the "HIV/AIDS war", as it should be referred to, is simply a war between the human race and the epidemic. This position is based on the human casualty rate of the epidemic since the 1980s, when it was first discovered, and its unquantifiable sociopolitical implications. No war in human history has claimed as many human lives as the HIV/AIDS epidemic has done and is still likely to do. Major attention is thus required in the same manner as for a real global war. In light of this, a total and overwhelming commitment of resources by the international community is needed to "win" the war. Consequently, it is imperative that no suggestion for tackling the global menace, no matter how bizarre it seems, should be rejected without trial.

In order to tackle the "HIV/AIDS war" effectively, the United Nations, the African Union and other related organizations should consider the development of crisis responses specific to the most vulnerable groups. By this, I mean that each of the most vulnerable groups (young and elderly people, homosexuals, sex workers, transgender individuals, detainees, migrant labourers, orphans, peacekeepers, refugees, HIV/AIDS outreach workers, civilians in conflict and post-conflict situations, and internally displaced persons) would be targeted by specific policy actions that recognize the particularity of each case and proffer a possible solution. This would allow for a thorough understanding of the needs and situations of members of each category. It would also facilitate the identification of the appropriate care and prevention methods required by each group. In the long run, this is far more advantageous than the current practice of attempting to address the crisis from a general perspective. Instead, each group identified as most vulnerable should be targeted by policy actions for specific care, prevention and treatment. My contention is that the strategies required by, for example, transgender individuals will differ significantly from those for prison inmates and HIV/AIDS outreach workers.

Similarly, it is obvious from current efforts by both the African Union and the United Nations to combat the epidemic that, whereas huge resources are committed to prevention, care and treatment, the search for a cure for the malignant epidemic seems to take a back seat. This is a serious omission. In committing resources to research a cure for HIV, all the relevant funding agencies should bring complementary and alternative medicines into the mainstream. This is a very important point for the African continent, bearing in mind that the continent is home to a large variety of herbs that have been found to have medicinal value. The African Union's recognition of traditional medicine at the Lusaka Summit in 2001 has yet to translate into meaningful action in respect of its being considered a possible source of a cure for HIV. So far, the Lusaka Declaration has resulted in limited progress: the development of a plan of action, which was adopted in April 2003; some achievements in research and development in the area of traditional medicine; the integration of traditional health practitioners into conventional healthcare facilities; and the recognition of 31 August as the African Day of Traditional Medicine.[29] Apart from African traditional herbal therapy, other categories of complementary and alternative medicine such as acupuncture and Tai Chi should be researched for potential cures for HIV.[30]

Given the potential that traditional herbal therapy offers for treatment, the African Union and the United Nations should have a specific policy framework regarding complementary and alternative medicine in the fight against HIV/AIDS. Equally important, the African Union must develop an action plan to combine resources (financial and human) to tap the continent's abundant herbal resources to combat the epidemic. Indeed, the current global trend of focusing on halving the number of victims of HIV/AIDS through prevention, treatment and care mechanisms, though laudable, tends to suggest a global institutional failure to source a cure.

Furthermore, and as part of an earlier suggestion for responses specific to particular vulnerable groups, it is imperative that the nature of peacekeeping operations be relaxed to accommodate the willing spouses of peacekeepers (both military and police). This is important because peacekeeping personnel have been identified as being some of the most vulnerable to the scourge. Although this assertion may not be surprising, the question it raises is how do peacekeepers contract the disease? The answer is not difficult to find. On the one hand, peacekeepers might have been infected before being deployed into the field. On the other, contraction can arise as the result of rape or sexual intercourse perpetrated by peacekeepers on local women, who are often emotionally vulnerable and seeking protection. In order to tackle the former case, pre-deployment testing appears to be the most feasible solution. For the latter, the question remains how to combat a situation that has become an embarrassment for the United Nations and the global community. Although the current efforts to sensitize and educate peacekeepers are praiseworthy, they should be supplemented with a policy by both the United Nations and the African Union to make it possible to accommodate spouses of peacekeeping personnel while on service. The direct implication is that peacekeeping operations would become more capital intensive but at the same time more flexible to allow leisure periods, and consequently more human intensive. This suggestion finds confirmation in the observation at the 2006 Abuja Special Summit that "an urgent and extraordinary problem requires an urgent and extraordinary response". The growing incidence of peacekeeping officials being involved in crimes of sexual and gender-based violence, which expose both the perpetrators and their victims to HIV/AIDS, may be avoided or reduced through the above-mentioned mechanism.

In addition, it is imperative that ARV therapy (ART) and other essential HIV drugs be available free of charge to victims. The African Union and the United Nations should develop a policy to this end that will ensure a regular and uninterrupted supply of ARV and other drugs. The experience gained from the "three by five" initiative in providing ART to people living with HIV/AIDS shows that, with a regular and unhindered supply of essential drugs, the scourge could be controlled. The result of the initiative in Africa shows that, "[o]f more than 4 million People Living With HIV/AIDS (PLWHA) needing antiretroviral ... drugs in Africa, 20% received treatment by the end of 2005. Three countries (Botswana, Namibia, Uganda) had reached the target of treating 50% of PLWHA needing ART by end 2005."[31] It can be argued that one major hindrance to effective treatment of HIV/AIDS patients, especially in Africa, is accessibility to essential drugs. In many places the drugs are unaffordable for local populations. In certain cases, the drugs are not available or are hoarded by drug peddlers and their sponsors so as to create scarcity and competition within the market. Consequently, it is necessary for the African Union and the United Nations, and the global community at large, to redirect attention in order to make HIV/AIDS drugs free and readily available. A policy implemented by the two bodies through which financial and material assistance can be made available to governments is desirable. This would also be provided in partnership with private organizations and willing donors to facilitate the production and distribution of essential HIV/AIDS drugs. In a similar fashion, I would recommend that latex condoms should not follow the trend in price increases and should be essentially free of charge. These suggestions are urgent in view of the fact that in Africa, as in other developing regions, poverty is facilitating the spread of the disease. So, while efforts are being made to tackle poverty at the state level through economic reforms, commodities such as condoms should be readily available to the whole population. To achieve this, member states of both the United Nations and the African Union are invited to ensure a free, regular supply or to discourage any profiteering from the sale of latex condoms and ARV and other essential drugs. The distribution network should be developed in such a way that all levels of government are supportive of the policy to distribute these drugs and materials free of charge.

In addition, much has been said in the literature about the need to protect and safeguard the human rights of people living with HIV/AIDS, but there is an apparent omission regarding the economic rights of the children orphaned by the virus. The basic truth is that HIV/AIDS causes significant social and economic dislocation and disruption in families. Often, it is the family breadwinners who more easily contract the disease. In such cases, the healthy members are often torn between taking care of the sick and looking for alternative sources of income. The elderly, children and young people are therefore more susceptible themselves to contracting the disease, because their economic disempowerment compels survival. For instance, young girls could be exposed to "trades" such as prostitution, survival sex, commercial sex hawking, and other forms of sexual and gender-based violence such as rape in their bid to secure a means of livelihood. In addition, socially frustrated individuals represent potential drug users.

Consequently, the United Nations and the African Union should encompass a policy agenda that encourages and assists member states to provide social security facilities to those orphaned by HIV/AIDS. Assistance should be in the form of, but not limited to, grants, long- and short-term interest-free loans and free vocational training supported by after-training kits. The African Union and the United Nations should make it a policy priority to set aside a special fund and encourage member states to have special trust funds set up in their respective states to cater for the economic needs of this class of people, particularly the "skip-generation families"[32] and the "child-headed families".[33] This will enhance the coping capacity of such people. One way of successfully executing this is for governments to partner at national level with the private sector and well-meaning individuals to establish the trust fund. Alternatively, an HIV/AIDS tax regime could be developed and levied on business organizations that are deemed important in the country.

Finally, it is an internationally recognized fact that sexual violence against women and girls, such as rape committed in the private or public sphere, is one means of contracting and spreading HIV. Since Africa accounts for no less than 40 per cent of global conflicts, it is necessary for the African Union and the United Nations to find a lasting solution to the problem of sexual violence, especially during armed conflict. A number of avenues can be explored. These would include sensitization programmes and sexual and gender-based violence and HIV/AIDS education in school curriculums from primary to tertiary levels. It is also important that sexual and gender-based violence is universally criminalized. Global criminalization through the United Nations should be replicated at the continental level by the African Union, and member states of the Union should be encouraged to criminalize sexual and gender-based violence at the national level. This effort should also include appropriate sanctions being put in place for perpetrators of the crime.

Conclusion

No stone should be left unturned and no effort should be deemed too great in the bid to combat and vanquish the seemingly all-conquering

HIV/AIDS epidemic. What is needed is the total commitment of the international community and the political will and determination of the entire human race not to withhold whatever it will take to fight the AIDS menace. Nothing – including HIV/AIDS – is insurmountable; what matters is simply the attention paid to it. So far the attention paid to the HIV/AIDS crisis by the United Nations and the African Union is inadequate. Political leadership is crucial as well as the development of effective public institutions to implement the policies. In all of this, the global (UN) and regional (AU) policy responses must complement one another in order to address the HIV crisis in Africa effectively.

Notes

1. "European Parliament Resolution on HIV/AIDS: Time to Deliver", ⟨http://www.europarl.europa.eu/sides/getDoc.do?pubRef=-//EP//NONSGML+TA+P6-TA-2006-0321+0+DOC+PDF+V0//EN⟩ (accessed 15 September 2011).
2. UNAIDS, "2004 Report on the Global AIDS Epidemic, Executive Summary", available at ⟨http://www.natap.org/2004/Bangkok/bangkok_05.htm⟩ (accessed 15 September 2011).
3. Ibid.
4. "European Parliament Resolution on HIV/AIDS: Time to Deliver".
5. Ibid.
6. Special Summit of African Union on HIV/AIDS, Tuberculosis and Malaria (ATM), Abuja, Nigeria, 2–4 May 2006, "Overview on the Theme: Universal Access to HIV/AIDS, Tuberculosis, and Malaria Services by 2010", ⟨http://www.africa-union.org/root/au/conferences/past/2006/may/summit/summit.htm⟩ (accessed 15 September 2011).
7. UNAIDS, *AIDS Epidemic Update: Special Report on HIV/AIDS: December 2006* (Geneva: UNAIDS & WHO, 2006), p. 10; available at ⟨http://data.unaids.org/pub/epireport/2006/2006_epiupdate_en.pdf⟩ (accessed 8 October 2011).
8. UNICEF, "HIV/AIDS and Children", ⟨http://www.unicef.org/aids/index_1.php⟩ (accessed 15 September 2011).
9. Ibid.
10. See UNICEF, "Children Orphaned or Made Vulnerable by HIV/AIDS", Childhood under Threat: The State of the World's Children 2005, ⟨http://www.unicef.org/sowc05/english/hivaids.html⟩ (accessed 15 September 2011).
11. United Nations Development Programme, "HIV/AIDS", ⟨http://www.undp.org/hiv/⟩ (accessed 15 September 2011).
12. See ILO, "ILO Programme on HIV/AIDS and the World of Work (ILO/AIDS)", ⟨http://www.ilo.org/public/english/protection/trav/aids/⟩ (accessed 15 September 2011).
13. See UNICEF, "HIV/AIDS and Children".
14. See UNAIDS, "About UNAIDS", ⟨http://www.unaids.org/en/AboutUNAIDS/default.asp⟩ (accessed 15 September 2011).
15. "United Nations Millennium Declaration", A/RES/55/2, 8 September 2000, ⟨http://www.un.org/millennium/declaration/ares552e.htm⟩ (accessed 15 September 2011).
16. See United Nations General Assembly Special Session on HIV/AIDS, "Declaration of Commitment on HIV/AIDS", A/RES/S-26/2, 2 August 2001, ⟨http://www.un.org/ga/aids/coverage/FinalDeclarationHIVAIDS.html⟩ (accessed 15 September 2011).
17. United Nations Security Council Resolution 1308 (2000) on the responsibility of the Security Council in the maintenance of international peace and security: HIV/AIDS

and international peacekeeping operations, S/RES/1308 (2000), 17 July 2000, ⟨http://www.un.org/docs/scres/2000/sc2000.htm⟩ (accessed 15 September 2011).

18. B. Gawanas, "African Union and Health Care Challenges in Africa: Strategies and Initiatives on Health Care Delivery", *African Renaissance*, July/August 2006, ⟨http://www.hollerafrica.com/showArticle.php?catId=1&artId=174⟩ (accessed 15 September 2011).

19. Ibid.

20. Ibid.

21. Ibid.

22. African Union, "Abuja Call for Accelerated Action Towards Universal Access to HIV and AIDS, Tuberculosis and Malaria Services in Africa" and "African's Common Position to the UN General Assembly Special Session on AIDS (June 2006)", available at ⟨http://www.africa-union.org/root/au/conferences/past/2006/may/summit/summit.htm⟩ (accessed 15 September 2011).

23. *Strategic Plan of the Commission of the African Union. Volume 2: 2004–2007 Strategic Framework of the Commission of the African Union*, May 2004, ⟨http://www.africa-union.org/AU%20summit%202004/volume%202%20final%20-%20English%20-%20June%202004.pdf⟩ (accessed 15 September 2011).

24. "Brazzaville Commitment on Scaling up Towards Universal Access to HIV and AIDS Prevention, Treatment, Care and Support in Africa by 2010", Brazzaville, Republic of the Congo, 8 March 2006, ⟨http://data.unaids.org/pub/BaseDocument/2006/20060317_UA_Brazzaville_en.pdf⟩ (accessed 15 September 2011).

25. Special Summit of African Union on HIV/AIDS, Tuberculosis and Malaria (ATM), p. 5.

26. Ibid.

27. Ibid.

28. Ibid., p. 2.

29. Gawanas, "African Union and Health Care Challenges in Africa".

30. For more information on complementary and alternative medicines, see National Center for Complementary and Alternative Medicine, ⟨http://nccam.nih.gov/research/results/#⟩ (accessed 15 September 2011).

31. Special Summit on HIV/AIDS, Tuberculosis and Malaria (ATM), p. 6.

32. The term is used to refer to families where the parent generation has succumbed to AIDS and AIDS-related illnesses and the families are made up of grandparents and orphaned grandchildren.

33. The term is used to connote families where not even grandparents are available to care for the orphaned grandchildren.

10

The Zambia Defence Force: Considerations on peacekeeping and HIV/AIDS

Lawson F. Simapuka

Overview: The United Nations, peacekeeping and HIV/AIDS

The United Nations (UN), established on 24 October 1945 in the aftermath of World War II, has since then been dedicated, in the enduring words of the UN Charter, to saving "succeeding generations from the scourge of war".[1] Since its creation, the United Nations has been called upon to prevent disputes from escalating into war, to persuade opposing parties to use pacific means rather than the force of arms to settle disputes. In over five decades, the United Nations has provided the multilateral forum to contain or end numerous conflicts, in many cases through the deployment of peacekeepers.

The United Nations' responses and approaches to actual and potential breaches of the peace as well as acts that threaten international peace and security have evolved steadily since the first peacekeeping operation of the United Nations in 1948. UN missions have grown in complexity and scope from largely military observer missions to multidimensional operations that oversee the implementation of comprehensive peace and ceasefire agreements. The military components of UN missions have become increasingly complex because conflicts in which they intervene no longer involve national armies alone but also irregular forces, guerrilla factions and even armed criminal gangs. International scholars argue that, since the end of the Cold War, most conflicts are intra-state and no longer inter-state.[2] Consequently, military operations under UN command have

HIV/AIDS and the security sector in Africa, Aginam and Rupiya (eds),
United Nations University Press, 2012, ISBN 978-92-808-1209-1

also evolved, and are no longer the armed intervention that was typical during the first 40 years of the United Nations.

The peacekeeping environment: Overview of challenges

The UN Department of Peacekeeping Operations (DPKO), which was established in 1992, is responsible for planning, managing, deploying, supporting and, on behalf of the UN Secretary-General, providing direction to all UN peacekeeping operations. It also performs similar functions in support of peace and security operations that are predominantly civilian, such as the United Nations Assistance Mission in Afghanistan. The DPKO works very closely with the Department of Political Affairs, which is the focal point in the UN system for conflict prevention, peacemaking and peacebuilding.

The DPKO currently manages several peacekeeping missions globally, fielding 100,000 troops, military observers, police and civilian peacekeepers from over 100 countries.[3] Peacekeeping missions are high-risk environments for the transmission of HIV owing to the constant rotation of troops, the structures and geography of deployment, challenging environments and limited medical care. Peacekeepers are usually also in the age group most heavily affected by the epidemic (20–40 years). Peacekeepers come from high- and low-prevalence regions, are deployed to mission in host countries with varying HIV prevalence and come from many different cultural backgrounds.[4] This implies different interpretations of risk and poses numerous challenges to achieving consistent and effective HIV prevention. In the presence of a peacekeeping mission, both host communities and peacekeepers are vulnerable to contracting HIV. It is hard to quantify the risk of transmission because conflict-affected settings rarely have sufficient baseline data to determine the impact of a peacekeeping presence, and most often no reliable data exist on prevalence rates among peacekeepers.

Although the DPKO does not have a policy of mandatory screening of peacekeepers for HIV, it encourages pre-deployment voluntary counselling and testing (VCT).[5] The majority of the troop/police-contributing countries (TCCs/PCCs), however, have mandatory pre-deployment testing for HIV. Whereas many countries exclude HIV-positive peacekeepers from being deployed to peacekeeping missions, others base their decision on whether or not to deploy an HIV-positive individual according to, for example, the infected person's CD4 counts.[6] Regardless of the testing policy of the individual TCC, the DPKO is normally not informed of test results. Recognizing that peacekeeping missions are high-risk environments for HIV transmission, UN Security Council Resolution 1308

(2000)[7] requested that comprehensive prevention and awareness programmes be put in place for all UN uniformed peacekeepers. The Resolution encouraged member states to offer peacekeepers VCT prior to deployment. Accordingly, all peacekeepers must receive education and training on HIV/AIDS and sexually transmitted diseases (STDs) and be sensitized to prevent sexual exploitation and abuse. Although predeployment training is mainly the responsibility of the TCCs/PCCs, the DPKO – in an effort to establish minimum standards – has developed a standard generic training module on HIV/AIDS, which member states can use in preparing military personnel for deployment. HIV/AIDS units have been established in large UN peacekeeping missions, while smaller missions have HIV/AIDS focal points.

Peacekeeping operations have a profound impact on people's lives. Women and girls, together with men and boys, benefit from the increased security and relative peace provided by peacekeepers as well as their role in the continuation of a peace process. The impact of peacekeeping operations can often be different for women and girls compared with men and boys. There is the potential for peacekeeping operations to have a positive impact on gender relations and inequalities. For example, initiatives supporting elections can facilitate women's participation as voters and as political representatives. Women and girls benefit when the peacekeeping effort is able to address and stop violence, including sexual violence. Civilian police elements of a peacekeeping mission may assist in the training, monitoring or restructuring of local law enforcement agencies and address violent crimes, including rape, domestic violence and other forms of gender-based violence, such as trafficking in women and girls.

The HIV epidemic – An overview

The HIV/AIDS epidemic has become a global emergency. Every day, thousands of people become infected with HIV, and equally thousands die of AIDS-related causes. HIV/AIDS remains one of the most serious communicable disease challenges faced by humanity in the millennium. Nonetheless, the current epidemiological assessment has encouraging elements since it suggests the following characteristics: (i) the global prevalence of HIV infection (the percentage of persons infected with HIV) is remaining at the same level, although the overall number of people living with HIV worldwide is increasing owing to the ongoing accumulation of new infections with longer survival times, measured over a continuously growing general population; (ii) there are localized reductions primarily in specific countries; (iii) there is a reduction in HIV-associated deaths, partly attributable to the recent scaling-up of treatment access; and (iv) globally there is a reduction in the number of annual new HIV infections.[8]

An examination of the global and regional trends suggests that the epidemic has developed along two broad strands: generalized epidemics diffused in the populations of sub-Saharan African countries, especially in the southern part of the continent; and epidemics spreading in the rest of the world, which are primarily concentrated among high-risk individuals, such as men who have sex with men, injecting drug users, and sex workers together with their sexual partners. HIV/AIDS has been recognized by the UN Security Council as a threat to international peace and security.[9] In addition to the direct impact on people living with HIV and AIDS, the epidemic undermines the foundations of state institutions through the huge number of deaths of parents, teachers, farmers, health and social workers, public and government officials, and traditional leaders and healers.[10] Sub-Saharan Africa remains the most seriously affected region, with AIDS as one of the leading causes of death.[11]

The Zambia Defence Force, peacekeeping and HIV: Lessons and experiences

The role of the Zambia Defence Force (ZDF) in international affairs began immediately after independence in 1964. At this moment in history, Zambia was surrounded by countries that were under either colonial rule or a dictatorial regime.[12] The then President Kenneth David Kaunda declared that there would be no peace in Zambia without the liberation of neighbouring countries. Throughout the 1970s and 1980s, Zambia harboured freedom fighters and actively participated in their struggles for political independence.

The ZDF participated in its first UN peacekeeping mission as part of the United Nations Iran-Iraq Military Observer Group (UNIIMOG), which was established in 1988. This mission was mandated to verify, confirm and supervise the ceasefire and withdrawal of all forces to the internationally recognized boundaries pending a comprehensive settlement. To date, the ZDF has participated in the following 12 peacekeeping missions:

- UNIIMOG
- United Nations Operation in Côte d'Ivoire (UNOCI)
- United Nations Mission in the Sudan (UNMIS)
- United Nations Observer Mission in Liberia (UNOMIL)
- United Nations Integrated Office in Sierra Leone (UNIOSIL)
- United Nations Angola Verification Mission (UNAVEM)

- United Nations Mission in Sierra Leone (UNAMSIL)
- United Nations Assistance Mission for Rwanda (UNAMIR)
- United Nations Assistance Mission for Iraq (UNAMI)
- United Nations Operation in Mozambique (ONUMOZ)
- United Nations Organization Mission in the Democratic Republic of the Congo (MONUC)
- United Nations Observer Mission in Angola (MONUA)

During these operations, Zambia recorded 68 fatalities owing to illness, accidents and malicious acts out of a total of 2,405 fatalities recorded by the United Nations from 1948 to 2007 (see Table 10.1). The highest number of fatalities occurred during UNAMSIL, where 34 troops were lost: four died in combat with rebels, six from bomb blast accidents, the rest from the Ebola virus, malaria and HIV-related illnesses. UNIIMOG, in contrast, was a relatively fortunate case as no fatalities were registered during this mission.

HIV was first reported in Zambia in 1984 and the first cases in the ZDF were reported in 1985. The country has one of the highest prevalence rates in the world, with the sero-prevalence rate for HIV-1 estimated at 16 per cent in 2002. Initially, HIV/AIDS cases were concentrated in urban areas, but it soon became clear that all regions were being affected. Since then, the scourge has moved on, with the 15–49 age group being the most likely target of infection.

Despite common beliefs, HIV transmission is mainly heterosexual. HIV infection has not spared the ZDF army either, although officers and troops serve with a high sense of discipline. It is generally believed that HIV infection might have claimed more lives than the wars for independence and those struggles in the neighbouring countries. It is believed that the prevalence rates are higher among defence force personnel than in the population as a whole, owing to their higher exposure to the virus.

Risk factors associated with the military

- *Age*: The majority of military personnel are young and sexually active. Because the military environment encourages risk-taking, young men and women in uniform may take part in risky sexual behaviour, such as non-protected sexual intercourse.
- *Financial superiority*: In some areas where ZDF men and women serve, they are better paid than their civilian counterparts, giving them power and influence over their potential partners, and consequently easier access to sex.
- *Military uniform*: The military uniform is considered to be highly attractive and those wearing it are generally admired by civilian women, who flock to them for security.

Table 10.1 Zambian fatalities in missions, 1948 – 31 October 2007

	Mission													Total
	UNOCI	UNMIS	UNMIL	UNIOSIL	UNAVEM	UNAMSIL	UNAMIR	UNAMI	ONUMOZ	UN Secretariat	MONUC	MONUA	
Casualties	1	2	1	1	7	34	3	1	13	1	1	1	66

- *Environment*: The conditions under which uniformed personnel live and work are often very stressful and expose them to HIV and other STDs. Isolation and the knowledge that they could at any time be placed in the firing line can create stress. As a result, the desire to look for comfort in alcohol or casual sex makes them vulnerable.
- *Exchanging sexual partners*: It is not unusual for different members of the military to have sex with the same partners, especially while on operations or under the influence of alcohol. In militaries where research has been done, high prevalence rates of HIV infection have been reported in civilian populations living near military installations or associated with the movements of service personnel. Service personnel often have a limited choice of sexual partners in areas where they have been deployed. This may force personnel from the same unit to share available partners over a period of time. Even if only a small number of the military personnel or their partners were infected initially, unprotected sex and the sharing of partners lead to the spread of HIV and other STDs.

Deployment

With the development of more effective treatments for HIV infection and related diseases, some soldiers who contracted the infection now continue productive careers for several years. In general, there is therefore no reason for an IIIV-positive person to be restricted from posts in a non-combat-related field. If soldiers with HIV infection are physically and mentally well enough to perform their duties effectively, then they should be permitted to do so. As a reasonable alternative, working arrangements should be made through a medical board. The HIV policy of the ZDF does not discriminate against troops according to their HIV status. Upon deployment, troops are screened for HIV and other infectious and non-infectious diseases. For those found to be HIV-positive, a CD4 count is done. The laboratories have standing orders to proceed and do a CD4 count on all HIV-positive samples. Post-test counselling is offered to all those with HIV-positive results. Deploying an HIV-positive soldier depends on the theatre of operation and laboratory indices. Contingent troops in non-combatant roles can be deployed according to the criteria in Table 10.2.

All soldiers and officers report to Maina Soko Military Hospital, the referral hospital[13] where the medical examinations are conducted under the supervision of the Commanding Officer. The final categorization for deployment is done by a consultant physician with specialization in HIV. From the referral hospital, the results are validated by the Director of Medical Services at Defence Force Medical Services headquarters, and

Table 10.2 Criteria for deploying HIV-positive troops

CD4 count	Comment
< 200	Not deployable
200–350	Deployable if on anti-retroviral drugs as a staff officer or observer and deploying in a non-hostile operational theatre. Review during Cadet Training Officer (CTO) leave at home
350–500	Deployable as a staff officer or observer. Review during CTO leave at home
500 >	Deployable as a contingent member, staff officer/observer. Contingent members reviewed by Unit Medical Officer

then the final list of "FIT" and "UNFIT" personnel is sent to the Command at defence headquarters. Since 2004, the ZDF has successfully deployed HIV-positive troops in both contingent and observer missions, and has done so without incident among the troops.

The challenges of deploying HIV-positive peacekeepers

Before the commercial release of anti-retroviral (ARV) treatments in 2004, unit commanders faced many challenges when deploying HIV-positive soldiers owing to the limited accessibility of ARV drugs. Several missions experienced increased attendance and referrals to higher-level hospitals as a result of HIV-related illnesses. Problems experienced following the commercialization of ARV treatments are usually the result of poor pre-deployment preparations and lack of adherence to advice by unit commanders, who sometimes impose soldiers of their liking on the contingent or observer mission. The rest of this section outlines of some of the challenges in the peacekeeping operations in which Zambia has participated.

Angola and Mozambique

During the operations in Angola and Mozambique in the mid-1990s, pre-deployment screening for HIV infection was not performed and very few medical officers in the unit had the knowledge and skills for managing HIV patients. Most of the clients were treated as cases of chronic malaria and repatriated. Following repatriation, however, there was minimal access to treatment, because only the referral hospital could test for HIV. Blood for CD4 counts was sent to South Africa in a few selected cases. Drug treatment was equally very expensive and not readily available on the local market.

Sierra Leone

Zambia deployed seven peacekeeping contingents of the ZDF to Sierra Leone from 2000 to 2004 and most of the challenges they faced were attributed to new infectious diseases such as Ebola. The harsh weather conditions and stress in the field affected soldiers known to be HIV-positive more than those who were HIV-negative. During the six-month tours of duty, there were three casualties and these were soldiers whose status was positive. Thus, the mission was very unsuitable for deploying HIV-positive troops. HIV infection contributed to most out-patient attendances and camp hospital admissions in the first months of deployment for persons known to be HIV-positive. Those needing treatment were referred to the Choithram Memorial Hospital, a Jordanian medical level III hospital in Freetown. All such referrals were HIV-positive. All soldiers who were repatriated owing to chronic ill health were also found to be HIV-positive and died within three months of arriving home.

Attitude of other nationals

Troops referred to the Choithram Memorial Hospital were subjected to an HIV test upon arrival, irrespective of the presenting complaints. Peacekeepers diagnosed with HIV at this hospital suffered discriminatory treatment protocols and isolation. Admissions and deaths at the hospital were liable to be broadcast on the UN website. Boards of Inquiry concentrated on the HIV-positive status of the deceased peacekeepers and totally disregarded any other circumstances that might have caused the death. Boards of Inquiry attributed blame to the troop-contributing countries for dispatching known HIV-positive peacekeepers as a way of avoiding or evading payment of a full compensatory package to the deceased's family.

Sudan

ZDF troops were deployed to Sudan in February 2000. The key issues and experiences encountered during the UNMIS deployment of the first Zambian Contingent (ZAMCONT I) are detailed as follows:

Poor pre-deployment preparation

ZAMCONT I was deployed in two phases, with two-thirds of the group being deployed in phase 1 and the other one-third in phase 2. The first group underwent comprehensive medical examinations and those who were not fit for deployment were not selected, in contrast to the second group, who did not undergo any form of medical testing and pre-deployment training. Some of the troops in this group were on sick leave during the time of deployment but found themselves ordered on a mission in the field. This led to frequent ailments among the troops and some were found to have serious illnesses that required referral to the medical level III hospitals in Khartoum.

Low-level care facilities

The contingent was accompanied by a level I UN clinic with very limited services and no HIV/AIDS treatment or support services such as laboratory facilities and ARV drugs. The clinic was set up in a remote part of southern Sudan with no higher level of care facility accessible nearby. This location could be reached only by air and the nearest UN facility was about 400 kilometres away by road.

Lack of professionalism by medical personnel

The medical officers at the level III hospitals in Khartoum and at the UN headquarters did not act professionally. They conducted HIV testing on all referrals without counselling or consent, and never discussed a patient's status with the individual patient. They instead opted to establish a repatriation procedure for all troops who tested positive, which led to the stigmatization of the contingent as a whole.

High rate of repatriation

During the first six months of deployment, seven repatriations were made, four of which were attributed to HIV infection. The majority of those repatriated were from the transport troop that arrived in the second phase of deployment.

High number of admissions and referrals

Owing to the high number of serious ailments experienced among the troops, there were increased clinic admissions and referrals to higher-level care facilities. Medical evacuations could be carried out only by air because the area was manned by different militias over a 400 kilometre stretch to the nearest UN town.

Gender

UN Security Council Resolution 1325[14] provides the most important mandate for mainstreaming gender perspectives in peacekeeping operations. It recognizes the contribution of women to the maintenance and promotion of peace and security, while acknowledging their specific concerns in armed conflict and its aftermath. Resolution 1325 also reaffirms women's roles in the prevention and resolution of conflicts and peace-building, stresses the importance of equal participation and full involvement in all efforts to maintain and promote peace and security, and highlights the need to increase their participation in decision-making regarding conflict prevention and resolution.

The ZDF UN peacekeeping missions were exclusively composed of male soldiers until 2001, when female soldiers and officers were first deployed as members of ZAMBATT 2 in Sierra Leone. Amongst the reasons for the non-deployment of female troops, the predominant factor was that they might become pregnant while serving in the operation area. Female soldiers have since been deployed as staff officers and observers. The medical treatments conducted for women include a pregnancy test. All those who test positive are not deployed. Instead, female soldiers who are pregnant serve at the battalion or contingent headquarters in non-combatant roles.

The impact of HIV infection on the deployment of female troops has not yet been investigated in the ZDF. Data on post-deployment HIV sero-prevalence are not available because the troops are not tested for HIV infection after returning from deployment. Because service personnel often have a limited choice of partners in the areas where they have been deployed, this may force personnel from the same unit to cohabit with fellow female service personnel over a period of time, consequently facilitating HIV transmission. This is still a grey area and a gender perspective regarding activities within the peacekeeping mandate warrants further investigation.

Conclusion

The military components in peacekeeping operations continue to evolve in response to new challenges and political realities. To maximize efficiency, troop contributors and the DPKO, with the assistance of donor governments, must work together to improve the readiness and capability of troops for the complex challenges of multidimensional peacekeeping. Regional militaries have not reached consensus on the way in which HIV-infected troops should be handled at times of operations. The DPKO does not have a policy of mandatory screening of peacekeepers for HIV. Instead, it encourages VCT. A large majority of TCCs/PCCs, however, have mandatory pre-deployment HIV testing. Most countries deploy troops in local operations and subject them to the same pre-deployment conditions and these countries do not deploy troops who are HIV-positive in international peacekeeping missions. In the Southern African Development Community region, only two countries have openly indicated that they do deploy stable troops with HIV infection in international peacekeeping missions. With the advent of highly active ARV therapy, healthy troops with acceptable CD4 counts should be allowed to be deployed in international UN operations. Deploying such troops would require rules and regulations for their deployment according to the security standards of the United Nations, the African Union and sub-regional organizations, which all troop-contributing countries should conform to. The absence of regulations has led to troops being discriminated against and stigmatized by other countries. It has also resulted in a higher level of healthcare in mission areas being offered to certain troop-contributing countries. There is a need to expand and upgrade the infrastructure of laboratory services and to improve knowledge and skilled human resources in the area of HIV/AIDS medicine. The medical examinations for UN operations should be conducted at referral hospitals to avoid lapses in the medical guidelines for deployment. Peacekeepers come from high- and low-prevalence regions and from many different cultural backgrounds, and are deployed on missions to host countries with varying levels of HIV prevalence. This implies different interpretations of risk and poses numerous challenges to achieving consistent and effective HIV prevention. In a peacekeeping mission, both host communities and peacekeepers are at risk of contracting HIV. Therefore denying HIV-positive peacekeepers deployment is discriminatory since host communities are equally able to transmit HIV infection to the peacekeepers. The solution is for all peacekeepers to receive education and training on HIV/AIDS and STDs and to be sensitized to eliminate sexual exploitation and abuse. Although pre-deployment training is the responsibility of the TCCs/PCCs, in an effort to establish minimum standards the DPKO has developed a standard generic training module on HIV/AIDS, which all UN member states should use in preparation for deployment. This is important because otherwise the TCCs may start refusing to deploy their troops to high-prevalence areas, which may result in a crisis that would take time to resolve.

The impact of HIV infection on the deployment of female troops needs to be investigated further, because a male-dominated operational theatre is liable to have a negative effect on female soldiers. Senior male counterparts may take undue advantage of their juniors, who may find it difficult to refuse, knowing the hierarchical way in which militaries operate. Prior to deployment, female soldiers should be educated about their rights. This sensitization should include creating awareness about the twenty-third Special Session of the UN General Assembly (New York, 5–9 June 2000) entitled "Women 2000: Gender Equality, Development and Peace for the Twenty-first Century", which reaffirmed the commitments made in the Beijing Declaration and Platform for Action and other relevant international instruments.[15] This General Assembly Special Session called for the full participation of women at all levels of decision-making in peace processes, peacekeeping and peacebuilding. All

TCCs, including the ZDF, should heed this call by mainstreaming gender into their operations and deploying Gender Officers at the mission head-quarters.

Notes

1. Preamble, Charter of the United Nations 1945.
2. Human Security Centre, *Human Security Report 2005* (Oxford: Oxford University Press, 2005); Allan Collins, ed., *Contemporary Security Studies* (Oxford: Oxford University Press, 2007).
3. DPKO, "Peacekeeping Fact Sheet", as of 31 January 2011, ⟨http://www.un.org/en/peacekeeping/resources/statistics/factsheet.shtml⟩ (accessed 16 September 2011).
4. See, generally, Stefan Elbe, "HIV/AIDS and the Changing Landscape of War in Africa", *International Security*, 27, 2002, p. 159; Duane Bratt, "Blue Condoms: The Use of International Peacekeepers in the Fight Against AIDS", *International Peacekeeping*, 9(3), 2002, pp. 67–86.
5. DPKO, "Questions and Answers on United Nations Peacekeeping: What Is Being Done to Address HIV/AIDS in United Nations Peacekeeping?", ⟨http://www.un.org/events/peacekeepers/2003/docs/qanda.htm⟩ (accessed 16 September 2011).
6. This refers to the number of "helper" CD4 T-lymphocytes in a cubic millimetre of blood. With HIV, the absolute CD4 count declines as the infection progresses. The absolute CD4 count is frequently used to monitor the extent of immune suppression in persons with HIV.
7. UN Security Council Resolution 1308 (2000) on the responsibility of the Security Council in the maintenance of international peace and security: HIV/AIDS and international peacekeeping operations, S/RES/1308 (2000), 17 July 2000, ⟨http://www.un.org/Docs/scres/2000/sc2000.htm⟩ (accessed 16 September 2011).
8. Joint United Nations Programme on HIV/AIDS (UNAIDS), *Report on the Global AIDS Epidemic 2010* (Geneva: UNAIDS, 2010).
9. Security Council Resolution 1308 (2000).
10. Food and Agriculture Organization of the United Nations (FAO), *The Impact of HIV/AIDS on Food Security* (Rome: FAO, 2001); International Food Policy Research Institute (IFPRI), *HIV/AIDS and Food and Nutrition Security: From Evidence to Action* (Durban: IFPRI, 2005); Jean Baxen and Anders Breidlid, eds, *HIV/AIDS in Sub-Saharan Africa: Understanding the Implications of Culture and Context* (Cape Town: UCT Press, 2009); Kondwani Chirambo, ed., *The Political Cost of AIDS in Africa: Evidence from Six Countries* (Pretoria: IDASA, 2008).
11. UNAIDS, *2008 Report on the Global AIDS Epidemic* (Geneva: UNAIDS, 2008), ⟨http://www.unaids.org/en/dataanalysis/epidemiology/2008reportontheglobalaidsepidemic/⟩ (accessed 8 October 2011).
12. Botswana, Angola, Zimbabwe and Mozambique were still colonies at the time Zambia gained independence; Namibia was governed as a trust territory by Apartheid South Africa.
13. A referral hospital is a major hospital that usually has a full complement of services.
14. UN Security Council Resolution 1325 (2000) on Women, Peace and Security, S/RES/1325 (2000), 31 October 2000, ⟨http://www.un.org/Docs/scres/2000/sc2000.htm⟩ (accessed 16 September 2011).
15. For information on the Special Session, see ⟨http://www.un.org/womenwatch/daw/followup/beijing+5.htm⟩ (accessed 16 September 2011).

11

A disorderly resolution of an organized conflict: The military dimension and the spread of HIV/AIDS in Sierra Leone

Olubowale Josiah Opeyemi

Introduction

The conflict in Sierra Leone in the late 1980s that eventually led to a full-scale civil war between 1991 and 2002 was not exclusively devastating to Sierra Leone. The conflict impacted heavily on the sociopolitical situation in the neighbouring countries of Guinea and Liberia. Liberia fought a civil war between 1989 and 2003, and Guinea became home to millions of refugees who fled the wars in Sierra Leone and Liberia. Instability, an ailing economy and suspicion owing to the influx of refugees transformed Guinea into a state of uncertainty. While this instability prompted some observers and international organizations to characterize Guinea as a "failed state", the conflicts in Liberia and Sierra Leone threatened the stability of the entire West African sub-region. However, among the most devastating results of the conflict, in both Sierra Leone and the region, were the human security implications of the ravages of the HIV/AIDS epidemic.

Sierra Leone is currently one of the countries in the West African sub-region with limited data on HIV/AIDS, but, according to projections and the number of reported cases, it is widely considered to have a very high rate of prevalence.[1] During the crisis, one major step taken by countries in the West African sub-region was the organization of the Nigeria-led Economic Community of West African States (ECOWAS) Monitoring Group (ECOMOG). Regrettably, the intervention of this multinational military force, with the mandate to restore peace to Sierra Leone, further

HIV/AIDS and the security sector in Africa, Aginam and Rupiya (eds),
United Nations University Press, 2012, ISBN 978-92-808-1209-1

escalated the dimension of the humanitarian crisis for the civilian population. Although ECOMOG was mandated to restore peace in Sierra Leone, its non-committal position on health security inadvertently undermined the already precarious situation in Sierra Leone, especially regarding the spread of HIV/AIDS. The mission in Sierra Leone had, as its priority, the resolution of the armed conflict between the warring factions, and it consequently neglected the human security dimension of the crisis. This chapter argues that the limits and failure of the ECOMOG mission to assess security in broader terms essentially escalated the HIV crisis in Sierra Leone.

Sierra Leone: A sequence of conflict

The history of Sierra Leone presents a country with a sequence of short- and long-term crises, often left unresolved. The establishment, in 1787, of a settlement of repatriated slaves by the British abolitionists rendered Freetown a hub for those enlightened people who had an awareness of freedom, in both economic and political terms. Present-day Sierra Leone moved further into the limelight of knowledge and influence when, in 1808, Freetown became a British Crown colony, as well as the centre of the colonial government overseeing the colonies of the Gold Coast (now Ghana) and the Gambia. The hinterland of the territory also became a British protectorate in 1896.[2] There was resistance to British colonial rule and to the Krio (an ethnic group in Sierra Leone, descendants of West Indian slaves from the Caribbean, primarily from Jamaica, and freed black American slaves from the United States), who were seen as British collaborators.[3] The colony and the protectorate formed an alliance in order to obtain political independence in 1961. Following this period, Sierra Leone experienced its first military coup d'état in 1967, when the government of President Siaka Stevens was toppled. Nonetheless, he was able to regain control through a counter-coup in 1968. Stevens remained in power as President under a one-party state until 1985, when he retired. The newly established government requested the presence of Guinean troops in Sierra Leone. Following a further attempt to overthrow the government, a number of people were arrested and executed. There was also an attempt in 1987 to overthrow President Joseph Seidu Momoh, who took over from Stevens, an event that led to the arrest and the eventual execution of those convicted, including Vice-President Francis Minah.

There were attempts at constitutional reform in 1990 to introduce multi-party democracy in Sierra Leone, but these were thwarted. Accusations of massive corruption against the government of Seidu Momoh and a lack of transparency in spending the vast revenue from the diamond trade, coupled with a decayed infrastructure, a breakdown of security in border areas, an increase in the sale and movement of weapons and drugs, and the Liberian civil war, culminated in the outbreak of civil war in Sierra Leone in 1991. The Revolutionary United Front (RUF), led by Foday Sankoh, immediately launched a brutal offensive against the government from the eastern region of the country.[4] Within months, much of the Eastern Province of Sierra Leone, bordering Liberia, was under the control of the RUF.

The Sierra Leonean crisis further deepened when, in 1992, young officers, led by Captain Valentine Strasser, toppled the government of Seidu Momoh and suspended the 1991 constitution, which guaranteed free speech, human rights and multi-party democracy. The Strasser regime also declared a state of emergency. The regime, supposedly meant to correct the failure of President Momoh to suppress the rebellion, established the National Provisional Ruling Council (NPRC), which was unable to settle the turmoil that was then affecting the capital, Freetown. In 1995, the NPRC hired a private security firm, Executive Outcomes,[5] which was surprisingly able to force RUF troops beyond the Sierra Leonean border within a short period of time. Following the expulsion of RUF rebels, the peace in the aftermath was short-lived. This was because the accountability of the NPRC government was soon undermined by a variety of scandals and accusations related to bribery and corruption. Some NPRC members, led by Brigadier-General Julius Maada Bio, staged a coup and dismissed Strasser from power. The new junta reinstated the constitution, organized elections and installed a civilian government led by President Ahmad Tejan Kabbah's Sierra Leone People's Party (SLPP). The Tejan Kabbah government was deposed, after a first failed attempt, by a group of soldiers led by Major General Johnny Paul Koroma,[6] who established the Armed Forces Revolutionary Council (AFRC) and invited the RUF, led by Foday Sankoh, to join the government. The RUF/AFRC government banned all political parties, suspended the constitution, shut down all private radio stations and banned all public demonstrations.

Waging peace: The ECOMOG intervention

There was widespread condemnation of the RUF/AFRC junta by the international community, and Tejan Kabbah, who had fled to Guinea, was able to rally enough support behind him. The governments of the United Kingdom, Nigeria and Guinea pledged their support for Tejan Kabbah and called for his immediate reinstatement as President of Sierra Leone. The Nigerian government subsequently dispatched troops to Sierra

Leone under the ECOWAS agreement establishing the ECOMOG intervention force. There were reports, however, that, before the deployment of the Nigerian troops, an agreement was reached between the United Kingdom's representative, the Guinean government and Nigeria to once again employ the services of Executive Outcomes.[7] The entry of ECOMOG (and perhaps Executive Outcomes) into the conflict in 1997 defined, to a large extent, the direction of not only the conflict but Sierra Leone as a country.

One outstanding characteristic of ECOMOG, particularly in its intervention in the Sierra Leonean conflict, was its ability to effectively exert control over the country, especially in Freetown. Equally, by intervening massively in terms of military strength, ECOMOG failed to safeguard the humanitarian aspect of the mission adequately, consequently neglecting the civilian population of Sierra Leone. This situation established the basis for the future health crisis represented by the spread of HIV not only in Sierra Leone but also in Liberia and Guinea. The epidemic remained unmonitored and no data were recorded until the United Nations Mission in Sierra Leone (UNAMSIL) was established in 1999, providing access to the country to other UN agencies.

Whereas there are numerous documented atrocities involving sexual violence by the RUF rebels, the issue of abuses perpetrated by ECOMOG troops against the civilian population was controversial because it was extremely difficult to prove these allegations. As Human Rights Watch reported: "Human Rights Watch has not documented any cases of rape by soldiers serving under ECOMOG, the Economic Community of West African States peace keeping force, or under UNAMSIL, the UN Mission in Sierra Leone."[8]

Unfortunately, the ECOMOG mission paid scarcely any attention to the humanitarian needs of civilians. The ECOMOG Command Headquarters (ECH), set up in Freetown, was a military office, meant to receive orders from the ECOWAS countries' home governments, Nigeria in particular. Considering its conduct and subsequent available reports, ECOMOG appeared to fulfil a single order: "reinstate Tejan Kabbah as President in Sierra Leone". ECH had no office dealing with humanitarian issues and the only non-military group it engaged with was the press. There is also evidence of documents produced by ECH about the health of its troops and civilians in the ECOMOG-controlled parts of Sierra Leone.

The absence of an office to address humanitarian issues and the civilian population made the ECOMOG troops prone to using their discretion in dealing with displaced people and the civilian population in towns and villages and in the bush. Although this chapter does not in any way condemn ECOMOG's political-military operation in Sierra Leone, my opinion is that ECOMOG's inaction in addressing humanitarian issues was reflected strongly in the post-conflict HIV/AIDS healthcare crisis in the country. The unilateral military agenda of ECOMOG, and its failure to collect data and make them available for civil society, created a social gap in a critical period that, although short in time, was very significant.

ECOMOG and HIV/AIDS: An unacknowledged relationship

The interactions between the civilian population in Sierra Leone and ECOMOG troops have been the subject of diverse accounts. There were incidences of sex workers who found it safer to patronize ECOMOG troops,[9] whereas other ECOMOG troops established families in Sierra Leone before they left.[10] This demonstrates the social interaction that often occurs between "peacekeepers" and civilians – a recurrent and conspicuous phenomenon in most conflict and post-conflict societies.[11]

Despite the HIV risks associated with military deployments in conflict situations, both the Nigerian government and the ECOMOG leadership were ill prepared to take proactive measures to address the potential impact of the epidemic on ECOMOG troops or the spread of the virus in the wider civilian population. ECOMOG troops were not tested either before or after deployment. There was no official HIV/AIDS policy or programme tailored to the needs of the ECOMOG mission in Sierra Leone.[12] ECOMOG operations, including HIV-related issues, were characterized as belonging to the military sphere and therefore deemed classified, confidential and a state secret. A review of available policy documents by the Nigerian military government of the late General Sani Abacha, under whose regime the ECOMOG mission was executed, revealed that there were no HIV data on the civilian population in Sierra Leone or their relationship with the ECOMOG troops. Although individual cases of death were communicated to the next of kin of the dead soldiers, there was silence on issues relating to the health or HIV/AIDS status of the soldiers.

Consequently, dealing with the HIV-infected ECOMOG troops who returned to Nigeria raised complex policy challenges in Nigeria. Although there is no official document acknowledging that returning troops were ill or HIV-infected, there were unofficial reports of an ECOMOG Army Commander, General Victor Malu, acknowledging the return to Nigeria of hundreds of HIV-infected troops.[13] Informal accounts by some of the soldiers who served in the ECOMOG mission in Sierra Leone and Liberia revealed that no HIV policy was in place prior to deployment and while in the field.

Subsequently, however, there were studies covering the 1990s, the period when HIV had gained a foothold in Nigerian society, which also coincided with the deployment of Nigerian troops for peacekeeping and enforcement action in the Liberian and Sierra Leonean conflicts. One such epidemiological study was conducted by Brigadier General A. Adefolalu, Commandant and Chief Consulting Surgeon at the Nigerian Army Medical Command School Headquarters in Lagos, Nigeria.[14]

Adefolalu concluded that HIV prevalence among Nigerian Army troops increased from less than 1 percent in 1989/90 to 5 percent in 1997, and by 1999 to 10 percent. The years 1998 and 1999 coincided with a return of troops from ECOMOG operational areas, and among them the HIV prevalence rate was 12 percent. The Adefolalu study also included a comparative analysis of HIV incidence and the lengths of soldiers' duty tours in the turbulent Operation Sandstorm area of Sierra Leone. Incidence rates among these troops increased from 7 percent after one year in the operational area to 10 percent after two years, and to more than 15 percent after three years of deployment, for a cumulative annual risk factor of about 2 percent.[15]

The presence of ECOMOG troops within Sierra Leonean borders complicated the crisis of HIV/AIDS in many ways. Although relative peace and stability were re-established within the country, this relative stability was threatened by the human security implications of the HIV crisis in post-conflict Sierra Leone. The difficulty of understanding how the interactions of ECOMOG troops and the civilian population drove the HIV crisis during the Sierra Leoncan conflict was rendered even more complex by the paucity of data and policy on testing before and after deployment in order to determine prevalence levels precisely and the exact time of infection. As Bratt argued, "in the case of ECOMOG, Sierra Leone argues that it was Nigerian peacekeepers who brought HIV/AIDS to their country. Nigeria, not surprisingly, argues that their military was not highly infected until it went to Sierra Leone."[16]

The implication of this is that not only did ECOMOG troops leave a population in disarray, they also returned home heavily infected. It remains unfortunate that the health issues of the civilian population in Sierra Leone, as well as of ECOMOG troops, were treated as a state secret that received virtually no policy attention from military administrators.

Concluding observations

The conflict in Sierra Leone, and the subsequent deployment of a Nigeria-led ECOMOG intervention force, had serious implications for the spread of HIV. The absence of any health policy as a component part of ECOMOG security/military operations complicated the HIV situation during the conflict. Admittedly, healthcare and institutions often break down during wars and conflicts, but there is a need for the military to devise ways of controlling the disease within its ranks during deployments to conflict situations. This was completely lacking in ECOMOG operations in Sierra Leone. The ECOMOG mission was treated as a military operation with the sole aim of reinstating the government of President Tejan Kabbah. Although the operation could be characterized as "militarily successful", it could be argued that it represented a massive humanitarian failure that, among other things, exacerbated the HIV/AIDS epidemic within the rank and file of the troops and the civilian population in Sierra Leone.

This chapter therefore recommends a novel approach to peacekeeping, especially with regard to data collection concerning serious health issues such as HIV. Peacekeeping missions should include a humanitarian department that, among other tasks, would have the capacity to collect information that should be used to address health issues as they emerge in conflict situations. This information should be shared widely by all relevant stakeholders, including civil society organizations. As African militaries face current and future peacekeeping and related military operations in Darfur and elsewhere, the lessons from the ECOMOG operations in Sierra Leone and Liberia should catalyse policy reform with respect to controlling the HIV/AIDS epidemic in the military. One lesson from the ECOMOG experience in Sierra Leone is that military operations should not ignore humanitarian concerns, especially those that relate to the crisis of HIV/AIDS, the greatest epidemic of modern times.

Notes

1. Central Intelligence Agency (CIA), "Africa: Sierra Leone", *World Factbook*, ⟨https://www.cia.gov/library/publications/the-world-factbook/geos/sl.html⟩ (accessed 16 September 2011).
2. Arthur Abraham, *Topics in Sierra Leone History: A Counter-Colonial Interpretation* (Sierra Leone: Leone Publishers, 1976).
3. An example of such resistance was the Hut Tax War of 1898, when the largest ethnic group in present-day Sierra Leone, the Temne, led by their chief, Bai Bureh, declared war on the British in Sierra Leone and many British officers and Krios were killed. Chief Bai Bureh was later captured and exiled to Ghana, but he was brought back in 1905 and installed as a chief over his people.
4. The Eastern Province of Sierra Leone contains most of the country's deposits of diamonds. Although there are arguments that the war was launched from the east because the RUF rebels were equipped and supported by President Charles Taylor of Liberia, within days of taking the Kailahun District the RUF took over all the diamond mines in the region and there were wide reports that Charles Taylor was compensated with diamonds from Sierra Leone.

5. Executive Outcomes was a South African security company founded by Lt-Col. Eeben Barlow, a former Apartheid regime Special Forces commander. It has been a focus of international condemnation for its interest in underdeveloped but mineral-rich failed states in Africa and Asia. For further reading, see Anthony C. LoBaido, "Executive Outcomes: A New Kind of Army for Privatized Global Warfare", *World Net Daily Exclusive*, 11 August 1998, ⟨http://www.wnd.com/?pageId=3290⟩ (accessed 16 September 2011); Christopher Wrigley, "The Privatisation of Violence: New Mercenaries and the State", Campaign Against Arms Trade, London, March 1999, ⟨http://www.caat.org.uk/resources/publications/government/mercenaries-1999.php⟩ (accessed 16 September 2011).

6. Johnny Paul Koroma was put in prison after he was arrested for the failed attempt to overthrow the government. After the successful toppling of the Tejan Kabbah government, Koroma was released from prison to head the new junta.

7. The reason given was that the Nigerian troops were still stationed in neighbouring Liberia and were to remain there till 1998. See Wrigley, "The Privatisation of Violence".

8. Human Rights Watch, "Sexual Violence within the Sierra Leone Conflict", New York, 26 February 2001, ⟨http://www.hrw.org/legacy/backgrounder/africa/sl-bck0226.htm⟩ (accessed 16 September 2011).

9. C. Reis, L. L. Amowitz, K. H. Lyons, B. Vann, B. Mansaray, A. M. Akinsulure-Smith, L. Taylor and V. Iacopino, "War-related Sexual Violence in Sierra Leone: Implications for HIV/AIDS", XV International AIDS Conference, Bangkok, 11–16 July 2004, ⟨http://www.iasociety.org/Default.aspx?pageId=79⟩ (accessed 16 September 2011).

10. Stefan Lovgren, "African Army Hastening HIV/AIDS Spread", *Jenda, A Journal of Culture and African Women Studies*, 1(2), 2001; Eboe Hutchful, "The ECOMOG Experience with Peacekeeping in West Africa", in Mark Malan, ed., *Whither Peacekeeping in Africa?*, Monograph No. 36 (Pretoria: Institute for Security Studies, April 1999).

11. On this, see Stefan Elbe, *The Strategic Dimensions of HIV/AIDS* (Oxford: Oxford University Press, 2003); Stefan Elbe, "HIV/AIDS and Security", in Alan Collins, ed., *Contemporary Security Studies* (New York: Oxford University Press, 2007), pp. 331–345.

12. On the policy challenges of HIV/AIDS and UN peacekeeping generally, see Michael Fleshman, "AIDS Prevention in the Ranks: UN Targets Peacekeepers, Combatants in War Against the Disease", *Africa Recovery*, 15(1–2), 2001.

13. Lovgren, "African Army Hastening HIV/AIDS Spread"; K. Ahmad, "Public Protests as Nigeria Bans Use of Untested HIV Vaccine", *The Lancet*, 356(9228), p. 493; John Harke, "HIV-AIDS and the Security Sector in Africa: A Threat to Canada", Canada Security and Intelligence Service, Commentary No. 80, 2001.

14. A. Adefolalu, "HIV/AIDS as an Occupational Hazard to Soldiers – ECOMOG Experience", unpublished paper presented at the 3rd All Africa Congress of Armed Forces and Police Medical Services, Pretoria, South Africa, October 1999.

15. Stuart J. Kingma and Rodger D. Yeager, "Military Personnel: On the Move and Vulnerable to HIV/AIDS and Other Infectious Diseases", Civil-Military Alliance to Combat HIV & AIDS, 2005, ⟨http://www.certi.org/cma/publications/000-Militar_Personnel-On_the_Move.pdf⟩ (accessed 16 September 2011).

16. Duane Bratt, "Blue Condoms: The Use of International Peacekeepers in the Fight Against AIDS", *International Peacekeeping*, 9(3), 2002, p. 75. See, generally, Obijiofor Aginam, "HIV/AIDS, Conflicts, and Security in Africa", in M. Ndulo, ed., *Security, Reconstruction, and Reconciliation: When the Wars End* (London: UCL Press, 2007), pp. 26–37.

Part III

HIV/AIDS: Perspectives on the police and prisons

12

Policing against stigma and discrimination: HIV/AIDS in the Zambia Police Service

Charles M. Banda

Introduction

Since 1988, the World AIDS Day has been celebrated annually with various themes in recognition of the global ramifications of the HIV/AIDS epidemic. In his message on "Leadership", the theme of the 2007 World AIDS Day, Peter Piot, the former Executive Director of the Joint United Nations Programme on HIV/AIDS (UNAIDS), stated that:

> [S]ustaining leadership and accelerating action on AIDS isn't something just for politicians. It involves religious leaders, community, youth and council leaders, chief executives and trade union leaders. It involves people living with HIV, and their families and friends. It involves you, me – each and every one of us – taking the lead to eliminate stigma and discrimination, to advocate for more resources to tackle AIDS.

> And it requires us all to focus on AIDS every day of the year. Only then can we hope to achieve the global goal of universal access to HIV prevention, treatment, care and support.[1]

This chapter highlights the trends of HIV/AIDS among the police in Zambia, and provides an outline of the benchmarks upon which policy development within the Zambia Police Service should be undertaken. This chapter stresses the importance and centrality of "leadership" in the implementation of the policy on HIV/AIDS, sexually transmitted infections (STIs) and tuberculosis by the Zambia Police Service. Recognizing

HIV/AIDS and the security sector in Africa, Aginam and Rupiya (eds),
United Nations University Press, 2012, ISBN 978-92-808-1209-1

the haphazard nature of most HIV/AIDS programmes so far undertaken by the Zambian police, this chapter recommends that the Zambia Police Service Medical Department document estimates of HIV prevalence within its ranks. In doing so, the Police Service should take into account effective intervention strategies to address the impact of the epidemic. Since the control of HIV/AIDS raises serious "governance" challenges, including issues of human rights, stigma and discrimination, the active involvement of the police in HIV/AIDS control is essential.

HIV/AIDS in Zambia: Overview of the prevalence rates

Zambia is located in southern Africa – the epicentre of the HIV/AIDS epidemic. The first case of AIDS in Zambia was identified in 1984. Since then, the government of Zambia has implemented programmes aimed at controlling HIV/AIDS, starting with the establishment of the National AIDS Surveillance Committee in 1986. At the end of 1999, with an estimated adult prevalence rate of 19.95 per cent, Zambia had the sixth-highest adult prevalence rate in the world behind Botswana, Zimbabwe, Swaziland, Lesotho and Namibia.[2] In 2001, UNAIDS estimated that about 1.2 million people were living with HIV/AIDS in Zambia.[3] In 2002, the Bureau for Global Health under the United States Agency for International Development (USAID) reported that, at the end of 2001, more than 1.2 million people in Zambia were living with HIV/AIDS. The demographic and health survey conducted in 2001–2002 confirmed that the infection rate in Zambia at that time was 16 per cent among adults of reproductive age (17.8 per cent for women, 12.9 per cent for men).[4]

In its 2010 global report, although UNAIDS listed Zambia as one of the largest epidemics in sub-Saharan Africa (alongside Ethiopia, Nigeria, South Africa and Zimbabwe)[5] that has stabilized or is declining, it nonetheless estimated Zambia's adult prevalence rate at the end of 2009 to be between 12.8 and 14.1 per cent. UNAIDS estimated that 59,000 adults were newly infected and 45,000 adults and children died of AIDS-related causes in Zambia at the end of 2009.[6]

HIV/AIDS and the Zambia Police Service

Although the impact of HIV/AIDS on the various sectors in Zambia – agriculture, mining, health, education, labour force, households and many others – is now fairly well documented,[7] these HIV national estimates and prevalence rates do not yet form an integral part of "policing" work in Zambia. Men and women in uniform, including the police, encounter certain risks in the course of their daily jobs that render them vulnerable to infection. The Zambia Police Service is hit hard by HIV/AIDS because, among other factors, policemen can target and afford sex workers since they work at night and often for long hours. They spend days away from their homes, and a considerable number of these officers are deployed in other countries as part of peacekeeping missions. These factors make them susceptible to engaging in casual sex while on mission or a posting away from home.

Because it is now widely accepted that the impact of HIV/AIDS has gone far beyond the household and community levels, the leadership of the Zambia Police Service is concerned about the rising number of HIV-positive police officers who are dying of AIDS and HIV-related diseases. All sections of the Police Service, including its operational command, are affected. Despite the impact of the epidemic on policing – an essential institution in the security sector – there has been no tangible policy intervention by the Zambia Police Service to address the epidemic. There are no effective benchmarks to indicate the number of police officers living with HIV. Even the policy trends outlined and discussed later in this chapter are haphazard policy pieces that lack proactive tools to address the epidemic. Policy responses aimed at addressing the impact of HIV/AIDS on the Zambia Police Service, where they exist, are merely reactive. This often leads to "stigmatizing" those who are already infected in ways that are clearly discriminatory.

HIV/AIDS statistics: Establishing the number of HIV-positive police officers

Despite the well-known fact that the HIV prevalence among police officers in Zambia is high, there are, for instance, no data on when the Zambia Police Service reported its first diagnosed AIDS case. The prevalence and incidence of HIV/AIDS among the police are unknown. This is partly owing to the fact that the police do not have a hospital of their own. Infected officers go to private or public hospitals. As a result, only very few (if any) officers who have been diagnosed with HIV and treated in those hospitals would inform the Police Command. If such cases were diagnosed in a police hospital, HIV-positive cases would form an important and credible estimate of the number of police officers known to be HIV-positive. The approximate number of police personnel who come forward for HIV testing would also be known. This has led to gross underreporting of the number of police officers living with HIV (prevalence) and the number of new infections each year (incidence). This distorts policy and makes planning extremely difficult.

In May 2005, Chendela Musonda, the then Commanding Officer of Lusaka Division of the Zambia Police, disclosed that "over 48 officers from Lusaka division died of HIV/AIDS-related diseases while over 1,000 others were already infected".[8] This is a fair reflection of the country-wide trend. At the national level, as many as 21 out of the Police Service's roughly 14,000 personnel may be dying of AIDS each month. This equates to approximately 254 personnel each year, with over 3,000 personnel having died of AIDS between January 1991 and April 2003.[9] The HIV prevalence rate within the Zambia Police Service is unknown but, since AIDS cases usually represent only a small proportion of the total number of people infected with HIV, prevalence is likely to be high.

Emerging trends

In Zambia, just as in most countries and regions, there are links between mobility and the rate of HIV infection. Depending on where people go, migration carries with it some HIV-related risks. The frequent movement of police officers from low- to high-prevalence areas might offer HIV an opportunity to move along with them. A considerable number of police officers are mobile, tending to be away from home for long periods. Away from home, "as in the case of migrant workers, loneliness, boredom and, sometimes, peer pressure may lead personnel to engage in casual or commercial sex and recreational drug use".[10] To worsen this situation, there is the likelihood that these officers exchange sexual partners, while, at the same time, spouses may also be having sexual relations with other partners. Conversely, the regular police officers (who are based in police stations and carry out general duties such as investigations, traffic and foot patrols) are quite settled. They are stationed in one duty station for longer periods of time.

Widows and newly graduated officers

Newly graduated police officers face many challenges in the Zambia Police Service. First, accommodation is scarce, and the presence of police widows living in police camps exacerbates the situation because some of them engage in survival sex (as the only source of income after the loss of the bread-winner). In such circumstances, new male officers, particularly single ones, sometimes cohabit with a widow before she is repatriated to her village. In October 2007, the *Monitor and Digest* newspaper published a story on widows of deceased police officers living in Lusaka's Sikanze Police Camp who had turned police servant quarters into brothels and taverns. According to the report, "some widows, who are still waiting to receive their deceased husband's benefits, are allegedly using the brothels and taverns in question to generate funds for their up-keep and to send their children to school".[11] Whenever this trend exists, it commonly leads to sexual relations between young officers and widows. Although largely consensual, this increases the risk of HIV transmission when sex is casual and unprotected.

"Policing" against commercial sex work is particularly problematic in Zambia. It remains debatable whether sex workers spread HIV because there is evidence that they are traditionally well informed about the use of condoms.[12] Nonetheless, the police leadership seems determined to accuse sex workers of spreading HIV, instead of focusing on officers who patronize the services of commercial sex workers.

Sexual relations between the wives of junior officers and their husband's supervisors are widespread, just as between junior female officers and senior male supervisors. This may not be true of all police camps, but it suggests some ways in which HIV is transmitted among police personnel, especially if these sexual relations are coerced and occur without condoms.

Police training facilities

At police training facilities, female recruits are often vulnerable to sexual exploitation or harassment. There exists a social pattern enabled by older male instructors – who are referred to as "bad eggs" – of luring young, new and unsuspecting female trainees into various degrees of sexual relationship. In this scenario, young women are locally labelled "village chicken". The misconception and naivety of this term reflect the idea that "a new person who comes into the area is not infected". Consequently, this mistaken belief puts both instructors and trainees at risk.

As part of its corrective measures, the police leadership, in accordance with Police College policy, has acted against convicted officers with warnings, transfers and even arrest. These strict measures are dictated by the sense of urgency regarding the spread of the infection. Even if just one training instructor engages in such behaviour each year, over a period of years this would result in many newly trained female officers contracting HIV. In this way, the chain of infection and re-infection continues.

Poverty and the vulnerability of local women

It is a well-known fact that in Zambia, as in many other developing countries, impoverished women fall victim to abuses of power by men, including male police officers. "A key component of women's poverty is their inability to obtain loans from banking institutions, which renders them less able to enter into safe, profitable economic activities."[13] Owing to their lack of monetary power, rural women are often unable to withstand sexual advances by police officers in return for money or favours. Consequently, this form of exploitation exponentially increases exposure and vulnerability to the virus.

Police "power" and abuse

Zambia is a patriarchal society where men have enormous social, economic and political power compared with women. The Zambia Police Service is a predominantly male-dominated institution, and officers wearing uniform are generally perceived as authoritarian members of the community. Consequently, female criminal suspects and sex workers can easily become victims of injustices and human rights abuses. On 23 May 2002, the British Broadcasting Corporation (BBC) reported that "[a] group of Zambian police officers could face the sack after being accused of sexually abusing prostitutes. The sex-workers said that they were repeatedly arrested and were only released after being raped by the policemen."[14]

According to Human Rights Watch:

> Even though prostitution is not illegal under Zambian law, it is illegal to solicit customers or to live off the earnings of someone engaged in sex work, and it is difficult for sex workers who suffer physical or sexual violence to report it to the police. Societal attitudes against sex workers and the stigma associated with them further discourage reporting. Police conduct round-ups of sex workers and charge them with loitering or indecent exposure. Usually, the women pay 10,000 kwacha (U.S.$2.30) and are freed in the morning; other times, the police take the women's money or demand sexual services as payment.[15]

Police culture

Culture represents the collective behaviour, way of life, beliefs and institutions of a people. In the larger Zambian society, there are diverse cultural and traditional practices across the 70+ ethnic groups in the country.[16] Within the Police Force, certain beliefs and practices put female personnel at risk of sexual harassment. These embedded beliefs and practices in turn make females vulnerable to contracting HIV. Peer pressure from colleagues and supervising officers may encourage engagement in risky behaviour, including unprotected sex, excessive drinking and, to a lesser extent, drug use.

The impact of HIV and AIDS

All diseases and medical conditions have repercussions on the social and economic life of the people affected by them as well as those close to them. The social, economic and political impacts of the HIV/AIDS epidemic have been devastating at the personal, family, community, national, regional and global levels. Because these impacts have been documented in the voluminous HIV/AIDS literature,[17] this chapter gives an overview of how the epidemic drives stigmatization and discrimination in police work and its impact on the cost of police recruitment and training.

The impact on individuals: Stigmatization and discrimination

All previous studies on HIV/AIDS in Zambia have concluded that stigma is one of the strongest factors driving the epidemic. Garbus observed that "misconceptions about HIV/AIDS persist and perpetuate stigma" within Zambian society.[18] Stigmatization often drives discrimination against HIV-positive persons based on negative thoughts, actions and other prejudices directed towards people living with HIV/AIDS (PLWHAs), either consciously or unconsciously. Quoting a Panos/UNICEF study, Elemu et al. define stigma as a "process of devaluation within a particular culture or setting where attitudes are seized upon and defined as discredible [*sic*] or not worthy".[19] Research suggests at least two types of stigma relating to HIV/AIDS: "felt stigma" (self-stigmatization), which is based on self-devaluation and internal feelings and perceptions of shame; and "enacted stigma", which refers to external negative thoughts and feelings against those perceived to be infected. In contrast to stigma, "discrimination" focuses – unfairly or unjustly – on the habits of the producers of rejection and exclusion.[20]

Although the "extreme forms" of stigmatization of HIV/AIDS and of discrimination against PLWHAs are no longer evident in most Zambian societies, Elemu et al. argue that "stigma remains high, and as long as it remains high, those who are infected would stay away from public participation".[21] The Zambia Police Service has been adversely affected by the HIV infection prevalence rate through indirect and direct stigmatization and discrimination. For example, infected officers are placed together in one office and assigned to similar "light duties". This is often done in a discriminatory way: the infected officers cannot share the same office space or be together with those who are presumed to be uninfected. The status of infected officers is often publicly declared, and this isolates them as a core group subject to stigmatization and discrimination. HIV/AIDS-based stigmatization and discrimination constitute a serious barrier to police officers in the performance of their duties. The multiple effects of stigmatization often include isolation and loneliness, rejection, stress, denial, blame, anxiety, disrupted relationships, suicidal thoughts, missed opportunities such as insurance, loss of respect, and flagrant violation of human dignity and human rights.

The cost of recruitment and training

As skill levels and service delivery decline drastically, police operations face increasing costs associated with recruiting and training new police officers to replace those who have become ill or died as a result of AIDS. In addition, fit and able-bodied police officers are outnumbered, overwhelmed or overburdened by work demands. With increasing crime levels, there are also increasing policing costs. Moreover, both foreign and local investments are likely to decline because the police presence is not adequate to provide security. As large numbers of police officers become ill and die, the reach and capacity of government institutions are reduced and the government budget is diverted to the health-related costs associated with the epidemic.

The continued loss of human resources to the epidemic is a disaster that should catalyse policy reform in the Police Service. The current loss is having a devastating impact as it equates to losing a battalion annually. A sick officer loses the physical ability and fitness to carry out the onerous and strenuous police work effectively. Police stations are not sufficiently staffed and the efficiency of those on duty is likely to be undermined by the epidemic. Accordingly, the fight against serious crimes, such as aggravated robberies, homicides and rape, is proving difficult to maintain. The Zambia Police Service urgently needs an effective HIV/AIDS policy to address the multiple challenges posed by the epidemic to police work. This policy framework is the subject of the next section.

Policy development

As already stated, there are no reliable data on HIV infection and prevalence levels in the police service. This lack impedes policy development and planning. Under a new HIV/AIDS policy, there is now a National HIV/AIDS Desk and HIV/AIDS committees operate at regional levels. Three functioning voluntary counselling and testing (VCT) centres at State Lodge, Livingstone and Sikanze Camp are serviced by a mobile VCT team from the Society for Family Health. Another VCT centre at Kamfinsa is not yet operational. Many officers have been trained to implement the policy, including the challenges to sensitization, workplace activities and peer education.

These policy developments target focused interventions aimed at keeping infection rates low and reducing the risk of and vulnerability to HIV in the police service. Prevention of HIV needs to focus on changing risky behaviours. Other critical prevention mechanisms and strategies would include, for example, shortening periods of night duty for police officers, reducing the duration of peacekeeping missions and other deployment away from home, encouraging police officers to go for VCT and seek early medical attention, and holding regular workshops, training programmes and sensitization/awareness campaigns. Further to prevention, there is a need for sustained care and support for those who are already infected. Stigmatization and discrimination should be discouraged by avoiding the practice of isolation and allocating light duties to infected officers. Treatment programmes should also offer free anti-retroviral drugs.

Conclusion

In examining HIV/AIDS in a culture such as the police, it is possible to identify a complex web of pre-existing prejudices and beliefs. This social context has serious implications for police officers infected with the virus. It is important to embark on a policy of comprehensive education of police officers about HIV/AIDS in order to de-mystify deeply held myths. On the positive side, techniques that challenge some of the police officers' unexamined beliefs and behaviours offer them the opportunity to work for a genuinely open and just society and the chance to examine and celebrate the diversity of human relationships.

This chapter has sought to propose a new conceptual framework in relation to the trends in HIV/AIDS infections and potential interventions to minimize the impact of the epidemic on "policing" in Zambia. This new framework could help improve understanding of the risk factors that lead to HIV infections and of the interventions to address them. Whatever policy is ultimately put in place, strategic interventions to address embedded stigmatization and discriminatory practices should proceed on three fronts: (i) identifying policies, programme elements and interventions that can contribute to effective responses to HIV/AIDS-related stigma and discrimination; (ii) identifying how these can best be implemented, including the likely outcomes of specific approaches; and (iii) improving understanding about how programme implementation and the potential for replication and "scaling-up" of successful approaches are influenced by broader policy and social contexts. Because these policy interventions require a legal and policy framework that protects the human rights of PLWHAs, leadership within the Police Service and beyond is needed. In line with the "leadership" theme of the 2007 World AIDS Day, the extent to which the battle with the HIV/AIDS epidemic in the Zambia Police Service is won or lost largely depends on leadership. It is up to the police authorities to establish coordinating mechanisms and to prioritize the necessary actions and intervention strategies to prevent HIV transmission, to care for those infected and to reduce the social and economic impacts of HIV/AIDS within its ranks.

Notes

1. UNAIDS, "Dr Peter Piot's Message on World AIDS Day 2007", ⟨http://www.unaids.org.vn/sitee/index.php?option=com_content&task=view&id=17&Itemid=66⟩ (accessed 16 September 2011).
2. Lisa Garbus, *HIV/AIDS in Zambia*, Country Policy Analysis Project, AIDS Policy Research Center, University of California, San Francisco, March 2003, ⟨http://www.ari.ucsf.edu/programs/policy/countries/Zambia.pdf⟩ (accessed 16 September 2011), pp. 20–21, quoting UNAIDS, *Report on the Global HIV/AIDS Epidemic, June 2000* (Geneva: UNAIDS, 2000) and *Report on the Global HIV/AIDS Epidemic, 2002* (Geneva: UNAIDS, 2002).
3. UNAIDS, *Report on the Global HIV/AIDS Epidemic, 2002*.
4. "Zambia: HIV/AIDS Country Profile", Bureau for Global Health, U.S. Agency for International Development.
5. UNAIDS, *Global Report: UNAIDS Report on the Global AIDS Epidemic, 2010* (Geneva: UNAIDS, 2010), ⟨http://www.unaids.org/en/media/unaids/contentassets/documents/unaidspublication/2010/20101123_globalreport_en.pdf⟩ (accessed 31 August 2011), p. 25.
6. Ibid.
7. See, for instance, Garbus, *HIV/AIDS in Zambia*, a 128-page study that covers the impact of the epidemic on various social and economic sectors in Zambia.
8. "Lusaka Police Launches HIV/AIDS Desk", *Times of Zambia*, Thursday, 12 May 2005, ⟨http://www.zamnet.zm/newsys/news/viewnews.cgi?category=30&id=1115888797⟩ (accessed 16 September 2011).
9. Southern African Regional Police Chiefs Cooperation Organization, Training Manual Module 3, "The Impact of HIV/AIDS on Human, National and Regional Security", quoting G. Chakulunta, *Data on School of Public Order Maintenance* (Zambia Police Service, 2003), p. 34.
10. Ibid.
11. The *Monitor and Digest* newspaper, Tuesday 16 October – Thursday 18 October 2007, Issue No. 274.
12. For a discussion of this, see Diane Richardson, *Women and the AIDS Crisis* (London: Pandora, 1989).
13. Garbus, *HIV/AIDS in Zambia*, citing the Zambian Ministry of Finance and National Planning, Zambia Poverty Reduction Strategy Paper.
14. "Sex-Workers 'Raped' by Zambian Police", *BBC News*, Tuesday, 23 April 2002, ⟨http://news.bbc.co.uk/2/hi/africa/1946107.stm⟩ (accessed 16 September 2011).
15. Human Rights Watch, *Suffering in Silence: The Links Between Human Rights Abuses and HIV Transmission to Girls in Zambia* (New York: Human Rights Watch, 2002), ⟨http://www.hrw.org/sites/default/files/reports/zambia1202.pdf⟩ (accessed 16 September 2011), p. 40.

16. Ibid., p. 20.
17. On the impact of HIV/AIDS on the various sectors in Zambia, see Garbus, *HIV/AIDS in Zambia*. On the impact of the epidemic on governance in Africa, see Kondawani Chirambo, ed., *The Political Cost of AIDS in Africa: Evidence from Six Countries* (Pretoria: IDASA, 2008), covering Namibia, South Africa, Tanzania, Zambia, Malawi and Senegal.
18. Garbus, *HIV/AIDS in Zambia*, citing a study by the Panos Institute on stigma and HIV/AIDS in rural southern Zambia.
19. D. Elemu, E. Rubvuta, A. Muunga and S. Mwase, "Zambia", in Chirambo, ed., *The Political Cost of AIDS in Africa*, p. 318.
20. Liz Sayce, "Stigma, Discrimination and Social Exclusion: What's in a Word?", *Journal of Mental Health*, 7(4), 1998, pp. 331–343.
21. Elemu et al., "Zambia", p. 316 (stating that, in the 1980s, PLWHAs were "chased out of homes", relatives abandoned them, leaving them without any support, and people would not share domestic utensils with them).

13

HIV/AIDS in Cameroon: The policy response of the police

Polycarp Ngufor Forkum

Introduction

This chapter examines the institutional framework adopted in Cameroon to fight the HIV/AIDS pandemic and how this framework related to the police. With the diagnosis of the first HIV cases in 1985,[1] the government embarked on a mission to control the scourge of HIV/AIDS, starting with its institutional and legislative framework. The approach has been holistic.[2] There are many factors that make those in uniform vulnerable to HIV. It is only recently that sector-specific measures, for example within the police, have been enacted. This chapter emphasizes the importance of a holistic approach because members of the police are part of the larger society. It also examines the mainstreaming of the police into the Ministry of Defence's HIV prevention plan and the resultant effects. It moves from the general to analyse efforts at the level of the police in Cameroon. The discussion does not intend to address the responses of other uniformed services, such as the armed forces and the penitentiary administration. Where these sectors are mentioned, it is purely for comparative purposes.

Geographical and demographic profile of Cameroon

The former French Cameroon and part of British Cameroon merged in 1961 to form the present Republic of Cameroon. Cameroon has gener-

HIV/AIDS and the security sector in Africa, Aginam and Rupiya (eds),
United Nations University Press, 2012, ISBN 978-92-808-1209-1

ally enjoyed stability, which has permitted the development of agriculture, roads and railways, as well as a petroleum industry. Despite slow movement towards democratic reform, political power has remained firmly in the hands of an ethnic oligarchy since 1982, headed by President Paul Biya. Cameroon is situated in Central and West Africa, with a coastline on the Bight of Biafra, and bordered by the Central African Republic, Chad, the Democratic Republic of the Congo (DRC), Equatorial Guinea, Gabon and Nigeria. Cameroon has an estimated population of about 20 million and its land area is slightly larger than that of the US state of California.

Overview of HIV sero-prevalence in Cameroon

Since the report of the first HIV/AIDS case in Cameroon in 1985, the sero-prevalence has been increasing steadily, making it the most dreaded disease in the country.[3] Between 1987 and 1998,[4] the sero-prevalence rose from 0.5 per cent to 7.2 per cent among the general population.[5] In 2000, it rose further to 11 per cent, and although in 2002 it was almost stagnant, with only a slight increase of 0.8 per cent, this still places the country among the 25 most-infected countries in the world.[6] The balance sheet of the disease between 1985 and 2002 shows 53,000 deaths, 210,000 orphans and 1 million people living with the disease.[7] In Cameroon between 1985 and 1998, the infection rate multiplied by 14.[8]

Between 1987 and 2002, there was a 23-fold increase, with the 20–39 age group being the most heavily affected. The most vulnerable groups within the population were: military personnel (15 per cent);[9] commercial sex workers (25–45 per cent); and truck drivers (18 per cent).[10] Other communities with high infection rates include those living along major highways and populations along the Chad–Cameroon pipeline.[11] On a gender dimension, women are more vulnerable, with statistics showing three infected women for every two infected men.[12] According to reports by both Cameroon's Minister of Health[13] and also the Technical Explanatory Note on the Third Cameroon Demographic and Health Survey (DHS-III), in 2004 there was a decrease of 5.6 per cent in HIV sero-prevalence among the sexually active population. The Permanent Secretariat of the Central Technical Group of the National AIDS Control Committee notes that the figures obtained from a representative national sample in the Technical Explanatory Note "reflect the real situation of HIV seroprevalence in [the] country" (that is, 6.9 per cent) and "fall within the range of the estimations for Cameroon by Joint United Nations Programme on HIV/AIDS (UNAIDS)",[14] which is understood to be between 4.8 per cent and 9.8 per cent.[15]

Scope and conceptual framework

Uniformed members in Cameroon comprise the armed forces, the police force and the penitentiary (prison) administration. However, this chapter examines solely the role of the police. As per the Police Act of Cameroon,[16] the word "police" is synonymous with employees of the national security force, who include personnel carrying out routine police duties such as the maintenance of law and order, investigation, intelligence-gathering and border control. They are also the subject of deployments in armed and unarmed missions of the United Nations (UN) and the African Union (AU). The entry age for the police is 18 years. Although some demographic statistics exist for the armed forces,[17] information about the police is scarcer, despite its huge number of personnel.

National responses

The approach to the HIV/AIDS epidemic in Cameroon has been generalized but ill focused, with little attention to the country's uniformed members and the police. Although officers are members of society equally with other citizens, they are particularly vulnerable to infection from the virus and are wanting in the fight against it.[18] When the government was concentrating on certain sectors of society rather than others, the police programme was – and is still – statutorily dependent on the military. The Discharge Commission of the Armed Forces and Police is the body appointed to safeguard the rights of police officers living with HIV/AIDS and other diseases (tuberculosis, cancer, poliomyelitis, leprosy and mental illness).[19] This inter-ministerial Commission is part of the Ministry of Defence and it oversees cases relating to both the police and the armed forces.

National legal framework

The national legal framework for HIV/AIDS control in Cameroon is very weak and is dependent on international and regional regimes for establishing norms.[20] The main pieces of legislation governing HIV/AIDS policy in Cameroon are those that establish various institutions that implement HIV/AIDS policy, and others governing specific issues, such as the cost of anti-retroviral (ARV) drugs and the decentralization of ARV treatment at the local level. The only law that specifically addresses HIV/AIDS is Law 2003/014 of 22 December 2003 regulating blood transfusion. In the absence of an effective legislative framework with a focus on HIV/AIDS, the relevant provisions in the 1996 Constitution,[21] the Penal

Code[22] and decisions of the courts (case law) may help set the legal framework for HIV/AIDS control in Cameroon.[23]

National strategies

In terms of strategies aimed at containing the pandemic, the government created the National AIDS Control Committee (NACC) in 1986. NACC, within the framework of the National AIDS Control Programme (NACP), successfully designed and implemented a number of policies. These comprised: a short-term plan, a first medium-term plan I running from 1988 to 1992, a second medium-term plan II running from 1993 to 1995, and a framework plan for HIV/AIDS control for the period 1999–2000.[24] Regrettably, the government itself has admitted that no satisfactory outcomes were reached through these programmes.[25] The shortcomings included poor coordination, inadequate involvement of other non-health sectors and insufficient resources.[26]

National AIDS Strategic Plan

The National AIDS Strategic Plan (NASP) was created as a result of the failure of the NACP. The authorities were expecting to reverse the epidemic's current trend, to reduce HIV-positivity to less than 10 per cent and to cut the incidence of HIV by 25 per cent among young people, uniformed personnel and women between 2000 and 2005.[27] The NASP was implemented within the context of a new and improved programme management that adopted a multi-sectoral approach, together with a policy of decentralized intervention.[28] In other words, it was managed by the NACC through its central, provincial outreach-level structures. The NASP was presented to the national and international community and adopted on 4 September 2000 with ratification by the Prime Minister.[29] Nonetheless, it is important to note that the control of AIDS is included in Cameroon's poverty reduction strategy as one of the country's priorities and this was described by UNAIDS as one of the best practices of this kind.[30]

Objectives of the National AIDS Strategic Plan

The NASP, implemented from September 2000 to 2005, had the following objectives:
- reducing the risk of child infection from birth to 5 years and educating children between the ages of 5 and 14 about healthy life skills and healthy sexual behaviour patterns;

- developing an information system geared towards monitoring sexual behaviour change in adults;
- reducing and preventing mother-to-child transmission;
- reducing the risk of contamination through blood transfusions; and
- increasing solidarity by developing national solidarity mechanisms with regard to people living with HIV/AIDS (PLWHA) and their families, assuring their medical coverage and psycho-social management, promoting and protecting their rights, and involving associations in this regard.[31]

The NASP envisaged, in addition, measures essentially aimed at attaining these objectives, through:

(i)   the construction of national and regional blood transfusion centres;
(ii) the establishment of HIV voluntary counselling and testing centres in all 10 provinces of Cameroon;
(iii) the promotion of condom use, mainly among the following vulnerable groups: students, military personnel, commercial sex workers and truck drivers; community mobilization; increased involvement of the public and private sectors, including religious denominations;
(iv) the promotion of interpersonal communication.

These objectives and accompanying measures were expected to be achieved through a five-stage process, clearly defined in the NASP.[32] The methods used to attain these objectives can be divided into control strategies on the one hand and control components on the other.

The control strategies included the following:

- development of medical and social mechanisms for the management of PLWHA;
- prevention of mother-to-child transmission, clinical management of sexually transmitted infections (STIs), and safe blood transfusion;
- promotion of voluntary counselling and testing and the use of male and female condoms;
- institution of a communication plan involving the public media (national radio stations);
- sensitization of youth in schools, universities and out-of-school contexts; women; workers; and the rural population.

The control components are mainly health responses, which form the central axis for HIV/AIDS control. They are embedded in the activities of the health sector, which aims at monitoring the evolution of the disease, reducing its spread and improving the quality of life for PLWHA and persons affected by HIV/AIDS. The attainment of these goals depended on the following: the securing of blood transfusions; prevention of mother-to-child transmission;[33] clinical management; psycho-social management and social de-stigmatization; epidemiological surveillance; voluntary counselling and testing; community response;[34] sector response;[35] funding;[36] private sector implication;[37] and the role of parliament.[38]

The expected outcomes of the implementation process of the NASP[39] were:

- to broaden the national response through the development of plans by various parts of the government's administrative arm (the Ministries of Defence,[40] National Education, Youth and Sports, Territorial Administration and Decentralization, Women's Affairs, Social Affairs, and Higher Education);
- to sign agreements with religious groups and private sector enterprises to wage the battle against HIV/AIDS within these communities, especially through preventive education, the promotion of condom use, and care for AIDS patients;
- to enhance local responses by setting up a process involving local authorities and communities by creating local non-governmental organizations (NGOs);
- to strengthen and organize programme management through the creation of a joint monitoring commission, which meets regularly; the creation of a multidisciplinary central management team; and capacity-building and improved logistical support for the central management team, as well the identification of offices for that team;
- to reduce the price of ARV drugs.

The new NASP 2006–2010

The 2006–2010 phase of the NASP, launched on 8 March 2006,[41] was an ambitious plan that marked a turning point in HIV/AIDS control in Cameroon.[42] Building on the relative success of the first NASP (2000–2005), the new plan aimed at preserving and maximizing the achievements of the first plan on one hand, and addressing its weaknesses on the other hand.[43] The central objective of this phase was to reduce the proportion of infected women and men to 50 per cent by 2010.[44] Attainment of this objective necessitated intervention in the following areas:

- counselling and voluntary screening to scale up awareness of personal serological status among women and men;
- prevention and control of STIs to reduce their prevalence;
- promotion of the use of condoms to 80 per cent (from 41 per cent for women and 54 per cent for men);
- blood transfusion safety;
- reinforcement of the prevention of HIV among children and women, and the reduction of mother-to-child transmission among breastfeeding babies to 50 per cent.[45]

There were five major strands of intervention strategies under the 2006–2010 NASP, which were aimed at correcting the shortcomings of the 2000–2005 NASP while addressing new challenges. These included:

- research and epidemiological surveillance;
- management of children affected by HIV/AIDS;
- access to medication;
- coordination, follow-up and evaluation;
- involvement of all sectors of society (that is, government, grassroots people, civil society, etc.).[46]

The strategy of involving all sectors[47] proved its worth in the 2000–2005 NASP, and it is within this framework that efforts at the Ministry of Defence, and thereby the police force, are being directed.

US Department of Defense HIV/AIDS Prevention Program (DHAPP)

The Walter Reed Johns Hopkins Cameroon Program is committed to providing technical assistance to Central African militaries to improve their HIV/AIDS prevention programmes.[48] In Cameroon, these interventions are organized by the military both for itself and for the police.[49] From November 2005 to January 2006, working sessions were conducted with the Cameroonian military health division and the HIV/AIDS prevention unit in preparation for launching the Cameroon component of the military-to-military HIV prevention project in Central Africa. In the second quarter of the programme, the military garrison at Ngaoundere was selected to host the one-year DHAPP project among the defence forces (including the police). A preliminary site visit was conducted in Ngaoundere garrison by the Director of Military Health and the HIV/AIDS focal point, during which the project objectives and implementation plan were presented to local military officers. This project received support from these leaders, as well as from local health authorities at the Ministry of Public Health.[50] Technical assistance was also provided to the military during the ongoing development of drafts of future materials to be used in this project.

The project was launched on 20 February 2006 in the presence of the United States Defense Attaché's Office in Cameroon, Walter Reed Johns Hopkins Cameroon Program staff for technical assistance, the Commandant of the 5th Military Region, the HIV focal point in the Cameroonian armed forces, the Director of Health of the General Delegation for National Security (Police) and the Provincial Delegate of the Ministry of Public Health in charge of the HIV/AIDS programme. This ceremony was followed by a three-day training of peer educators.[51] A total of 50 people were trained on the various aspects of HIV/AIDS.[52] Among the peer educators trained, 10 were police officers, 5 were civilians and the remaining 35 were from the armed forces. Given the imbalance between the three representative groups and some misunderstandings over the allocation of resources and facilities, it is arguable that a police-specific strategy may be required. In addition, a range of educational materials were produced as part of this project.[53] The educators were encouraged to provide HIV/AIDS prevention messages whose focus went beyond abstinence and/or fidelity. One indigenous organization was provided with technical assistance for strategic information and institutional capacity-building. Three individuals received training in capacity-building, and all 50 peer educators received training in communication techniques to address behavioural change and the promotion of HIV counselling and testing in the community.[54]

The Cameroonian police and the HIV/AIDS challenge

Legal framework for the control of HIV/AIDS in the police

Articles 36(2), 37 and 142 of the Police Act give the powers of managing PLWHA to the Discharge Commission of the Armed Forces and the Police. Accordingly, a police officer suffering from HIV/AIDS or other serious diseases[55] is placed on extended leave following the opinion of the Discharge Commission.[56] This body rules that the person in question has taken six or more months of leave over a 12-month period and has still not recovered.[57] During the extended leave, the officer should receive full remuneration.[58] In addition, the state provides free medical consultations and healthcare in public establishments, as well as providing reimbursement for those officers who have borne such expenses.[59] Also, time spent on extended leave is valid in consideration for promotion to seniority and may count towards retirement.[60] In other words, full remuneration during extended leave, free medical care and reimbursements are the statutory rights of police officers living with HIV/AIDS in Cameroon. Through these measures, the parliament brought HIV/AIDS on a par with the approach taken to other terminal diseases.

Survey of HIV sero-prevalence in the Cameroonian police force

Although precise official data based on studies of HIV/AIDS in the police sector are lacking, the estimates are worth noting. For the period from January 2004 to December 2006, HIV/AIDS accounted for 80 per cent of police deaths.[61] Of the 9,700 new police officers recruited in 2003,

811 tested HIV-positive.[62] The HIV-positive recruits were subsequently rejected following the results of the medical examination. In dubious circumstances, these same recruits were later returned to the training school by the then Delegate-General for National Security (i.e. the Minister of Police), for what he considered "political reasons".[63]

These episodes represent a major source of concern given the increasing participation of the Cameroonian police in peacekeeping operations. These include but are not limited to the United Nations Interim Administration in Kosovo, the United Nations Mission in Sierra Leone, the United Nations Mission in the DRC and several armed and unarmed missions of the African Union.[64] Prior to deployment, there is a comprehensive medical examination, which includes a mandatory HIV test. Of the 1,239 shortlisted police officers who underwent pre-deployment HIV testing between 2003 and 2006, 203 people (or 16.38 per cent) tested positive.[65] The police force was until that time a part of the overall NASP. However, owing to their high risk of exposure, it became necessary to conceive a strategy for the security sector as a whole. This strategy, which was essentially performed by the military leadership, resulted in discrimination in resource allocation at the expense of the police, as explained above. These conditions compelled the creation of the project outlined below, designed by the police themselves, together with experts from the NGO and government sectors.[66]

The police project

The police project is based on the following guidelines: the drafting of a budget for the plan to fight HIV/AIDS; the designation of focal points; the creation of a central coordination committee; the organization of educational talks; free screening exercises in police units; the training of educators; and general training/sensitization in police academies. To concretize these guidelines, the police published a manual entitled "Police: Training Manual for HIV/AIDS", which was adopted on 9 August 2007.

"Police: Training Manual for HIV/AIDS"

Elizabeth Mosima, quoting the Permanent Secretary of the General Delegation for National Security, Police Commissioner Victor Ndoki, observed that:

> Studies have shown that the prevalence rate of the HIV/AIDS virus in the police corps is higher than in the general population. This is because policemen and women are in contact with the population. Worse still, they are out of their homes most of the time. This puts them at high risk of the pandemic.[67]

This higher infection rate among the police force is the raison d'être for adopting the manual to train police personnel about HIV/AIDS, a decision that was made during a one-day workshop at the National Advanced Police School in Yaoundé. At the workshop, Police Commissioner Ndoki stated that HIV/AIDS is not only a major public health problem but also a crucial development problem for African countries. The lethal disease affects families, businesses and governments, and police officers are not exempted. He praised the idea of adopting a training manual on HIV/AIDS in the police corps and said that counselling and communication for behavioural change in the police corps contribute to the success of the NASP. The existence of the training manual in the police units is an asset for the police corps.[68] The "Training Manual for HIV/AIDS" is a way forward towards a more central and efficient approach. The training manual has two major parts: the first consists of basic knowledge about HIV/AIDS and anatomy; the second section focuses mostly on communication techniques. There is also a trainer's guide.[69] The training manual and trainer's guide are intended to be adopted in the country's police training centres. A notable achievement of this police project was the training of trainers and counsellors in January 2008.

In the long run, the success of the police HIV/AIDS project will depend on a number of factors, including the sustainability of its funding and budget and the justification of the project spending in the preceding year in parliament.[70] If the parliament gives approval, the next indicator is whether the disbursements are made in a timely fashion and whether there is accountability and transparency in the management of the budgeted funds. This chapter addresses these challenges in the following sections. Overall, the greatest success in the Cameroonian HIV/AIDS control efforts is the provision of increased access to free ARV drugs for people living with HIV and AIDS. Access to free ARV treatment benefits every patient, the police included.

The move to free ARV treatment in Cameroon

The drop in the cost of ARV treatment from 600,000 Communauté Financière Africaine francs (XAF) (approximately US$300) per month in 2001 to zero in May 2007 came as a result of concerted efforts on the part of government and donors. The shift to the provision of free drugs was not easy. The Ministry of Health stated that Cameroon adhered to the "Access to Treatment" initiative, which was geared principally towards the reduction of ARV prices. The commitment of scientific laboratories during the first phase of the 2000–2005 NASP played a significant role in achieving a one-third price reduction. In 2002, within the framework of the introduction of generic drugs, the monthly prices were reduced from XAF 70,000–100,000 to about XAF 21,000–22,000. Subsequent direct state subvention facilitated a reduction to XAF 15,000–18,000.[71] In 2003, the Global Fund provided a subvention of up to 50 per cent on top of the state subvention. In 2004–2005, there was a general reduction in the price of medical examinations, and free treatment and HIV/AIDS screening tests were provided to pregnant women, children, tuberculosis patients, prisoners and other vulnerable groups.[72] In 2006, ARV prices remained between XAF 3,000 and XAF 7,000 for the first and second sets of treatment.[73]

In 2001, when ARV drugs cost XAF 600,000, it was estimated that only 600 patients were receiving treatment. By 2008, 31,000 were receiving treatment, and the officials of the Ministry of Health hoped that 43,000 adults and 4,000 sick children would have access by the year's end. According to the Minister of Health, ARV drugs were funded by the government and grants from the Global Fund and the Clinton Foundation. The 2008 programme was expected to treat approximately 47,000 people at a cost of about XAF 5.5 billion (US$11.9 million).[74] These measures give some hope for the future, in spite of the epidemic nature of HIV/AIDS.[75]

These developments are the result of a joint concerted effort in which the Cameroonian government promised to "reduce the price of antiretroviral drugs".[76] On Thursday, 19 April 2007, the then Minister of Health, Urbain Olanguena Owono, as part of the 2006–2010 NASP, announced imminent free treatment for all HIV/AIDS patients starting from 1 May 2007.[77] This measure, according to the World Health Organization, ranked Cameroon among the states to adopt a sweeping, all-access programme to ARV drugs, following Brazil, Senegal, Ethiopia, Tanzania and Zambia.

Major challenges in the fight against HIV/AIDS

State reporting

Cameroon has a poor history of fulfilling its reporting obligations to relevant international organizations. For example, Cameroon submitted its initial report to the UN Committee on Economic, Social and Cultural Rights only in 1998, and the report was presented in 1999 at the Committee's 21st session.[78] Although accepted, Cameroon's report was criticized for lacking form and substance. Information relating to the right to health was scant, specifically about HIV/AIDS. The report did not provide statistics on PLWHA, prevalence rates or other related infectious diseases.[79] At the regional level, Cameroon succeeded in presenting its belated initial report only at the 31st session of the African Commission on Human and Peoples' Rights in Pretoria in 2002. Owing to Cameroon's lack of consistent reporting, the success of the country's HIV/AIDS policy cannot be objectively ascertained. It is not enough that policies seem to be working from a national perspective. They need to be frequently tested against international standards, independent stakeholders' assessments and experiences from other countries.[80]

Rights and obligations of PLWHA

Just like women, children, the disabled, refugees, non-citizens, internally displaced persons and victims of crime, PLWHA constitute a vulnerable group in need of special protection. The right to health is a needs-based right that further enhances life's raison d'être – the full enjoyment of all rights.[81] Access to ARV treatment and drugs for the treatment of opportunistic infections is essential for PLWHA to enjoy their right to life.[82] In order to strengthen the framework for the right to health in Cameroon, including the rights of PLWHA, comparative judicial experience from countries such as South Africa will be extremely useful.[83] Specifically, PLWHA should not be subjected to any form of stigma and discrimination, and they should be guaranteed fair and equal treatment in the workplace. Within the police force, there is a challenge in striking a just balance between respecting the right to employment of PLWHA on the one hand, and maintaining a healthy and efficient police corps on the other.

Sensitization

In the words of Dr Atangcho Nji Akonumbo, "sensitization about HIV/AIDS in Cameroon has been relatively effective".[84] It is estimated that over 90 per cent of the population, both rural and urban, know about HIV/AIDS, its mode of transmission and prevention methods.[85] In October 2004, at the signing of the cooperation agreement with the International Partnership Against AIDS in Africa, the Minister of Health, who also chairs the NACC, noted that "the silence has so far been successfully broken. Nowadays, programs educate the population, especially women and children who are most vulnerable to the epidemic."[86] In spite of this apparent success in awareness-raising and sensitization, the fact remains that this success is not reflected in sexual behaviour patterns, especially in the use of condoms or abstinence.[87] The adoption of the "Police: Training Manual for HIV/AIDS" stands out as a breakthrough in the culture of silence, particularly for uniformed members. Within the command structure, talking about HIV/AIDS is perceived to be akin to a command.

Cooperation and research

Cooperation on HIV/AIDS in Cameroon involves multiple actors – public, private, bilateral and multilateral donors, civil society and NGOs. The private sector has been instrumental in HIV/AIDS control. This is demonstrated by the actions of the Cameroon Employers' Federation, which is engaged in the promotion of rights for HIV/AIDS workers. It has collaborated with private companies to develop a health-related social security policy for their workers and family members. Some private sector employers have drawn up HIV/AIDS action plans. There is now a trend towards this approach by many business enterprises.[88]

Whereas there has been significant success in terms of cooperation between various stakeholders, this has not been the case with research. HIV/AIDS research in Cameroon is largely uncoordinated. Although research is undertaken in the public and private spheres, it is mostly led by individual researchers.[89] Public research has been conducted by the Ministry of Health and the Ministry of Higher Education in partnership with the Faculty of Medicine and Biomedical Sciences, University of Yaoundé 1. Private research is very promising, but has remained rather isolated. HIV/AIDS research in Cameroon lacks a collaborative and coordinated approach. For instance, the Centers for Disease Control and Prevention in Atlanta, United States, has separate projects with the Cameroon Ministry of Defence, and the Faculty of Medicine and Biomedical Sciences sometimes has separate research projects with the Institute of Tropical Medicine in Antwerp, Belgium, and the London School of Hygiene and Tropical Medicine. In all of these projects, the Home Ministry – the ministry in charge of scientific research – is not involved directly, but rather has a protocol agreement with the NACC.

At the individual level, the late Professor Victor Anomah Ngu, a medical researcher and former Minister of Health in Cameroon, made clinically tested breakthroughs in this field that have led to impressive clinical management of PLWHA. The visit to an HIV/AIDS research centre in 2003 by an eminent researcher of the deadly Ebola virus, UNAIDS Executive Director Dr Peter Piot, was recognition of Cameroon's efforts in HIV/AIDS control.[90] Thus, one finds public institutions of the same system engaged in isolated and perhaps competing struggles on an issue of national and even international interest. This is a serious dilemma since it weakens national efforts on HIV/AIDS research and confuses private donors who may not know where and how to channel their support.[91]

Management of funds and accountability

The most important issue in HIV/AIDS control that calls for concern is not only funding but, more importantly, the rational use of available funds. The more funding by the various actors (the state, the private sector, bilateral and multilateral donors) increases, the more doubt increases over the use of funds.[92] As Transparency International noted, the health sector is prone to corruption because of imbalances in information, uncertainty in health markets and the complexity of health systems.[93] The types of corruption in this sector include embezzlement and theft, corruption in procurement, corruption in payment systems, corruption in the pharmaceutical supply chain, and corruption at the point of health service delivery.[94] Considering the prevalence of corruption in Cameroon, there should be a sound regulatory framework to combat corruption[95] – arguably the greatest challenge to the police, which is perceived to be the most corrupt sector in Cameroon.[96]

Lack of statistics

The lack of statistics on sero-prevalence within the police force is a serious problem in terms of budgetary planning and success of the HIV/AIDS initiative in this sector. It is recommended that the police leadership should break the culture of silence and authorize and sponsor a study to uncover the real facts about the scourge of HIV/AIDS within its ranks. Such a needs assessment study will be useful for planning, policy development and monitoring as well as ensuring adequate budgeting for HIV/AIDS programmes in the police.[97]

Conclusion

The chapter has discussed the achievements and limits of HIV/AIDS control in Cameroon, focusing on the programmes of relevant public agencies and institutions. The activities of the NACC and the NACP reached a decisive stage with the launching of the NASP for the period 2000 to 2005. The hallmark of the second phase (2006–2010) of the NASP was the effort to mainstream the fight within various sectors. Previous efforts – in which the police were treated as part of the Ministry of Defence, and as part of the Walter Reed Johns Hopkins Cameroon Program – led to problems of discrimination and under-funding by their military colleagues. This, in turn, led to a re-framing of the police programme itself, which featured a draft budget for the fight against HIV/AIDS. This also included the designation of focal points, the creation and implementation of a central coordination committee, sensitization programmes, trainer trainings, and free screening exercises in police units.

The most notable HIV/AIDS success story in Cameroon was the attainment of free ARV treatment in May 2007. In spite of this landmark achievement, measures to avoid corruption during the process of distributing drugs are still fraught with serious challenges. For the police, a specific and critical challenge is the lack of statistics on the impact and trends of HIV/AIDS. It is recommended that: (i) a needs assessment study be carried out on the Cameroon police force; and (ii) the fight against HIV/AIDS in Cameroon be carried out in a more coordinated and coherent manner. Efforts must be made to overcome the challenges of timely disbursements and accountability in the management of available funds.

Notes

1. "Report of the State of Cameroon to the 31st Session of the African Commission on Human and Peoples' Rights" held at Pretoria, South Africa, 5 May 2002, para. 289.
2. "Addressing the Unmet Need for HIV/AIDS Prevention, Cameroon 1993–96", *Mini-Compendium of HIV/AIDS Interventions*, Advance Africa Best Practices Unit, Advance Africa Virginia, 2004, pp. 5–11.
3. Atangcho Nji Akonumbo, "HIV/AIDS Law and Policy in Cameroon: Overview and Challenges", *African Human Rights Law Journal*, 6(1), 2006, p. 87.
4. At various times during that decade, the sero-prevalence rate was 1.04 per cent in 1988; 2.0 per cent in 1992; 3.0 per cent in 1994; 5.0 per cent in 1995; and 5.5 per cent in 1996.
5. In 1986, there were 21 diagnosed cases; in 1998, 6,843 new cases were officially registered, bringing the total number to 20,419. See Programme National de Lutte contre le SIDA (PNLCS), "Plan stratégique de lutte contre le SIDA au Cameroun 2000–2005", Yaoundé, Cameroon, October 2000, p. 9.
6. Comite National de Lutte contre le SIDA (CNLS), *Le Cameroun face au VIH-SIDA: Une réponse ambitieuse, multisectorielle et décentralisée* (Yaoundé, Cameroon, 2005), p. 8.
7. See CNLS, *La riposte du Cameroun au VIH-SIDA: L'expérience de la prise en charge par les ARV* (Yaoundé, Cameroon: ColorSprint, 1994), p. 6. See also National AIDS Control Committee (NACC), *Impact of HIV/AIDS in Cameroon* (Yaoundé, Cameroon, 2000).
8. PNLCS, "Plan stratégique de lutte contre le SIDA au Cameroun 2000–2005", p. 5.
9. "Report of the State of Cameroon", para. 292.
10. PNLCS, "Plan stratégique de lutte contre le SIDA au Cameroun 2000–2005".
11. See CNLS, *La riposte du Cameroun au VIH-SIDA*, p. 8. See also NACC, "Impact of HIV/AIDS in Cameroon".
12. Ibid.
13. E. Tumanjong, "Health Survey Shows AIDS Rate of 5.5% in Cameroon", *Associated Press*, 28 October 2004; see ⟨http://www.thebody.com/content/art26028.html⟩ (accessed 11 October 2011).
14. Central Intelligence Agency (CIA), "Africa: Cameroon", *The World Factbook*, as at 4 July 2011, ⟨https://www.cia.gov/library/publications/the-world-factbook/geos/cm.html⟩.
15. Ibid. The adult prevalence rate now stands at 5.3 per cent (based on 2009 estimates). See also Akonumbo, "HIV/AIDS Law and Policy in Cameroon", p. 88.
16. Decree No. 2001/065 of 12 March 2001 lays down the special rules and regulations for employees of the national security corps.
17. CIA, *The World Factbook*. Manpower available for military service for males aged 18–49 is 3,525,307; manpower fit for military service for males aged 18–49 is 1,946,767

and for females aged 18–49 is 1,834,600 (2005 estimate); manpower reaching military service age annually for males aged 18–49 is 191,619 and for females aged 18–49 is 187,082 (2005 estimate); military expenditures stood at 1.3 per cent of GDP (2006).

18. See Bunmi Makinwa and Mary O'Grady, eds, *The Civil-Military Project on HIV/AIDS: An International Joint Venture for HIV/AIDS Prevention* (FHI/UNAIDS Best Practices in Prevention Collection, 2001), p. 248. On peacekeeping and HIV transmission, see Rodger Yeager, "Military HIV/AIDS Policy in Eastern and Southern Africa: A Seven-Country Comparison", Civil-Military Alliance to Combat HIV and AIDS, Occasional Paper Series No. 1 (1996), p. 2, ⟨http://www.certi.org/cma/articles/cma1a.pdf⟩ (accessed 11 October 2011).

19. Decree No. 2001/065, Article 142.

20. Akonumbo, "HIV/AIDS Law and Policy in Cameroon", p. 92.

21. The Constitution, in the preamble, clearly gives full effect to the fundamental rights and freedoms spelled out in the Universal Declaration of Human Rights and all duly ratified international conventions relating thereto under separate headings.

22. The Penal Code was adopted in the late 1960s, a time when the most criminally reprehensible conduct of the present time was not foreseen. It can only be interpreted to make provision, by analogy, for HIV/AIDS-related criminal conduct.

23. Akonumbo, "HIV/AIDS Law and Policy in Cameroon", p. 93.

24. Ibid., p. 100.

25. "Report of the State of Cameroon", para. 293.

26. PNLCS, "Plan stratégique de lutte contre le SIDA au Cameroun 2000–2005", p. 9.

27. "Report of the State of Cameroon", para. 294.

28. Ibid., para. 295.

29. Akonumbo, "HIV/AIDS Law and Policy in Cameroon", p. 101.

30. CNLS, *Le Cameroun face au VIH-SIDA*, p. 11.

31. PNLCS, "Plan stratégique de lutte contre le SIDA au Cameroun 2000–2005", p. 11.

32. Ibid., pp. 12–16.

33. CNLS, *Le Cameroun face au VIH-SIDA*, p. 12. In 2003, a total of 62,817 pregnant women received counselling, of whom 42,872 were tested; 7.7 per cent of the women tested were HIV-positive; 80 per cent of the 1,432 HIV-positive women were given Nevirapine during pregnancy and continued to take it at delivery; 1,303 babies born of such mothers were treated with Nevirapine.

34. A total of 2,442 action plans by local communities have been supported technically or financially by the programme within this framework.

35. This initiative proved very successful in ministries of higher education, national education and women and social affairs, religious communities, private institutions, universities and research institutes, but had little success at the Ministry of Defence.

36. Apart from foreign aid, the government has achieved a progressive increase in its HIV/AIDS budget. The Ministry of Health's budget for HIV/AIDS was only US$13,000 in 1995, but by 2001 it had risen to US$1.8 million. US$9 million was budgeted from the HIPC (Heavily Indebted Poor Countries) Initiative for HIV/AIDS within the framework of the execution of Poverty Reduction Strategy Papers 2000–2004. Some of these funds were allocated to ARV procurement, thereby reducing the average monthly cost of treatment for PLWHA to US$34. See CNLS, *Le Cameroun face au VIH-SIDA*, p. 14.

37. The government has opted for a decentralized and multi-sectoral approach, actively involving the private sector, since it is evident that a single-handed fight cannot be effective. Paragraph 23 of the Abuja Declaration on HIV/AIDS, Tuberculosis and Other Related Infectious Diseases of April 2001 enhances this approach "through a comprehensive multisectoral strategy which involves all appropriate development sectors of our governments as well as a broad mobilisation of our societies at all levels", including the private sector, civil society and non-governmental organizations.

38. See also Akonumbo, "HIV/AIDS Law and Policy in Cameroon", pp. 102–109.
39. "Report of the State of Cameroon", para. 296.
40. As stated earlier, as far as the fight against HIV/AIDS is concerned, the Ministry of Defence includes the police force.
41. CNLS, *Le Cameroun face au VIH-SIDA*.
42. Akonumbo, "HIV/AIDS Law and Policy in Cameroon", p. 119.
43. Ibid.
44. Ibid.
45. Ibid.
46. Ibid., pp. 119–120.
47. For a sector analysis, see *HIV/AIDS Guide for the Mining Sector* (Care, Golder Associates and International Finance Corporation of the World Bank Group, 2006), ⟨http://www.care.ca/userfiles/file/AIDS-MiningGuide.pdf⟩ (accessed 16 September 2011).
48. On security sector HIV/AIDS programmes, see S. J. Kingma et al., *Winning the War against HIV and AIDS: A Handbook on Planning, Monitoring and Evaluation of HIV Prevention and Care Programmes in the Uniformed Services* (Hanover, NH: Civil-Military Alliance to Combat HIV and AIDS, 1999).
49. S. J. Kingma, "HIV and the Military: Prevention Education is the Key to Protection", unpublished Address to the First International Conference of Military and Police Medicine, Yaoundé, Cameroon, 23–24 February 1995 (on file with this author).
50. US Department of Defense, "DoD HIV/AIDS Prevention Program: Cameroon", ⟨http://www.dhapp.org/subPage.php?sp=21⟩ (accessed 11 October 2011).
51. US Department of Defense HIV/AIDS Prevention Program (DHAPP), "Cameroon", in *2006 Annual Report* (January 2007), pp. 21–23; available at ⟨http://www.dhapp.org/library/file/DHAPP/Reports/2006%20Annual%20Report.pdf⟩ (accessed 11 October 2011).
52. The trainees were instructed on the following topics: STIs and HIV/AIDS, common STIs and their consequences, methods of transmission and prevention of HIV/AIDS, counselling in HIV prevention, the national programme on HIV care and treatment and the different treatment centres, and communication techniques and role play in peer education.
53. The materials produced included 500 brochures, 500 posters, 500 uniforms for peer education and 50 artificial penises for demonstration.
54. For more on HIV and the armed forces, see Tan Sokhey, *Mainstreaming HIV Prevention in the Military: A Case Study from Cambodia* (Bangkok: UNDP, 2004).
55. Examples include tuberculosis, cancer, poliomyelitis, leprosy and mental illness.
56. Decree No. 2001/065 of 12 March 2001, Article 37.
57. Ibid., Article 36(2).
58. Ibid., Article 39(2).
59. Ibid., Article 13.
60. Ibid., Article 41.
61. Focused discussion with Mme Ngo Babang Eugénie, Chef de Service des Grandes Endémies, MST/SIDA, 2008.
62. Statistics are from the Service de la Securité Civile.
63. Focused discussions with Commissioner Ngounte Robert, Chief of Service for recruitment, 2008.
64. Renata Dwan and Sharon Wiharta, "Multilateral Peace Missions", in *SIPRI Yearbook 2004* (Oxford: Oxford University Press, 2004), ⟨http://www.sipri.org/yearbook/2004/04⟩ (accessed 16 September 2011).
65. Communication with Onana Louis Ndongo, Senior Laboratory Technician at the National Security Medical Centre, Yaoundé, Cameroon.

66. The police project evolved through cooperation between the police and development partners, notably the US Embassy and NGOs such as CARE and Health Program, among others.
67. Elizabeth Mosima, "Police: Training Manual for HIV/AIDS Approved", *Cameroon Tribune*, 10 August 2007, 〈http://www.cameroon-info.net/cmi_show_news.php?id=20102〉 (accessed 16 September 2011).
68. Ibid.
69. DGSN/US Embassy/Care and Health Program, "Police: Training for HIV/AIDS. Trainers Guide" (Yaoundé, 2007).
70. Cameroon runs a budgetary year that corresponds to the calendar year. The last session of the parliament in November is devoted to voting on the state budget where the heads of ministerial departments are invited to justify their budgetary allocations and, more challengingly, to justify the expenditures of the previous year. The degree of accountability of the previous year is a very serious consideration.
71. Alain Tchakounte, "Traitement du Sida: désormais gratuit", *Cameroon Tribune*, 21 April 2007, 〈http://www.cameroon-info.net/cmi_show_news.php?id=19227〉 (accessed 16 September 2011).
72. Ibid.
73. Ibid.
74. Emmanuel Tumanjong, "Cameroon to Give Free Treatment for AIDS", *Associated Press*, 19 April 2007, 〈http://ap.lancasteronline.com/4/cameroon_aids〉.
75. Tchakounte, "Traitement du Sida".
76. "Report of the State of Cameroon", para. 296.
77. Tchakounte, "Traitement du Sida".
78. UN Document E/C.12/Q/CAMER/1 of 17 December 1998.
79. See Article 12 of UN Document E/1990/5/Add.35 on the list of issues to be clarified in Cameroon's initial report on socioeconomic rights defined in the 1966 International Covenant on Economic, Social and Cultural Rights.
80. Akonumbo, "HIV/AIDS Law and Policy in Cameroon", p. 110.
81. Ibid., p. 111.
82. Office of the United Nations High Commissioner for Human Rights, "General Comment 6: The Right to Life", 1982, para. 5.
83. See A. Hassim, M. Heywood and J. Berger, *Health and Democracy: A Guide to Human Rights, Health Law and Policy in Post-Apartheid South Africa* (Cape Town: Siber Ink, 2007). See also Akonumbo, "HIV/AIDS Law and Policy in Cameroon", pp. 111–112.
84. Akonumbo, "HIV/AIDS Law and Policy in Cameroon", p. 113.
85. Republic of Cameroon, *National HIV/AIDS Strategic Framework 2000–2004* (Yaoundé, Cameroon, 2000), p. 39.
86. Martin Nkematabong, "AIDS: Steps to Intensify Preventive Action", *Cameroon Tribune*, 15 November 2004, 〈http://allafrica.com/stories/200411150553.html〉 (accessed 16 September 2011).
87. Akonumbo, "HIV/AIDS Law and Policy in Cameroon", p. 114.
88. Ibid.
89. Ibid., pp. 114–116.
90. Irene Morikang, "Fighting AIDS: Cameroon's Efforts Recognised", *Cameroon Tribune*, 19 June 2003, 〈http://www.hartford-hwp.com/archives/35/205.html〉 (accessed 16 September 2011).
91. Akonumbo, "HIV/AIDS Law and Policy in Cameroon", pp. 114–116.
92. Ibid., pp. 117–119.
93. Transparency International, *Global Corruption Report 2006: Special Focus – Corruption and Health* (London: Pluto Press, 2006), p. xvii.

94. Ibid.

95. Akonumbo, "HIV/AIDS Law and Policy in Cameroon", p. 118.

96. For a study on police corruption in Cameroon, see Polycarp Ngufor Forkum, "Police Corruption in Cameroon and Uganda: A Comparative Analysis", unpublished Master of Laws dissertation, University of Pretoria, South Africa, 2007; available at ⟨web.up.ac. za⟩ (accessed 11 October 2011).

97. An example of such a study has been carried out in the Nigerian armed forces. See S. B. Adebajo et al., *Knowledge, Attitudes, and Sexual Behaviour Among the Nigerian Military Concerning HIV/AIDS and STDs* (Armed Forces Programme on AIDS Control, Final Technical Report, 2002). See also M. Rupiya, ed., *The Enemy Within: Southern African Militaries' Quarter-Century Battle with HIV/AIDS* (Pretoria: ISS, 2006).

14

Policy challenges on HIV/AIDS and prisons: Towards a southern African template

Martin R. Rupiya

Given the high financial, social and ethical costs of imprisonment, the data should prompt policy makers in every country to consider what they can do to limit the size of their prison population. Excessive use of imprisonment does nothing to improve public safety.[1]

Introduction

Over the past decade, our understanding of the complexities of HIV/ AIDS – associated with awareness, spread, care and treatment, home-based care, orphans and medical protocols – has dramatically improved. This has occurred as a result of sustained research and committed political leadership, coupled with dedicated local and international financial support systems. However, while acknowledging this impressive contribution before the final cure is found, there is one area that appears to have drawn little or no significant attention and research interest: the prisons. Focusing on the southern African region, this chapter explores the policy challenges of HIV and prisons.

The prison environment

The 2009 World Prison Population List put the prison population at 9.8 million people held in penal institutions throughout the world, mostly as pre-trial detainees (remand prisoners) or as sentenced prisoners in 218 independent countries and dependent territories.[2] As the World Prison

HIV/AIDS and the security sector in Africa, Aginam and Rupiya (eds),
United Nations University Press, 2012, ISBN 978-92-808-1209-1

Population List also showed, almost half of these inmates were in the United States of America, followed by Russia and China. The other 50 per cent was shared amongst the rest of the world. Of these figures, Africa was host to just under 1 million inmates, and had an annual turnover of 2.7 million.[3]

In Africa, among the 47 states in which the epidemic has hit hardest, five countries from the southern region are represented in the highest prison population category. For instance, South Africa leads the continent with 160,026 inmates, followed by Tanzania with 40,111, the Democratic Republic of the Congo (DRC) with approximately 30,000, Zimbabwe with about 15,000, and Zambia with 15,544.[4] Significantly, holding facilities in the southern African region, as elsewhere, fall well below the United Nations suggested standard of 100,000 per national population. On occupancy rates in southern Africa, Zambia takes the lead with an actual prison population that is 207.3 per cent over-capacity. In Tanzania, the occupancy rate is 145.1 per cent; in Malawi 197.6 per cent; and in Botswana 131.5 per cent. The existence of such a large group of prison inmates, comprising old and young people, males and females, and members of every race and ethnic group, represents a major source of concern. This is because prisoners often participate willingly or under coercion in sexual acts within a violent prison environment, thus requiring detailed research to determine the complex and intricate relationships that stem from this pathological social condition and HIV/AIDS. Furthermore, the continued neglect of these trends of overcrowding, lack of facilities and high prison populations can be addressed through the adoption of a penal policy that discourages the practice of remands in custody for long periods awaiting trial.

Table 14.1 presents a statistical picture of the situation in southern African prisons as at February 2010. The following categories are captured: the number of facilities; the official capacity compared with the actual numbers of prisoners; and the categories of prisoners in the facilities. The main purpose of this chapter is to raise awareness and recommend the adoption of common policy and practice. Evaluating the implications of these statistics should be done against the broader social context, for example, what happens within a cell and within prison walls, as well as the linkages of inmates with the outside and the relationships between national poverty, criminality and the ability of prisons to deliver on their primary goals.

Social norms and practices in the prisons

Social norms across detention facilities often occur amongst a group that has unique characteristics:

Table 14.1 Template of prisoners in southern Africa as at February 2010

	Country	No. of establishments	Official capacity	Actual prison population	Occupancy level (per cent)	Remand (per cent)	Female detainees (per cent)	Juveniles (per cent)
1	Angola	22	6,000	8,300	138.3	58.9	3.3	5.0
2	Botswana	23	3,967	5,216	131.5	17.0	4.1	5.6
3	DRC	213	?	30,000	?	?	3.2	?
4	Lesotho	12	3,002	2,276	86.3	21.1	2.9	2.4
5	Malawi	31	6,070	11,996	197.6	18.5	1.7	4.2
6	Madagascar	82	10,199	17,703	173.6	47.9	3.9	2.1
7	Mauritius	9	2,058	2,163	104.0	29.9	6.5	0.9
8	Mozambique	73	8,346	15,249	191.7	26.9	2.2	?
9	Namibia	13	4,347	4,064	93.5	7.9	2.7	5.5
10	Seychelles	1	400	323	80.8	63.0	3.7	8.3
11	South Africa	239	118,154	160,025	135.4	29.0	2.2	0.6
12	Swaziland	12	2,838	2,623	92.6	27.5	2.6	0.7
13	Tanzania	126	27,653	40,111	145.1	48.5	3.3	3.9
14	Zambia	54	7,500	15,544	207.3	35.3	2.6	2.2
15	Zimbabwe	46	17,000	15,000	88.0	30.0	3.0	1.8
	Total	956	217,534	330,599				

Note: Table collated using data from the International Centre for Prison Studies, "World Prison Brief: Africa", ⟨http://www.prisonstudies.org/info/worldbrief/?search=africa&x=Africa⟩ (accessed 17 September 2011).

[G]iven to using illicit drugs, unsafe injections, tattooing with contaminated equipment against a background of violence, rape and engaging in unprotected sex. These factors are then exacerbated by overcrowding facilities, poor nutrition, limited access to health care and high rates of air-borne and blood-borne diseases amongst the community.[5]

Specifically in Africa, there are certain cultural taboos that impede efforts aimed at engaging prisoners emotionally. This is largely owing to societal constructs around the idea of masculinity, and common myths associated with male rape and the subsequent veil of secrecy that permeates these behaviours. There is a widely held view that prisoners should bear whatever happens to them because they are getting their "just deserts" and must, therefore, not complain.[6]

Research on HIV/AIDS and the prison system in southern Africa is important at the local, national and regional levels because the epidemic has led to higher mortality and morbidity burdens in this region than in the other regions of the world. However, the challenge lies in the fact that, in every prison, there are foreign nationals who may introduce foreign or exotic species of HIV that combine with local strains to form a deadly combination of the pathogen. This remains a major challenge to be tackled by the local administration.

There exists a paucity of data analysing the social dynamics inside detention facilities and amongst guards, or regarding interactions with the outside. This lack of research – apart from the lack of interest – has occurred because there is lack of access to and testimony from credible informants. This seems to be the consequence of political and security considerations, the impenetrable nature of the prison environment and related legal constraints on gaining access. A number of countries have banned regular access to and interaction with the detainee community, providing as a rationale for this decision the assumption that those condemned do not deserve a voice because they have lost their claims to fairness, humane treatment and basic human rights. This assumption partly explains the cursory government attitude to the myriad issues that affect prisoners. This assumption, among others, supports the prevailing view that homosexuality does not exist in prisons because it has been legislated against. The existence of paper regulations takes precedence over the reality that permeates prisons.

Public officials often decide not to provide condoms within the prisons. To do so, they argue, would be tantamount to encouraging promiscuity. This is part of the official attitude that refuses to recognize and deal with the reality. And yet, curiously, such executive decisions, which clearly emerge from ignorance, do enjoy the full support of societies, themselves steeped in deep cultural idiosyncrasies and beliefs. In these instances, the prison community is seriously discriminated against and denied basic rights and the "legal" voice to challenge a plethora of such ill-informed decrees. Conventional wisdom demands that even inmates who are serving jail terms for committing the most heinous crimes deserve to be treated as humans with certain rights during confinement.

Against the attempts to move "prisons" out of the mainstream view, however, evidence emerging from the penal institutions confirms the long-held perception that HIV/AIDS prevalence rates are in fact high in prisons. The pattern(s) of its spread in the prisons include widespread homosexual relationships, tattooing using contaminated instruments and the shaving of heads with shared razor blades. Although both the authorities and the majority of the public appear to be supportive of the mainstream view, there is a school of thought that is sympathetic to focusing more attention on researching HIV/AIDS and the prisons because studying these interactions would ultimately make a difference to public health dynamics in terms of understanding the best policy interventions to address the epidemic.[7] Against these presumptions, this chapter delves into this often-neglected aspect of HIV/AIDS research and advocacy in Africa. Simply put, whatever has been achieved so far in the area of HIV/AIDS control remains flawed if data from the prison system in general are excluded – consciously or otherwise – from the national policy of each country.

Evidence from the prisons should be made readily available as part of the comprehensive response mechanism to the HIV/AIDS epidemic. For this to happen, a massive attitudinal change in terms of the societal perception of prisons and inmates is needed. African countries are facing a grave danger by refusing to allow an open investigation of HIV/AIDS in the prisons, in effect foreclosing the opportunity to reverse the raging spread of the epidemic "behind the walls" of prison facilities. Critical research issues in this area would include attempting to identify and isolate the relationships amongst prison inmates, between prison inmates and warders, and within detention facilities as an institution, and how they relate to the rest of the community in the sensitive areas of sexual networks, intimacy, opportunity and interaction.

This chapter has been prompted by the lack of policy guidelines in relation to the challenges of HIV/AIDS and the prisons. At the 8th Biennial Conference of Eastern, Southern and Central African Prison Chiefs, 8–10 August 2007, in Swaziland, under the theme "Towards Regional Integration and Harmonization in Corrections/Prisons: The Need for an All African Correctional Organization for Effective Penal Institutions", it was noted that virtually all the participating countries had no policy frameworks in place to address HIV/AIDS and prisons. This was a major indictment of HIV/AIDS control in southern Africa, reflecting the complexities of the epidemic and the ability of political elites to be dismissive of its impact on the prison system. This chapter provides insights into the existing challenges and seeks to use the scant available empirical and anecdotal evidence on prisons and HIV/AIDS in the southern African region to make policy recommendations. Focusing on this region is extremely important because it has remained the epicentre of the epidemic in the past three decades. This chapter seeks to develop a policy template on HIV/AIDS, the prison community and society as a way to link the control of the epidemic in the prisons with the comprehensive public policy responses to the epidemic by states.

Evolution of the prison system: An overview

Since the establishment of the state system during the Peace of Westphalia, 1648, detention facilities, as an institution, have become an integral part of the state apparatus. The main purposes of prisons, which are located within the justice and penal system of each country, have evolved over time as a means: (i) to safely secure inmates in state custody until lawfully released, (ii) to hold the inmates in order to instil socially approved behaviour in preparation for reintegration with society,[8] and (iii), where possible, to generate revenue on a cost-recovery basis through the judicious employment of prisoners.[9]

Depending on the country, there is a different nuance placed on the holding of detainees. This generally falls between rehabilitation in preparation for reintegration and a more punitive and retributive approach that tends to lack acknowledgement and effort towards eventual return to society. One system encompasses the correctional services approach, which is characterized by a readiness to forgive once a sentence is served and an expectation that the person will reintegrate in society. This system also offers rewards for good behaviour to categories of prisoners who do not present a threat or danger. The second type of prison system emphasizes punishment, with little incentive for or expectation of reintegration into the society. These forms of detention either are deliberately designed to serve this purpose or actually degenerate to these retrograde levels. For instance, an Amnesty International report on the Nigerian criminal justice system,[10] which included a study on detention, stated that it is a "conveyor belt of injustice, from beginning to end".[11] Despite various Nigerian governments recognizing the inhumane treatment of inmates and making several pledges to reform the system, Amnesty International notes that 65 per cent of detainees have never been convicted of any crime, and others spend up to 10 years awaiting trial in poor conditions that are detrimental to mental and physical health.[12] The same report also assessed the conditions of prison staff in Nigeria, and found that personnel were working in extremely poor conditions. They were grossly underpaid and in some instances had worked for months without payment. In addition, complaints raised by staff were neglected. This has resulted in collusion between guards and detainees, together with episodes of officers delegating authority to prisoners. Consequently, prisoners took a leadership and disciplinary role in order to control facilities while officers are generally away.

"Prison culture" and conditions and the transmission of HIV

Detention conditions and the system of imprisonment have both established a connotation of "prison culture" and the norms associated with the life within these environments. Although global trends exist, the local conditions, culture and history of the society temper each country's "prison culture". For instance, the prison culture within the US detention system differs from the patterns in China or Russia, although there are some common lines that run through each because they are drawn from the similar framework of transgressing national laws. Granted that it is extremely problematic to generalize patterns of "prison culture" across African countries, nonetheless benchmarks do exist in the declarations of regional and sub-regional organizations such as "The Kampala Declaration on Prison Conditions in Africa",[13] as well as the assessment of prison conditions in each specific country offered by the United Nations agencies and related intergovernmental and non-governmental organizations.[14] The Kampala Declaration confirmed, among others things, that African prisons are overcrowded and inadequately resourced. The prison commissioners acknowledged that bad prison conditions may result in life-threatening health conditions as a result of poor sanitation, inadequate provision of food, overcrowding, staff shortages and warders with low morale.[15] Since the Kampala Declaration in 1996, not much has changed in the prison conditions of most African countries. As the United Nations Office on Drugs and Crimes (UNODC) noted in its report on Nigerian prisons, human resources and dilapidated infrastructure are serious challenges to prison reform.[16]

There exists a clear link between harsh prison conditions and impoverished countries. Of the 31 most impoverished countries cited by the United Nations *Human Development Report 2006*, 11 are located in eastern and southern Africa. These include Angola, Mozambique, Malawi, Kenya, Tanzania, Burundi, the DRC, Zambia, Lesotho and Zimbabwe.[17] The link between poverty, inequality and criminality is a shared phenomenon impacting on the criminal justice systems of these countries, which have all failed to respond adequately to the challenges of HIV/AIDS in the prisons. These systems, which are predicated on common law, civil law or Roman-Dutch law frameworks according to the respective colonial heritage and customary traditions of the country, have evolved along different lines with respect to command and control and the philosophy underpinning the institution. In other words, they emphasize either the correctional or the punitive route. For instance, prisons in Angola, Botswana, Malawi, Tanzania and Zambia fall under the Minister of Home Affairs, whereas Zimbabwe's institutions are within the jurisdiction of the Minister of Justice and Legal Affairs. Meanwhile, prisons in Namibia, Swaziland and South Africa fall under a separate Correctional Service, whereas prisons in Mozambique, like those in Uganda, are split between a separate National Director of Prisons as part of the Justice Ministry and yet another component, the Prisons Department, under the Minister of Home Affairs. In terms of prison management in southern Africa, there appears to be a hybrid system of three models from which it is possible to harmonize and standardize approaches.

At the International Seminar on Prison Conditions in Africa, held at Kampala in 1996, it was observed that poor prison conditions were not a direct result of the increased criminality of African people or a reflection on the (in)efficiency of the court system in sentencing offenders. The reason, instead, relates to neglect by policy-makers. For instance, increased incarceration rates are a direct result of the deliberate use of detention and imprisonment as a tool by the state and its organs. In most cases, 50 per cent of all detainees are actually on remand and awaiting their chance to appear before the courts. When most remand prisoners eventually appear before the courts, the charges are dismissed and prisoners are freed. The question therefore is to address not imprisonment per se but the culture of abusing imprisonment by political leaders and public officials. In Nigeria, "prison capacity is at about 42,000 detainees, slightly above the (about) 40,000 registered prisoners. One endemic problem is that of overcrowding, particularly in urban prisons, which results from high percentages (60% and higher, depending on prison/state) of inmates awaiting trial".[18] Evidence dating back to the 1990s shows that Angola, Madagascar and Mozambique have the greatest proportion of pre-trial detainees across the southern African region.[19] As regards the problem of overcrowding, "[i]n Kenya, the prison population exceeds official capacity by 230 per cent; in Zambia the figure stands at 160 per cent; and in Uganda and Tanzania the figure is 100 per cent above the capacity. These are all among the top ten African countries with the worst levels of prison overcrowding".[20] Overcrowding, together with inadequate staffing levels and resources, results in increased stress and burden on the prison population.

Southern African leaders and institutions appear still to be beholden to the archaic idea that a homosexual relationship is a foreign ("un-African") cultural practice that does not take place, even in prisons. In most countries in the region, legislation that criminalizes homosexual acts still exists, and the prevailing perception is that effective enforcement will curb the practice and ultimately stamp it out. Similarly, the established leadership is convinced that the distribution of condoms is likely to encourage promiscuity, and thus they are not made readily available. These attitudes led to an intense debate at the International Conference on HIV/AIDS in African Prisons held in Dakar, Senegal, 16–18 February 1998. The position of a sub-group of participants – the southern African prison commissioners – was that: (i) condoms encourage prisoners to have sexual relations and therefore must not be made available in the prisons; (ii) the use of condoms is against moral codes, customs and religion; and (iii) homosexuality is rare in Africa.[21] As a corollary to this position, this sub-group argued that the law forbids homosexual activity and therefore, by implication, legal coercion and sanction can successfully curb the practice, and have done so. Generally, the prison commissioners have the ability to strictly enforce supervision and stamp out (minor) cases of "unnatural offences".[22] These recommendations represent the dominant psyche and mindset of many officials and members of the political elite in southern Africa. Consequently, any progressive HIV/AIDS-related policies to be implemented within the penal and prison system are "stigmatized" from the outset. The combination of the positions enunciated by the prison commissioners and held true by governments has continued to have adverse effects on efforts aimed at combating the HIV/AIDS epidemic. It is significant to note that not much has changed since 1998. In a statement in 2010, Tom Moyane, the Secretary of the African Correctional Services Association, observed that "corrections or prison systems across the continent face high levels of overcrowding, prevalence of HIV and AIDS, archaic prison infrastructure, sluggish management of awaiting trial systems which contribute in building instead of reducing high rates of overcrowding".[23]

The transmission of HIV within prisons

How is HIV transmitted within the prisons? Following the insightful work by Jolofani and DeGabriele on Malawian prisons,[24] it is useful to analyse how the virus penetrates the "impenetrable" prison walls. Starting with a template that is common to all prisons, it can be seen how a facility is divided for the purposes of holding inmates. Further divisions are arranged according to the seriousness of the crimes committed. Each facility is typically divided into blocks: Block A for male adults and those serving over five-year terms; Block B for male adults on remand; Block C for female prisoners; and Block D for juveniles. On average, cells that were constructed during the colonial era are meant for 22–25 inmates.

In each cell there are complex, life-threatening and thinly disguised formal and informal lines of command and control. In the Malawian case study, guards appoint a cell leader, locally known as *nyapala*, who acts as the delegated authority of the prison system among prisoners. Not only does the *nyapala* represent the common view of inmates but all instructions from the prison staff are communicated through this person. In a crowded cell, where inmates sometimes spend over 18 hours or more locked up, the *nyapala* is king. The *nyapala* is known to take bribes for favours, including sexual ones from new inmates, especially juveniles, in exchange for protection.[25] Furthermore, even within this formal arrangement, when wealthy and influential people have been incarcerated, they are always prepared and willing to pay for connections within and outside the prison. Given the poor conditions of service, wealthy people also manipulate a different set of lines of communication with warders as well as with criminal networks already operating inside the prisons.

In Malawi for instance, the three major prison-holding centres are located in Zomba (Central Prison), Blantyre (Chichiri Prison) and Lilongwe (Maula Prison). A significant aspect of each of the prisons, especially the Zomba Central Prison, is that, despite the limited holding capacity of just under 2,000 persons, by the end of each year each facility will have hosted at least five times this number. For Zomba Central Prison, the turnover of inmates in a single year (1996–1997) was over 10,666.[26] Add to this the turnover in the other prisons in Lilongwe and Blantyre and one begins to see the actual level of direct interaction between the prison population and the wider society at any one time. Furthermore, significant sections of each prison are taken up by the kitchen and clinic areas. In Malawi, only one prison – the Chichiri facility in Blantyre – had a medical officer and an assistant in place; the other prisons had a single medical assistant staffing the clinic.

In analysing the model of HIV transmission, the first point to acknowledge is that there were, and still are, inmates who arrive in prison already HIV-positive. The next question to understand is how homosexual relations occur and develop, particularly within the detention environment. The reasons vary, but the most common that have emerged from both anecdotal and preliminary evidence are:
1. Amongst detainees there are gay individuals who continue their sexual activity in the relatively conducive prison environment.

2. When the opposite sex is absent, homosexual sex is associated with prison culture.
3. Male prostitution (voluntary) may continue once in detention.
4. "Brothel runners" make use of prison and warder networks. One of the common "tools" that they employ is inflicting life-threatening violence, including gang rape, on reluctant new recruits.
5. Poorly paid prison officers, both male and female, may collude with wealthy inmates, including participating in sexual activities themselves. Collusion practices comprise receiving expensive items such as jewellery from relatives on behalf of inmates and agreeing to sell these for a substantial commission before delivering the cash.
6. Impoverished state resources reduce both warders and inmates to finding alternative ways to survive.

A further trend that hitherto remained relatively unnoticed is HIV transmission from ex-inmates, mostly prisoners on remand or awaiting trial, who are now suffering from a high incidence of HIV and AIDS after exposure, even temporarily, because of the contaminated conditions in the facility: poor sanitation, poor diet and the presence of HIV in extremely overcrowded conditions.[27]

The main mode of transmission in prisons is attributed to unprotected anal intercourse between men. Evidence from juveniles, scarred with perianal abscesses, underlines the widespread practice in the clinics within the Malawi prisons. The following factors could explain why and how such practices involving juveniles occur:

1. Sex is consensual between inmates and between warders and inmates.
2. There is a demand side, able to "order" preferred young males as "wives" or "short time" through the networks run by *nyapalas*, warders, cooks, and library, medical and clinic staff. For example, a single warder may "escort" up to 20 or 30 seemingly sick juveniles to a clinic, some of whom then disappear from the queue to see the single medical assistant and are smuggled into the adult prison blocks. This practice is known as *kuika mulaini* in Malawi, meaning that such "transactions" take place with the connivance and knowledge of the warders. The juvenile can spend months or years in the adult block from where they are eventually handed over or rented out to others. Only when very occasional, perhaps half-yearly, inspections are carried out do the prison authorities "discover" juveniles living among the long-term criminals and inmates. When this happens, everyone denies responsibility – the prison personnel, the *nyapalas* and even the juveniles themselves. Many of the "volunteering" juveniles, when they arrive, are quickly broken by the *nyapalas* by being denied blankets, plates, soap, food and opportunities to rest without constant harassment, including death.[28]

3. The lack of relatives or an external social support system places new inmates in even more vulnerable positions in which they are threatened by warders, *nyapalas* and their networks alike.

The problem of overcrowding

Overcrowding is a phenomenon that has continued to characterize the detainee population in southern Africa.[29] Only two countries in the region have prisons that are not over-capacity. The existing prison population in the region is approximately 200 per cent of the capacity of the holding facilities.[30] This state of affairs is clearly one of the major causes of the spread of HIV within prisons. The reality, however, is that HIV transmission does not remain within the confines of the cell or prison walls. As the Malawi Central Prison experience of 1996–1997 showed, some 10,000 people – in a rapid revolving door manner – went through the 2,000-capacity prison facility before re-entering society. In the case of Zambia, an evaluation of the distribution of prisoners among the existing facilities may be one way of responding quickly in order to decongest the facilities before proposing appropriate HIV/AIDS-related policies.

The challenge of remand and pre-trial inmates

The majority of detainees in southern African nations fall into the pre-trial and remand category. Government action(s) and inaction have contributed to prison congestion and inhibited the criminal justice system from operating more efficiently. Consequently, the system is overwhelmed and prisons are overburdened. It does not cost much to improve the prison facilities in terms of human resource needs, as supported by the findings of the UNODC study on Nigeria.[31] Dealing with the problem, however, requires massive attitudinal change in order to begin to rely less on custodial instruments and more on non-custodial sentences of community service, fines and suspended penalties.

Angola, the DRC, Mozambique and Tanzania, among other countries, continue to have high numbers of pre-trial prisoners who remain in custody for months, and sometimes even years, before they are tried and sentenced. Inmates have died in custody while awaiting trial. The issue of pre-trial incarceration should be addressed because this would very likely lead to dramatic decongestion in the prisons.

Juvenile incarceration and protection

The protection of juveniles during incarceration presents serious challenges in many countries. In most societies, imprisonment tends to lead to inmates coming out as hardened criminals. Prisons, therefore, are not always a correctional institution that will reform criminals – an ideal that society would hope for.[32] However, the so-called "beardless" "soft-bottom" "wives", referring to young juveniles off the streets and thrown into prison for the first time, are, according to Jolofani and DeGabriele, the most sought-after commodity by the long-term and hardened inmates.[33] Once imprisoned, the juveniles are subjected to violence, "escapes" and "smuggling", as well as being "rented out" for short-time sex (to quote Jolofani and DeGabriele) from their designated facilities to other sections of the prison, and, curiously, including even outside the prison walls, all for a price.[34]

In Mozambique, for instance, about 30 per cent of imprisoned juveniles are below 19 years old. Given that the country is still developing a competent and effective criminal justice system, the country's society is at high risk. This risk is associated with the post-detention dynamics of the re-entry of these young inmates into society and the impact they are likely to make in transmitting the virus if they had contracted it in prison.

Foreigners in regional prisons

Prisons in the tiny southern African state of the Kingdom of Lesotho hold foreign prisoners from many countries including Nigeria, China and South Africa.[35] The implication of this in terms of HIV transmission is twofold. First, there could be several strains of HIV emanating from the prisons in Lesotho, as in many other countries holding foreign prisoners, which are different from the local and regional strains. Second, the possible introduction of new strains of HIV/AIDS via prisons means that policy-makers and practitioners should factor these global and regional dynamics into their national HIV/AIDS policies.

Summary of findings

This chapter sets out the broad relationships between HIV/AIDS and the prison system, by looking at inmates, prison warders and how the sexual tendencies and networks found within prisons relate to the wider society.

The first finding is that there is a rampant and rapidly increasing incidence of sexual intimacy within southern African prisons. This is in spite of the existing psychological stigma surrounding homosexuality in southern African countries, driven by legislation that criminalizes such acts, and periodic exhortations by public officials against such practices. Most prison employees are aware of these practices yet remain powerless to stop risky sexual activities. It is recommended that southern African states provide better resources for adequate and humane prison facilities. Overcrowding, poor conditions and inadequate diets have become breeding grounds for infectious diseases, including deadly strains of TB. In order to address this challenge, concerted efforts are required to employ and train new staff, while providing adequate facilities, food and standards of hygiene for detainees. As the World Health Organization (WHO) stated: "HIV/AIDS are a more concentrated and aggressive threat in prisons than outside, and prisons are serving as foci for the development of high levels of drug-resistant communicable diseases."[36]

If sustainable changes are to occur, it follows that attitudes and approaches to the penal system among those in charge also need to be radically transformed. Presently, the prevailing assumptions that laws against sexual intimacy inside prisons are being observed fail to recognize the reality. Also attitudes that do not recognize the importance of condom distribution need to change. In order to bring about the changes required, two strands of process need to develop in parallel: a change of attitude, and the provision of adequate and sufficient resources for prison staff.

The second major challenge concerns those awaiting trial and pre-trial detention, and the related issue of the over-use or misuse of imprisonment as a form of punishment. Two problems can be identified here. The first is the failure of the criminal justice system to respond to the numbers of accused who appear in the courts. The second relates to instances where an accused is placed on remand. Here, most states tend not to follow up adequately on such cases and, by so doing, overburden the judicial system with detainees without concluded trials. The Nigerian case study,[37] where people have spent 7–10 years awaiting trial, is illustrative of this problem, which is prevalent in most southern African countries. To address this problem, the judicial system has to be provided with better resources. At the same time, the courts should proactively release detainees whose cases are not prosecuted by the state within a reasonable time-frame.

The third challenge relates to prison overcrowding and occupancy rates. As shown in this chapter, prison facilities in many southern African countries are grossly inadequate for the number of prisoners held in the facilities. Tackling overcrowding requires a recognition by policy-makers that it directly contravenes the UN-recommended standard of hygiene and humane conditions in prisons. Related to overcrowding are other causal factors that would compel each country to urgently address serious gaps and pitfalls that overburden the judicial and criminal justice system.

The fourth challenge relates to the fact that southern African prisons are holding foreign nationals from various parts of the globe. Given the prison culture of tattooing, constant shaving using shared instruments, and frequent sexual activity – all being methods through which HIV is transmitted – various other countries may be affected. For instance, in the prisons of the Mountain Kingdom of Lesotho, Chinese, Nigerians and South Africans are incarcerated for long periods together with the Basotho. Meanwhile, West Africa, India and parts of China are reportedly host to the less widespread although more virulent Type 2 HIV variant. In southern Africa, Type 1 is generally more prevalent. The implication here is that the challenge of HIV/AIDS and prisons is complex and multifaceted.

There is a possibility that a hybrid type of HIV will emerge from the mixing of the two types that are currently known, with unknown impact and implications. Any policies that are put into place requiring the provision of drugs, health knowledge and related matters should take into account the existence of the two types of HIV. This is a huge challenge that requires the cooperation of the southern African regional states. Notably, the support that these states receive from donor and funding agencies ignores HIV/AIDS in the prisons. To then ask states to generate resources to address the new complexity of a possible hybrid strain of HIV is an added burden that many may not be able to afford. Stemming from this observation, it is important to treat the implications of foreign nationals within prisons in the Southern African Development Community as an issue that deserves urgent attention.

The fifth challenge relates to the protection of juveniles in prisons. No prison system is capable of offering full and maximum protection to prevent youth inmates from being abused within the prison system. Available evidence suggests a ready and easy collusion between prison staff and inmates over the exchange and control of juveniles for sexual exploitation.

Conclusions

This chapter has focused on the conditions in African prisons against the backdrop of the HIV/AIDS epidemic that has ravaged the continent, with its epicentre in southern Africa. Presently, there appears to be very little or even no awareness about the connection between HIV/AIDS and the prison system among governments of southern African countries. This is manifest in the lack of resources allocated by governments to prisons and the near absence of pragmatic and forward-looking policies on HIV/AIDS and the prisons.

The perceptions and widely held beliefs across southern African societies complicate the evolution of a sustainable HIV/AIDS policy. The refusal to distribute condoms in prisons, for instance, is predicated on the perception that doing so would encourage homosexuality and that homosexuality is an exotic behaviour that contravenes African moral and cultural norms.

Imprisonment has been used and abused as a form of punishment by state officials, resulting in huge populations being confined within the prison walls – and not always with good reason. Clearly, this trend has further undermined the already overburdened judicial system in most of Africa. In moving towards alternatives to incarceration, this chapter calls for urgent consideration of existing non-custodial sentencing options such as warnings, fines and community service orders. The onslaught of the HIV/AIDS epidemic means that, until measures are found to eradicate the virus, the only viable option, with respect to the prisons, is to evolve effective policy interventions to control the spread of the virus among inmates. Poor working conditions, lack of professionalism among warders, pressures from inmates, among other problems, mean that the prison environment is a breeding ground for the virus. Authorities must begin to acknowledge the adverse impact of HIV/AIDS, as well as the difficulties of keeping order inside prisons, and start providing adequate resources to these woefully neglected institutions throughout Africa.

Finally, this chapter is part of an initial research initiative that calls for sustained interest and attention to developments within the prison system in southern Africa. If successful in raising awareness, it is hoped that this effort could then be extrapolated to other regions in order to reflect a broader, continental picture. The ultimate purpose of this chapter is to catalyse in-depth research that, hopefully, addresses the emerging trends of the deadly conspiracy between the conditions in African prisons and the transmission of HIV.

Notes

1. Rob Allen, Director of the International Centre for Prison Studies, commenting on the publication in January 2009 of the "World Prison Population List (8th Edition)". See Press Release 16/09, 26 January 2009, available at ⟨http://www.kcl.ac.uk/news/news_details.php?news_id=993&year=2009⟩ (accessed 8 October 2011).

2. Roy Walmsley, "World Prison Population List (8th Edition)", International Centre for Prison Studies, King's College London, January 2009, ⟨http://www.kcl.ac.uk/depsta/law/research/icps/downloads/wppl-8th_41.pdf⟩ (accessed 17 September 2011).
3. Lukas Muntingh, "Responses to Combating HIV/AIDS in Prisons through Consideration of the WHO Guidelines: Establishing a Common Approach", unpublished paper presented at the Conference of Eastern, Southern and Central African Prison Chiefs, 8–10 August 2007, Swaziland, p. 1 (on file with this author).
4. International Centre for Prison Studies, "World Prison Brief: Africa", ⟨http://www.prisonstudies.org/info/worldbrief/?search=africa&x=Africa⟩ (accessed 17 September 2011).
5. Muntingh, "Responses to Combating HIV/AIDS in Prisons", p. 2.
6. P. Mashabela, "Victims of Rape and Other Forms of Sexual Violence in Prisons: News Highlights, Prison Report 11/07, World Prison Population Still Growing", paper delivered at the 11th International Symposium on Victimology, 13–18 July 2003, Stellenbosch, South Africa.
7. Dorothy Jolofani and Joseph DeGabriele, *HIV/AIDS in Malawi Prisons: A Study of HIV Transmission and the Care of Prisoners with HIV/AIDS in Zomba, Blantyre and Lilongwe Prisons* (Paris: Penal Reform International, 1999), p. 4; a pdf copy of the book is available at ⟨http://www.penalreform.org/publications/hivaids-malawi-prisons-0⟩ (accessed 17 September 2011).
8. Some states emphasize this by designating the institution a "correctional service" and not simply a "prison".
9. In Malawi, according to official reports, because of the intervention of the International Committee of the Red Cross after the 1994 election, citing international law and guidelines on the use of prisoners for work, inmates have been stopped from working on state farms where they were producing up to 30 per cent of their own food; they have since been starving because the government lacks adequate resources to feed the increasing prison population. See Jolofani and DeGabriele, *HIV/AIDS in Malawi Prisons*, p. 19.
10. Amnesty International, *Nigeria: Prisoners' Rights Systematically Flouted* (London: Amnesty International, 2008).
11. Amnesty International, "Nigeria: Criminal Justice System Utterly Failing Nigerian People; Majority of Inmates Not Convicted of Any Crime", Press Release, 26 February 2008,   ⟨http://www.amnesty.org/en/for-media/press-releases/nigeria-criminal-justice-system-utterly-failing-nigerian-people-majority⟩ (accessed 17 September 2011).
12. Ibid.
13. "The Kampala Declaration on Prison Conditions in Africa", adopted at the International Seminar on Prison Conditions in Africa, held in Kampala in September 1996. Available at the Penal Reform International website, ⟨http://www.penalreform.org/publications/kampala-declaration-prison-conditions-africa⟩ (accessed 17 September 2011). The Kampala Declaration was adopted by ministers and prison commissioners from 40 African countries.
14. See, for instance, United Nations Office on Drugs and Crimes (UNODC) Nigeria, "Improving the Nigeria Prisons Service (NPS) Adherence to International Standards in the Treatment of Prisoners through Human Resource Development", ⟨http://www.unodc.org/nigeria/en/t52prisons.html⟩ (accessed 17 September 2011). See also UNODC Nigeria, "Criminal Justice Reform: Prisons", ⟨http://www.unodc.org/nigeria/en/criminal-justice-reform.html⟩ (accessed 17 September 2011), citing the 144 prisons and 83 satellite prisons originally established in 1961 but still reflecting the poverty and overcrowding as of April 2010.

15. "The Kampala Declaration on Prison Conditions in Africa".
16. UNODC Nigeria, "Criminal Justice Reform: Prisons".
17. United Nations Development Programme, *Human Development Report 2006. Beyond Scarcity: Power, Poverty and the Global Water Crisis* (New York: UNDP, 2006), Table 1.
18. UNODC Nigeria, "Criminal Justice Reform: Prisons".
19. See the successive annual reports of Penal Reform International, ⟨http://www.penalreform.org/pri-annual-report⟩ (accessed 8 October 2011).
20. Penal Reform International, *Annual Report 2006* (London: PRI, 2006), p. 8.
21. Despite the position taken by a majority of southern African prison commissioners, South Africa remains one country in the region that regularly makes condoms available in prisons.
22. Jolofani and DeGabriele, *HIV/AIDS in Malawi Prisons*.
23. South African Government Information, "Correctional Services National Commissioner Moyane Calls for Activism in Corrections to Address Perennial Challenges Facing Prisons in Africa", 26 September 2010, ⟨http://www.info.gov.za/speech/DynamicAction?pageid=461&sid=13180&tid=19548⟩ (accessed 17 September 2011).
24. Jolofani and DeGabriele, *HIV/AIDS in Malawi Prisons*.
25. Ibid.
26. Ibid., p. 5.
27. South African Government Information, "Correctional Services National Commissioner Moyane Calls for Activism in Corrections".
28. Jolofani and DeGabriele, *HIV/AIDS in Malawi Prisons*.
29. South African Government Information, "Correctional Services National Commissioner Moyane Calls for Activism in Corrections".
30. This is the case even when the statistics for at least two country-related figures are not available.
31. UNODC Nigeria, "Improving the Nigeria Prisons Service (NPS) Adherence to International Standards".
32. See, generally, Marvin D. Krohn, Alan J. Lizotte and Gina Penly Hall, eds, *Handbook on Crime and Deviance* (New York: Springer, 2009), p. 354.
33. Jolofani and DeGabriele, *HIV/AIDS in Malawi Prisons*.
34. Ibid.
35. Author's conversation with the Commanding Officer of Lesotho Prisons, 18 October 2007, at the ISS Conference "Policy Challenges for the Management of HIV/AIDS in the Armed Forces in Southern Africa" in Maseru, Kingdom of Lesotho, 17–19 October 2007.
36. Paola Bollini, ed., *HIV in Prisons: A Reader with Particular Relevance to the Newly Independent States* (WHO Regional Office for Europe, 2001), ⟨http://www.penalreform.org/files/rep-2001-HIV-in-prisons-en_0.pdf⟩ (accessed 17 September 2011).
37. UNODC Nigeria, "Improving the Nigeria Prisons Service (NPS) Adherence to International Standards".

15

HIV/AIDS among Cameroonian prison staff: Response to a deadly challenge

Tayou André Lucien

Introduction

Before the 1980s, HIV/AIDS was unknown to people throughout the world. The discovery of AIDS first raised doubts across society, especially as it was said to have no specific symptoms, to be partly or mostly related to sex (and therefore a taboo topic and source of shame and stigma) and to be incurable. Today, no country can honestly claim to be exempt from the HIV/AIDS scourge. Moreover, within a given community, some social or professional groups are more exposed to the epidemic for reasons related to either education, culture, age, sex or mental attitude. Sub-Saharan Africa is known to be the region worst hit by the epidemic. The impact of the epidemic on uniformed defence and security sectors in Africa is worth examining not only because of the high risk of infection within these groups, but also because of the devastating impact of the disease on the economy, the defence capacity and the security alertness of the countries concerned. Along with the rest of this book, this chapter seeks to contribute to the efforts being made to understand the policy dynamics as African countries strive to address the impact of HIV/AIDS on the uniformed, defence and security forces in Africa.

Prison personnel in Cameroon are quite different from members of the military and police forces, and yet they are part and parcel of the national defence and security forces.[1] The harsh conditions of enrolment and training, the military-based discipline and the very strict obligations to which Cameroonian prison staff are bound are sufficient indication of

HIV/AIDS and the security sector in Africa, Aginam and Rupiya (eds),
United Nations University Press, 2012, ISBN 978-92-808-1209-1

their involvement in matters regarding security in the country. In addressing HIV/AIDS among Cameroonian prison staff, the intention is not only to advance the study of the epidemic within the defence and security forces in Cameroon, but also to make a critical appraisal of the responses that have so far been suggested as attempts to combat HIV/AIDS.

To this end, I first delineate the historical, geographical, human and health particularities of Cameroon before and after the advent of HIV/AIDS. I then focus on the strategies and other responses to the disease nationwide, particularly vis-à-vis the prison staff. Finally, the responses to the problem are critically examined, and recommendations to improve the efficiency of the fight are proposed.

Overview of the land and the people of Cameroon

Situated in Central Africa, Cameroon is easily recognized by its triangular shape, which extends from the Atlantic coast to Lake Chad and the fringes of the Sahara Desert. Comprising dense forests in the south, light vegetation in the centre and the threatening desert in the north, Cameroon also hosts a very diverse population: the Pygmies, the Sawas, the Tikar, the Bamileke and Fang-Bulu in the South, and the Sahelo-Sudanese people in the northern part of the country.

Factors driving the spread of HIV/AIDS in Cameroonian society

Illiteracy

Cameroon has a population of about 20 million, of whom more than 50 per cent are less than 30 years old.[2] Though efforts are made by the government to provide basic education to all citizens (including free primary education in all public schools since 2000, the construction of hundreds of schools throughout the country and special incentives to children from remote areas), the national rate of people receiving a basic education is still below 80 per cent. This situation has serious consequences for the general capacity of Cameroonian nationals to understand and perceive the magnitude of health problems such as HIV/AIDS. This poses a great challenge, especially as most illiterate people live in their traditional settlements, which are by no means isolated from HIV/AIDS. Moreover, the absence of means of communication (radio and TV signals) in the majority of rural areas contributes to keeping populations unaware of relevant information on the disease and the general strategies planned to combat it.

Poverty levels

The arrival of HIV/AIDS in Cameroon coincided with the widespread economic crisis that affected the country and all sectors of society for over 15 years. Many industrial companies were closed down and thousands of jobs were lost. Meanwhile, as agro-pastoral products such as coffee, cocoa and cotton were unable to be sold or were sold at give-away prices, the rural exodus increased in volume. As a result of very high unemployment rates, the urban areas became overcrowded. There were millions of jobless people, and a significant percentage of them resorted to petty activities in order to survive. Many women were forced into commercial sex work as a result of the harsh economic conditions.

Psychosocial attitudes

HIV/AIDS is generally known in Cameroon to be mostly transmitted through sex. Like other sexually related matters, the disease has been considered taboo for a long period. It is traditionally believed in Africa in general, and in Cameroon in particular, that every question relating to sex must be kept secret. As a result, sexually transmitted infections (STIs) are considered to be shameful conditions that imply marginalization and stigma, and should in no way be known by anybody apart from one's medical practitioner. Within this context of social taboo, HIV/AIDS managed to spread very silently and quickly throughout the nation.

In the early years of the HIV/AIDS epidemic in Cameroon, several people made fun of those who were trying to demonstrate how deadly the disease was. For instance, they ironically turned the French acronym for AIDS, "SIDA" (Syndrome d'Immunodéficience Acquise), into "Syndrome Imaginé pour Décourager les Amoureux", which translates as "syndrome dreamed up to discourage love makers".

Various sectors of society openly supported their natural preference for unprotected sexual intercourse because they considered the use of condoms to be "artificial and disgusting". Others said, "on ne peut pas sucer le bonbon avec son plastique", meaning that one cannot enjoy the taste of sweets if they are still covered with their plastic packaging. This generally negative response to HIV/AIDS was also reinforced by doubts over the existence of the disease. The absence of a particular symptom to identify the syndrome doomed many attempted responses to failure. The first AIDS patients were thought to be suffering from a slow poison, symptoms of which could include ongoing diarrhoea, cough and malaria. People were reluctant to admit that the cause of the sickness was the actual virus.

The traditional role of women

Most African societies, including Cameroon, are highly patriarchal. Women play a secondary role in almost all matters regarding political, social and even family life. They are expected to obey and follow the decisions of men. This is even more the case in matters regarding their sexual life. Customarily, women do not have the right to suggest to their male partners the use of condoms or any other contraceptive method. To do so may lead to divorce, which carries a lot of stigma in most African societies. This submissive attitude prevents women from taking an active part in the prevention of HIV/AIDS and therefore exposes them to a high risk of contracting the virus. African cultural practices impede women's self-determination when it comes to making decisions on matters of sexuality.

Proliferation of sexual activities

The mutable and continuously changing patterns of social behaviour of the past 20 years have favoured a more uninhibited approach to sexual activities. Along with the ongoing modernization of the country, commercial sex has become a consistently widespread activity, thus paving the way for the diffusion of HIV. The extent of the sex industry is evidenced by the increasing number of hotels, inns and unregulated facilities serving alcohol and provided with bedrooms. These buildings can be found in the major streets of the cities. In addition, several bars and dance clubs are open 24 hours a day and serve a large quantity of alcoholic beverages. These activities represent triggering factors for unprotected sexual activity, consequently facilitating infection with HIV.

The media have also played a role in facilitating the spread of HIV/AIDS in Cameroon. Radio and TV stations have taken a fancy to suggestive songs and dances broadcast day in and day out, and to music clips and films that are not only morally offensive to some people but also seductive to others, who later try to emulate the actions they have seen or heard. With the utopian aim of breaking all sex-related taboos, the media, either consciously or unconsciously, is contributing to the development of attitudes and activities favourable to the diffusion of the disease.

The response to HIV/AIDS in Cameroon

The initial response

As in almost every African country, Cameroonian society paid little attention to the threat during the early years of the spread of the virus.

Many Africans thought that their own country could not be affected. Meanwhile, patients who clearly showed HIV/AIDS symptoms were taken to traditional healers who claimed to cure HIV/AIDS. The first HIV/AIDS cases in Cameroon were discovered in 1985. As the number of cases increased, some initiatives were taken by the government, first to raise awareness regarding the existence of HIV/AIDS, and second to promote more mindful sexual habits and attitudes.

The national response

The first nationwide response to the HIV/AIDS issue was awareness-raising and education. In fact, to bring a community so rooted in its traditions to a new *modus vivendi* was a difficult challenge in itself. The awareness-raising phase was conducted through radio, television and the written media. The challenge was to persuade the general public to accept that HIV/AIDS was a reality in the country and that many Cameroonians were already dying of the disease. Short messages, sketches, songs and other radio announcements were repeatedly broadcast and published to increase individual and general consciousness of the epidemic, especially in light of the absence of a cure.

As for the principal modes of transmission, another challenge was to explain to the public that sex is one, albeit the main, mode of HIV transmission in Cameroon. With sexual issues being generally considered taboo, nobody could imagine that he or she might become a victim of the disease. Even if someone were to suffer that fate, they would prefer to die in secret and in silence rather than let anybody know that they were affected by AIDS. It must be noted that the awareness-raising process was very difficult because of the lack of precise information about HIV/AIDS at the time. Journalists had to work hard to find relevant sources in an environment in which even medical doctors still knew little about HIV/AIDS.

The second stage of the national response involved the Ministry of Health in the fight against HIV/AIDS. By this time, the government response started to be more practical and the strategies more realistic. The first strategy dealt with the establishment of a national committee, made up of competent doctors, to tackle the problem in a professional manner. The objective of the committee was to stop the rapid progress of the epidemic through greater communication, research and prevention strategies. With the technical and financial assistance of specialized health organizations, the National AIDS Control Committee carried out various research programmes, intensified radio and TV programmes on HIV/AIDS, and even initiated medical research that could lead to the discovery of active constituents that could be used for the treatment of the illness.

The contributions of private researchers

During the second stage, private researchers contributed significantly in the national effort to fight HIV/AIDS, although the results did not always meet expectations. Professor Victor Anomah Ngu, a former Minister of Health, attracted the attention of the international medical community with his promising research. His VANHIVAX formula is a vaccine prepared from the viruses contained in the blood of a person infected with HIV. It is re-administered to the patient concerned as a therapeutic auto-vaccine, and a prototype of the vaccine was intended for use as a preventive vaccine against HIV.[3]

The involvement of traditional healers

The national strategy set up by the government also includes traditional healers. The objective here is twofold: (i) to make traditional doctors aware of the existence of HIV/AIDS, to educate them about anti-retroviral (ARV) therapy and the modes of transmission of the disease and to caution them not to use razor blades, syringes, etc., on more than one person; (2) to encourage them to take an active part in research on ways and means to cure HIV/AIDS.

Practical responses

Stage three of the national HIV/AIDS strategy seems to be more practical than ever before. In the administrative sector, the National Committee was reorganized to improve its productivity. At the provincial level, the National Multisectoral Strategic Plan for HIV/AIDS for 2000–2005 created Provincial Technical Groups, whose main role is to coordinate the activities of local committees, composed of young men and women trained in the techniques of combating the disease. The role of these committees is to train as many people as possible at the grassroots level, so as to increase their awareness of the existence of the epidemic, show them the preventive methods and encourage them not to stigmatize those who may be infected or affected.

The National Committee also designed posters in the two official languages of French and English, and supervised their distribution all over the country. These posters called on people to be careful whenever coming into contact with blood or engaging in sexual activities, to go for confidential and anonymous HIV/AIDS testing, and to take proper care of relatives who have tested positive. Special emphasis is placed on pregnant women, who are constantly encouraged to undergo prenatal check-ups and systematically submitted to HIV/AIDS screening.

The training of counsellors and peer educators

Another important phase of the national response to HIV/AIDS has been the training of counsellors and peer educators. A group of selected volunteers was offered training on how to handle HIV/AIDS cases, how to encourage people to undergo an HIV/AIDS test and psychologically prepare candidates for the test, and how to provide moral and medical support to those who happen to be HIV-positive. During seminars, conferences, meetings and working sessions, people from a wide range of backgrounds, including medical practitioners, defence and security officers, business people, retailers, students, party and religious leaders, unemployed young men and women, teachers and parents, were and still are offered free training according to the level and nature of the task expected from them.

The distribution of teaching and prevention materials

To meet the needs of trained counsellors and of peer educators for materials to make their actions more effective, they were given posters and other written documents intended to provide more information about HIV/AIDS. For demonstrations of how to use a condom, wooden penis-shaped tools were given to educators, and millions of condoms were distributed free of charge to everybody during awareness-raising sessions. The price of single-use syringes fell in pharmacies, so as to enable everybody to afford them whenever needed.

Investigation and sectoral responses

While awareness-raising programmes were going on, many studies were carried out in order to have reliable basic indicators of Cameroonians' health conditions in general and of the national and sectoral prevalence of HIV/AIDS in particular.[4] According to the 2004 edition of the Cameroon Demographic and Health Survey,[5] the average national HIV/AIDS rate stood at 5.5 per cent (6.8 per cent for women and 4.1 per cent for men); in urban areas, the average rate was 6.7 per cent (8.4 per cent for women and 4.9 per cent for men), whereas in rural areas it was 4.0 per cent (4.8 per cent for women and 3.0 per cent for men); see Figure 15.1. Women became infected at an earlier age than men. Prevalence for both women and men increased with age until reaching a peak – for women at age 25–29 (10.3 per cent) and for men at age 35–39 (8.6 per cent); see Figure 15.2.

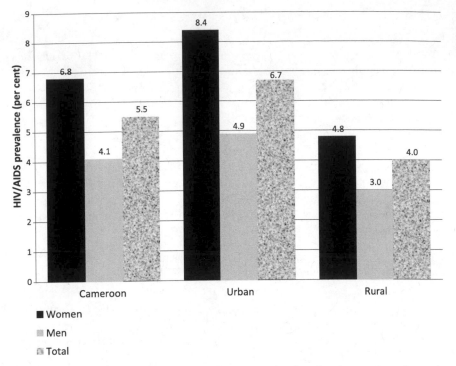

Figure 15.1 HIV/AIDS prevalence in Cameroon (national, urban and rural rates). *Source*: National Institute of Statistics in collaboration with the National AIDS Control Committee, "2004 Cameroon Demographic and Health Survey: HIV Prevalence and Associated Factors", ⟨http://www.measuredhs.com/pubs/pdf/HF2/Cameroon_HIV_factsheet.pdf⟩ (accessed 8 October 2011).

Though these rates are not as high as in other African countries, it should be remembered that they were two times higher just a few years prior to the rates recorded in the 2004 survey. This result is an indication that the various responses to the disease have had some success.

Sectoral responses

In 1998, with the assistance of the World Health Organization, the national HIV/AIDS policy included a new orientation for the existing strategies. It was decided that the fight against the epidemic would be carried out within predefined sectors, each corresponding to a separate ministry. Each sector (ministry) had to draw up a five-year plan of action to fight HIV/AIDS in the communities that fell within its area of competence. Financial support was given to sectors to help implement their strategies and programmes. In 2001, the Prison Department was given financial

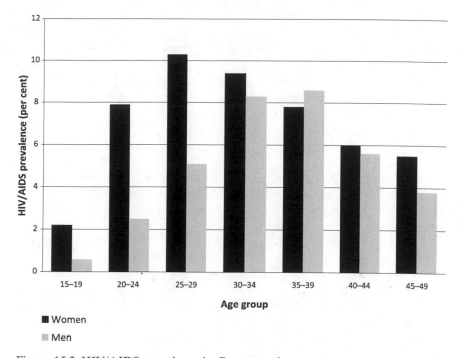

Figure 15.2 HIV/AIDS prevalence in Cameroon by age group.
Source: National Institute of Statistics in collaboration with the National AIDS Control Committee, "2004 Cameroon Demographic and Health Survey: HIV Prevalence and Associated Factors", ⟨http://www.measuredhs.com/pubs/pdf/HF2/Cameroon_HIV_factsheet.pdf⟩ (accessed 8 October 2011).

support, as it was by then part of the Ministry of Territorial Administration and Decentralization.

Free HIV/AIDS tests and ARV treatment

Nowadays, Cameroon has reached a stage where HIV/AIDS tests are given free of charge to anybody willing to undergo the process; this is also the case with ARV treatment. The research aimed at discovering a drug that can cure the disease is still ongoing in medical research institutes such as the Yaoundé University Hospital Centre, the Centre Pasteur du Cameroun, the Chantal Biya Foundation, the Military Garrison Hospital Centre, Professor Anomah Ngu's clinic and other centres for traditional medicine. One may say from the above-mentioned results that Cameroon has come a long way in its HIV/AIDS general policy and strategy. In the sections that follow we shall see how far the fight has come in the prisons and among the defence and security forces.

HIV/AIDS in Cameroon's prisons

An overview of the Cameroon prison system

The first unified legal document governing Cameroon's prisons was published in 1973,[6] 13 years after independence. Cameroon currently has 74 prisons, which are divided into three main categories:
* Central Prisons (10)
* Principal Prisons (47)
* Secondary Prisons (17)

Statistics for 2008 showed that 22,734 people were detained in Cameroonian prisons[7] – 96.8 per cent male and 3.2 per cent female. Moreover, 85 per cent of the inmates were aged between 18 and 45 years.[8] The main characteristics of Cameroonian prisons are:
* overcrowding: some prisons are more than 10 times over their designated capacity;
* old structures: more than half of the prisons were built before independence in 1960;
* hard living conditions: as a result of overcrowding and insufficient financial resources, prisoners are exposed to malnutrition, sexual promiscuity, long pre-trial detention and other problems.

Inmates and HIV/AIDS

Although there are no official data on HIV/AIDS prevalence in Cameroonian detention facilities, studies were conducted in some of the major prisons between December 2006 and July 2007. Sponsored by GTZ, a German non-governmental organization (NGO), investigations in the Yaoundé, Douala and Bafoussam Central Prisons gave the following HIV-positivity results:[9]
* Yaoundé: 21.3 per cent of female subjects and 7.2 per cent of male subjects;
* Douala: 28.21 per cent of females; 5.88 per cent of males;
* Bafoussam: 20.0 per cent of females; 15.1 per cent of males.

This high HIV prevalence rate among prisoners has many causes, the most important of which are:
  (i) Some prisoners are infected before they are brought to the prison. The case of *The People* vs *K.E.H.L.*[10] clearly shows how an HIV/AIDS-infected woman is sentenced to a prison term for having knowingly infected other people.
  (ii) Inmates are infected while inside the prison, either through unprotected homosexual practices[11] or through tattooing and shared use of syringes.

Even before the results of the GTZ-sponsored study were available, the Cameroonian government had taken some specific measures to combat HIV/AIDS among prisoners. The general strategies already mentioned above were also applied in the prisons, especially from 2001, with awareness-raising and education programmes, the training of inmate peer educators and counsellors, and free ARV care and treatment of STIs.

HIV/AIDS and the uniformed forces

Defence and security are important yet sensitive sectors of the institutional apparatus of a nation. When these sectors are adequately handled, they constitute a guarantee of peace and stability, which are necessary and sufficient conditions for sustained economic growth and social development. For these crucial reasons, the defence and security forces need to be in permanently good health, so as to be ready at any time to carry out their duties without complaint.

The strategy adopted by Cameroon to fight HIV/AIDS within the uniformed forces went through the following three stages:

- *1985–1998*: No specific programme was used for defence and security forces, as the strategy was general and involved all Cameroonians.
- *1998–2001*: It was decided that the fight would be continued in "sectors", with every ministry being defined as a sector; the army therefore fell under the control of the Ministry of Defence, the police were to be taken charge of by the General Delegation for National Security and the prison staff were overseen by the Ministry of Territorial Administration.
- *2001–2006*: A joint commission in charge of the control of HIV/AIDS among the uniformed forces was created; its mission was to explore all ways and means through which the epidemic could be curbed within these forces.

The Cameroon prison staff

The Cameroon prison staff are divided into four cadres according to the four categories of the Cameroon Public Service. The subdivisions within the cadres are called grades.

1. The cadre of Prison Warder is open to holders of the First School Leaving Certificate or any equivalent certificate, and corresponds to category D of the Public Service.
2. The cadre of Prison Chief Warder is open to holders of the General Certificate of Education (GCE), Ordinary Level or any equivalent certificate, and is equivalent to Category C of the Public Service.

3. The cadre of Superintendent of Prisons is open to holders of the GCE, Advanced Level or any equivalent certificate, and corresponds to Category B of the Public Service.
4. The cadre of Administrator of Prisons is open to holders of a bachelor's degree, preferably in law or human sciences; it is equivalent to Category A of the Public Service.

All prison personnel are trained at the National School of Penitentiary Administration (ENAP) in Buea, in the south-western part of the country. The first three months of the training are essentially based on military rules and exercises. The shortest training time is one year (for Prison Warders) and the longest is two years (for Administrators of Prisons). The Cameroonian prison service is made up of 2,572 men and women from all grades,[12] many of whom are aged between 20 and 40 years.

The main factors exposing Cameroon prison staff to HIV/AIDS

In addition to the general factors mentioned above that favour the spread of HIV/AIDS in Cameroonian society, the following more specific factors can be credited with spreading HIV/AIDS among uniformed personnel and the Cameroon prison staff.

Professional environment

Detention officers work every day in close proximity with prisoners who comprise mostly young men and women who have been leading a risky life inside or outside the prison, often engaging in homosexual or unprotected sex, other times committing sexual abuses, and practising scarification and tattooing. The daily contact that guards have with such prisoners, especially with sick or injured inmates, exposes them to the risk of infection. The increasing number of tuberculosis cases among detention guards in recent years may, to a certain extent, be partly explained by this occupational hazard.

Age

Over 70 per cent of prison staff are under 50 years old and more than 50 per cent are aged below 40. This is the age when people tend to be more sexually active and aggressive.

Military way of life

Prison staff in Cameroon maintain the institutional patterns of a military corp. The training they have received, the uniform they wear, the constant contact with guns and their barracks lifestyle have contributed to distorting their opinions on events that they encounter daily. For instance, unprotected sex (the so vividly called "full contact game"), multiple sexual partners, risk-taking and death-challenging attitudes are considered to be acts of bravery. Precautions to avoid HIV/AIDS are considered to be cowardly.

Financial privilege

Uniformed personnel in Cameroon receive some of the highest salaries among civil servants. Accordingly, prison staff, together with the army and the police, enjoy some financial advantages that other civil servants have been refused since the beginning of the economic crisis. This gives them an advantage over other members of the community when looking for a partner.

Resistance to HIV/AIDS tests

Despite the claims of bravery and courage, prison guards are often uneasy about undergoing HIV/AIDS screening, even when they are given assurances that it will be free, confidential and anonymous. They pretend not to be sure of the confidentiality of the test or the anonymous character of the results. This premise suggests that they are conscious of the danger and the devastating consequences of HIV/AIDS. By refusing voluntary testing, prison workers frustrate any attempt to collect reliable data on their HIV/AIDS status and on HIV/AIDS prevalence rates in the corps as a whole.

Responses to HIV/AIDS in Cameroon's prisons

Health promotion in prisons

The prison environment has not been excluded from the national strategies set up to combat HIV/AIDS. It should be noted here that these strategies were divided into two main groups: the inmates group and the prison staff group. In 1992, a sub-directorate in charge of health in the prison population was created in the Ministry of Territorial Administration and Decentralization, which at that point still had control of Cameroonian prisons. Later, in 2000, eight fully fledged medical doctors were recruited and trained at ENAP, with the objective of deploying them to the Central Prisons. In addition, many other prison workers were sent to national medical training centres, and prison medical centres were created or given official status. Today, every detention facility has a dispensary, a provision that had often been lacking in the past; and every dispensary has at least one trained nurse from the prison corps. Though these medical structures are not yet well designed and equipped, the government's willingness to improve prison health conditions can be observed over time. For instance, since 2006, every prison has a budget line for prisoners' healthcare. In other words, the government has committed a certain degree of resources to tackle this vital issue.

Strategies for fighting HIV/AIDS in the prisons

Before 2001, no measure had been taken to combat HIV/AIDS specifically in the prisons or among the prison workers. In 2001 and 2004, three crucial events rang the alarm bell for HIV/AIDS in prisons, as a consequence of which more attention was paid to prison life in general and to the prison staff in particular.

1. The results of research carried out by Colonel Dr Mpoudi Ngole[13] in 1999 and 2001 on HIV/AIDS prevalence among the Cameroon uniformed defence and security forces were released. The studies, which were financially backed by the United States Agency for International Development, revealed that in 1999 the prevalence of HIV/AIDS among uniformed men was 15.6 per cent and that by 2001 it had risen to 23.3 per cent.[14]

2. A plan of action was drawn up by the Ministry of Territorial Administration and Decentralization to fight HIV/AIDS in the sector. Because the Prison Department was still part of this ministry at that time, a series of measures were planned to tackle HIV/AIDS not only among prison staff and at the prison training school but also among inmates. For instance, all prisons were given the status of local HIV/AIDS-fighting committees.

3. The introduction of HIV/AIDS testing into the pre-enrolment assessment of prison warders in 2004 brought the attention of higher authorities to the alarming situation among prison workers. Of the 700 recruits who underwent testing, 97 were found to be HIV-positive (59 male and 38 female), giving an HIV/AIDS prevalence rate of 13.9 per cent. Higher prison officials ordered that those recruits who tested HIV-positive should be allowed to continue the training programme. The result was that three of them died while undergoing training (within one year); others, who were mostly sent to the Yaoundé Central Prison, died a few years later. In recent times, it has been reported that less than half of them are still alive. This shows how profound the HIV/AIDS issue is among prison staff. It also shows the importance of a clear policy and well-planned strategies.

Concerning the prison staff, the creation in 2001 of a national board to fight HIV/AIDS among the uniformed defence and security forces gave a decisive impetus to concrete awareness-raising and education actions aimed at prison workers. The first person appointed to chair the board was the sub-director in charge of health in prisons. This person organized seminars all over the country to raise awareness among high-ranking military, police and prison officers about the significance of HIV/AIDS.

The second stage was to train peer educators, put up posters and distribute condoms in army, police and prison units and barracks all over the country.

The third phase was the most difficult and delicate one, as uniformed agents were invited to undergo HIV/AIDS screening. Having already been warned about the lack of a cure and the various modes of transmission of the disease, and knowing well what they had done so far in terms of sexual promiscuity, many of them dreaded hearing that they were HIV-positive, information that they thought would be catastrophic to their lives and their career. So, this phase was not as successful as the previous ones, except in the army where an HIV/AIDS test has been introduced as part of the mandatory pre-employment and pre-training testing.

The fourth stage was free HIV/AIDS testing and free ARV treatment in prisons. In 2006, the minister in charge of public health published a list of the first beneficiaries of this "privilege", including the prison units. This stage was also characterized by the intensification of partnerships with international and non-governmental organizations specializing in the fight against HIV/AIDS. In this respect, the NGO "Care and Health Program" is worth mentioning. Having signed a partnership agreement with the Cameroon Ministry of Public Health, the National AIDS Control Committee and the Global Fund, this NGO has, since 2005, been organizing training sessions on counselling techniques to tackle STIs and HIV/AIDS in prison units and within the military and the police. It has also been providing prisons with some free STI drugs and testing materials.

The strategies used by the prison officials to combat HIV/AIDS can be summarized as follows. Initiated by the National AIDS Control Committee, the National Multisectoral Strategic Plan 2000–2005 had three priority domains: prevention (sex, blood and transmission from mother to child); medical and psychosocial care for HIV-positive people; and coordination, follow-up and evaluation of activities.

The first strategy deals with communication and awareness-raising (training of counsellors and peer educators, awareness-raising of individuals and families, promotion of voluntary testing, promotion of the use of condoms). The second strategy concerns the promotion of collective protection through the creation of hygiene and HIV/AIDS-fighting committees in prisons and the promotion of single-use syringes. The third strategy lays emphasis on the medical and psychosocial care of HIV-positive people in prisons. Free medical care is given to all STI patients. The fourth strategy deals with the promotion of partnerships with NGOs with a view to coordinating their activities so as to achieve more successful outcomes.

In conclusion, there is no doubt that a lot has already been done to combat the epidemic, not only within the Cameroonian population but also among defence and security staff. The fact that the HIV/AIDS prevalence rate dropped from 7.7 per cent to 5.5 per cent over the five years of the plan[15] is testimony to the hard work that has been carried out to alleviate the burden of this scourge. Despite all these efforts, much still needs to be done.

Critical appraisal and recommendations

Consistent efforts have been made in Cameroon to alleviate and reduce the spread of HIV/AIDS transmission and infection. The awareness-raising phase has had some success, given that almost everyone aged 10 years old and over in Cameroon today knows about HIV/AIDS. The drop in the sero-positivity rate to 5.5 per cent is another sign of the success of the approach. The initial idea of a strategic plan of action for army, police and prison personnel was very good but, in the longer term, things have changed such that every section of the defence and security services is waging a solitary war against a common enemy. There is still no legal framework to provide clear guidelines on how to coherently manage the various policies, strategies and programmes that exist to fight HIV/AIDS.

More emphasis is laid on the promotion of condom use but almost nothing is said or done to promote moral virtues. In fact, it has been noted that during awareness-raising sessions much time is spent on how to use condoms, whereas the words "faithfulness" and "abstinence" are only sporadically mentioned. As regards the prison staff, little or nothing has so far been said or written about how HIV/AIDS is affecting this category of security agents: there has been no specific study and no official data currently exist. Moreover, the actions carried out with respect to prisons seem to be intended solely for the benefit of prisoners. There is no specific programme for prison staff and, if there were to be one, it should be not only focused on the prison agent but also extended to family members.

Nothing has so far been done about a pre-enrolment HIV/AIDS test for potential prison staff. Yet the 2004 experience could have provided the opportunity to solve that problem once and for all. In the same vein, the introduction of mandatory HIV/AIDS testing in the prison service, not with a view to causing discrimination or exclusion but with the aim of providing early and efficient care to those testing positive, should be urgently reviewed. A specific board should be established to follow up and issue reliable, comprehensive data at regular intervals so as to remind every prison staff member that his or her life is at stake in any unprotected sex venture.

Conclusion

As a general conclusion, the HIV/AIDS epidemic poses a serious challenge to humankind as a whole. Like previous plagues, it has come and settled in Africa where it counts its victims in the hundreds every day. Since the 1980s, every African country has been struggling to close its frontiers to the deadly disease. Unfortunately, the epidemic recognizes no frontier or barrier, so every country has to construct its own strategies to fight against – and maybe one day overcome – the common enemy.

The strategies arrived at in Cameroon have yielded some results already. The enemy is being beaten on some fronts, but others are still vulnerable, such as prison personnel who are in urgent need of reinforcement. The prison service is part and parcel of the defence and security structure of a country. Of what use is a country whose prisons are wide open because guards are unable to work?

The government has undoubtedly taken some steps to fight HIV/AIDS in the defence and security sectors and in the ranks of prison staff in particular. Despite these efforts, more needs to be done to improve the quality and efficiency of the fight against HIV/AIDS, which still has a long way to go, at least as long as the search for a drug to cure the disease continues.

Notes

1. Article 2 of Decree No. 92/052 of 27 March 1992, Special Rules and Regulations Governing Prison Staff in Cameroon.
2. National Institute of Statistics, *Basic Socio-Demographic Indicators in Cameroon* (Yaoundé: National Office of Statistics, 2006).
3. V. A. Ngu, "VANHIVAX, an auto-vaccine for the treatment of HIV", paper presented to AIDS 2006 – XVI International AIDS Conference, 13–18 August 2006, ⟨http://www.iasociety.org/Default.aspx?pageId=11&abstractId=2194257⟩ (accessed 8 October 2011).
4. The following are some of the important studies that were carried out: 1987 General Population and Housing Survey, 1992 Cameroon Demographic and Health Survey, 1998 Cameroon Demographic and Health Survey, 2004 Cameroon Demographic and Health Survey.
5. National Institute of Statistics in collaboration with the National AIDS Control Committee, "2004 Cameroon Demographic and Health Survey 2004: HIV Prevalence and Associated Factors", ⟨http://www.measuredhs.com/pubs/pdf/HF2/Cameroon_HIV_factsheet.pdf⟩ (accessed 8 October 2011).
6. Decree No. 73/774 of 11 December 1973 lays down the rules and regulations governing prisons in Cameroon.
7. Roy Walmsley, "World Prison Population List (8th Edition)", International Centre for Prison Studies, King's College London, January 2009, ⟨http://www.kcl.ac.uk/depsta/law/research/icps/downloads/wppl-8th_41.pdf⟩ (accessed 17 September 2011).
8. Ministère de l'Administration Territoriale, "Mise en place d'une banque de données carcérales: Recensement au 31 Août 2000", Yaoundé, February 2001.

9. M. T. Mbeng, sub-director in charge of health in prisons, Ministry of Justice, Yaoundé, 13 November 2007.

10. K.E.H.L. was given the death penalty in the Nkongsamba High Court for having intentionally transmitted HIV through infecting two of her former boyfriend's children, in retaliation for his unilateral decision to end their love affair. High Court, Nkongsamba, 25 June 2003.

11. For example, *The People* vs *M.E.O. and N.E.F.* The latter were sentenced to terms of 2 years and 9 months, respectively, on grounds of homosexual practices. High Court, Nkongsamba, 28 December 2004.

12. Ministry of Justice, Prison Department, Yaoundé, 2007.

13. E. Mpoudi Ngole, "Prévalence du VIH/SIDA chez les hommes en tenue", Rapport Yaoundé, 2000.

14. Ibid.

15. National Institute of Statistics, *Basic Socio-Demographic Indicators in Cameroon.*

Part IV

HIV/AIDS: Gender and other emerging issues

16

HIV/AIDS and women in the Zimbabwe Defence Forces: A gender perspective

Getrude P. S. Mutasa

Introduction

This chapter explores the lived experiences of women in the Zimbabwe Defence Forces (ZDF) in the fight against HIV/AIDS. The chapter offers a gender perspective on how HIV/AIDS programmes have responded or failed to respond to the needs of the ZDF women. Research on HIV/AIDS and the military predominantly focuses on the serving members, the majority of whom are male. Women in the military are often overlooked as a subject of analysis in academic and policy literature. In addition, they are scarcely represented in the policy-making and resource-allocation echelons of military institutions. Consequently, male counterparts tend to overlook the important needs of women. Experience has shown that responses to women's needs are typically planned and managed reactively rather than proactively. Based on this observable phenomenon, this chapter explores the perceptions of how the needs of women have been met in the ZDF's fight against HIV/AIDS. It is hoped that the experiences of the ZDF women may be useful to other militaries in the Southern African Development Community (SADC) region.

Definitions and use of terminologies

When discussing "women in the armed forces", it is common practice to refer only to female serving members. This chapter broadens this term to

HIV/AIDS and the security sector in Africa, Aginam and Rupiya (eds),
United Nations University Press, 2012, ISBN 978-92-808-1209-1

include both "female serving members" and the "spouses of male serving members". The reason for this is twofold. First, those women currently married to male soldiers are inseparable from their husbands, and are often vulnerable when it comes to issues such as sexuality, health conditions, and protection from and prevention of HIV. Second, in the ZDF, spouses and children of serving members are automatic beneficiaries of free healthcare and treatment, and as such any military HIV/AIDS programme/policy ought to take them into consideration.

"Gender" refers to the socially determined personal and psychological characteristics associated with being male or female, namely masculinity and femininity, which affect a person in all aspects of life. In Zimbabwe, power is highly gendered in favour of men, as indicated in the National Policy on HIV/AIDS for Zimbabwe.[1] Sexually transmitted infections (STIs) that affect the spouses of serving men are likely to equally affect the husbands of serving women, since postings and deployments away from home have an impact on both females and males regardless of gender. This chapter will specifically examine the situation of women in this context. Taking into account the national and organizational responses to HIV/AIDS, it seeks to analyse the experiences and perceptions of ZDF women and health services personnel regarding the way in which women's needs have been addressed. The study centres on the two life-saving and complementary actions that must be taken in order to defeat the HIV/AIDS epidemic.[2] The first is to ensure that uninfected persons take the necessary preventive measures so that they remain uninfected, and the second relates to ensuring that those who are already infected live as long and good-quality lives as possible through treatment, care and support.[3] In successive Reports on the Global HIV/AIDS Epidemic, the Joint United Nations Programme on HIV/AIDS (UNAIDS) has affirmed that these complementary actions are achievable through relevant policy interventions that empower all stakeholders to become HIV/AIDS-competent.

Zimbabwe: Colonial, cultural, social and religious contexts

Until independence in 1980, Zimbabwe (previously known as Rhodesia) was under British colonial rule for more than 100 years. The Rhodesian colonial laws in many ways subordinated women to men and regarded females as inferior beings, whereby only their father, male guardian, husband or adult sons could represent them in legal tenders and related matters. The Zimbabwean women's pasts are built on both the colonial and the cultural patriarchal practices that sidelined them in the decision-making processes on matters that directly affected them. At best, the male-dominated communities planned for, rather than planned with, women.[4]

In Zimbabwe, there exist harmful and risky cultural practices and traditions that impede the prevention of HIV infection. These practices increase concern over the already acknowledged and unique challenges of HIV/AIDS among the spouses of male soldiers.[5] Such examples include the practice of polygamy and levirate (the local customs and tradition that compel a widow to marry her late husband's brother against her wishes).[6] Also common are the pledging of girls for marriage to older men, intra-vaginal practices or "dry sex" (a sexual practice of minimizing vaginal secretions to please men), and postmenopausal abstinence for women, during which the husband may have sex with other partners.[7] In effect, Zimbabwean women have been enduring the male, cultural and colonial patterns of repression. One approach to the prevention of HIV is to encourage people to follow more closely the precepts of their religion.[8] The predominant religion in Zimbabwe nationally, and in the ZDF in particular, is Christianity, which accepts sex only within – and not before – a monogamous marriage.[9]

Reforming colonial laws

The story of women in the ZDF is told in the context of the past and ongoing efforts by the government of Zimbabwe to reform the laws inherited from colonial rule. On attaining independence in 1980, there was a concerted effort to address the situation by removing the oppressive laws and regulations that marginalized women and silenced their voices[10] and by passing more amenable laws that have the potential to empower the voiceless.[11] Such laws included the Legal Age of Majority Act 1982, which defines adults as "all persons" who are aged 18 years and above regardless of sex; the Matrimonial Causes Act, Section 5(13), which guides issues of divorce; the Prevention of Discrimination Act, Section 8(16), which regulates against discrimination on any grounds, including gender; and the Domestic Violence Bill, Section 5(16), which regulates against domestic violence.

Methodology

As a narrative discourse, this chapter is based on knowledge obtained through participation "with" the subjects, not merely based "on" the "suffering others". Using the narrative approach, as espoused by White and Epston,[12] I am mindful of being respectful and non-judgemental, and regarding the research participants as experts in their own lives.[13] This chapter is based on information derived from two focus group discussions composed of participants who were selected based on their availability at the time of the studies. The group discussions were an effort to document the story of ZDF women. The study aimed to engage the two groups in a participatory activity in which they collectively searched for knowledge based on contributions from all members of the groups.[14]

Focus group discussion with the Zimbabwe Army Wives and Women's Association

The first focus group discussion comprised 12 members of the Zimbabwe Army Wives and Women's Association (ZAWWA). The women were assembled for a National Executive Committee meeting at the ZDF Headquarters. ZAWWA is an association that comprises the wives of the Zimbabwe National Army (ZNA) male members and also ZNA female members. The Commander of Defence Forces established ZAWWA in October 1995 with the goal of economically empowering its members, most of whom are not gainfully employed and rely solely on their husband's income. Regarding HIV/AIDS, ZAWWA women have themselves been, to varying extents, affected by the epidemic. They have also witnessed the pain and suffering inflicted by HIV/AIDS in the cantonments.[15]

Because of the lived experiences of its members, ZAWWA is an organized and credible source for evaluating the performance of the ZDF in meeting the needs of women in the fight against HIV/AIDS. Facts from the first focus group discussion with ZAWWA members were the basis of the policy recommendations articulated in the paper entitled "HIV/AIDS and Women in the Military in Zimbabwe: A Review of Response Activities Hitherto",[16] which was first presented at an SADC Policy Advisory Group Meeting convened by the Centre for Conflict Resolution (a think-thank based in Cape Town) in Windhoek, Namibia, in 2006. The seminar was held ahead of the anticipated formulation of policy for the management of HIV/AIDS for the SADC Standby Brigade. Perspectives from ZAWWA members were included in the policy recommendations contained in the Centre for Conflict Resolution's report.[17]

The second focus group: ZDF Health Services personnel

The second focus group discussion comprised 41 male and female members of the two arms of the ZDF Health Services. Nurses, environmental health officers and health promotion officers who undertook a certificate course in systemic counselling in October 2007 participated in the discussion. The inclusion of male and female members and different health disciplines from both the ZNA and the Air Force of Zimbabwe was intended to bring plurality as well as participatory rather than prescriptive approaches.[18] Some of the health professionals have a wealth of experience in witnessing the devastating nature of HIV/AIDS on a daily basis as they go about their work. In line with the canons of participatory action research, the findings were presented to some of the members to enable them to validate the representations of their words.[19]

Additional sources of information

Narrative practitioners posit that there are many possible directions that a conversation can take, and that the participants play a significant part in determining the direction that is taken.[20] In this narrative involving the ZAWWA women, contributions that were made in a confidential manner were privileged. The findings of the second focus group discussion received further input in a peer group review workshop convened in Johannesburg, South Africa, on 3–4 December 2007 by the Institute for Security Studies. In addition to validation by the research participants, the findings were reviewed by other professionals and researchers, including the Directors of Medical Services of both arms of the ZDF and one AIDS Programme Manager at services level.

The national responses to HIV/AIDS in Zimbabwe

National statistics

The first case of HIV infection was diagnosed in Zimbabwe in 1985.[21] Zimbabwe is in southern Africa – a region that is within the epicentre of the global HIV epidemic. Although Zimbabwe continues to be counted among the countries with the highest HIV infection rates in the world, it is the first in the region to have recorded a decline in HIV prevalence, from 26.0 per cent to 18.1 per cent.[22] A further decline from 18.1 per cent to 15.6 per cent was announced by Dr Owen Mugurungi, the head of the AIDS and Tuberculosis Unit in the Ministry of Health and Child Welfare, at the end of 2007.[23] The prevalence of HIV/AIDS in Zimbabwe and many other sub-Saharan African countries has either stabilized or declined. In its *Report on the Global AIDS Epidemic 2010*, UNAIDS stated that "the largest epidemics in sub-Saharan Africa – Ethiopia, Nigeria, South Africa, Zambia, and Zimbabwe – have either stabilized or are showing signs of decline".[24] Moreover, "[f]ive countries – Botswana,

South Africa, United Republic of Tanzania, Zambia, and Zimbabwe – showed a significant decline in HIV prevalence among young women or men in national surveys".[25]

National policies and guidelines that impact on women

The National AIDS Council Zimbabwe spearheads government responses, and is guided by a multi-sectoral board comprising 13 members, including people living with HIV/AIDS.[26] The National AIDS Council was created through an Act of Parliament in 1999 and started operating in 2000.[27] Through it, the government has pronounced a number of HIV/AIDS policies and guiding principles. For example, Section 7 of the 1999 National Policy on HIV/AIDS[28] makes the following acknowledgement about the gender implications of HIV infection:

> In most societies masculinity takes precedence over femininity and may lead to discrimination and oppression. Societal norms and values, and society's ability to handle change and challenges have to be considered when looking at gender issues. The feminine gender, when accorded a low status is disadvantaged or marginalized. Gender roles and gender relationships further dispose females to HIV/STIs because of unequal power relations.[29]

Similarly, Section 3 of the Zimbabwe National HIV and AIDS Strategic Plan 2006–2010 has specific gender-relevance provisions.[30] These policies are supplemented by the Prevention of Mother-to-Child Transmission (PMTCT) programme, which was initiated for expectant mothers, first as a pilot project and now at all levels.[31] The PMTCT programme was declared a public health priority, and in 2001 a national scale-up of the programme was initiated within the wider Antenatal Care Services.

International and national funding

Zimbabwe has been placed under punitive sanctions by international funders for HIV/AIDS owing to the political crisis surrounding its land reform programme. For example, the country received as little as US$4 per HIV-positive person in 2004, against Zambia's US$187.[32] Other funders have, however, maintained their support, such as the United Nations Educational, Scientific and Cultural Organization, the United Nations Children's Fund and the Elizabeth Glaser Pediatric AIDS Foundation, which are all cooperating with the Ministry of Health in a PMTCT project. To address the funding cuts, the government introduced the National AIDS Trust Fund, commonly known as the "AIDS Levy", which has been acknowledged as an innovative approach to mobilizing funds in southern Africa. The AIDS Levy is collected from a 3 per cent tax on all taxable income and is controlled and disbursed by the National AIDS Council. Management and utilization of the funds are decentralized to provincial, district, ward and village AIDS action committees. In the ZDF, the National AIDS Council funds are administered by HIV/AIDS coordinating committees headed by Brigadier General Administration Staff of the ZNA and by the Director-General Supporting Services of the Air Force of Zimbabwe, and also decentralized to the smallest units.

When the government declared the lack of access to anti-retroviral (ARV) treatment to be an emergency in 2002, it was able to import locally manufactured generic ARV drugs as well as.[33] The national ARV rollout plan was launched in April 2004 and national guidelines were developed the same year. Treatment providers were trained and by the end of 2005 more than 40 ARV centres were registered in Zimbabwe. Furthermore, the government provided a budget line for the ARV programme of up to ZWD 10 billion a year. The Ministry of Finance, through the Reserve Bank of Zimbabwe, put in place a facility for the Ministry of Health and Child Welfare to access up to US$ 1 million a month for the ARV programme. By the end of 2005, some 25,000 Zimbabweans, or only about 7 per cent of those in need, were receiving ARV treatment. Fortunately, by the beginning of 2008, ARV treatment was being dispensed free of charge by the Ministry of Health.

ZDF response activities

Response activities that have been performed to date include a baseline knowledge, attitudes, perceptions, beliefs (KAPB) survey in 1989, and a follow-up survey some five years later. Scores of information, education and communication (IEC) conferences and seminars have been held around the country for all ranks. Some of the recommendations from the participants at the conferences and seminars form part of the current organizational policy guidelines. To date, a number of voluntary counselling and testing (VCT) centres have been established around the country. Anti-retroviral therapy (ART) programmes within the confines of national guidelines commenced and are currently running. In addition, opportunistic infection (OI) management centres have been established. The seconding of doctors for relevant courses in and outside Zimbabwe has assured capacity-building for the management of these centres. Other disciplines have also undergone training in ART and OI management relevant to their particular field, including counselling. Support groups have been established under the management of people living with HIV/AIDS.

230 GETRUDE P. S. MUTASA

The participants' stories

The results of this study are classified under the key strategies and targets for fighting HIV/AIDS as outlined in the Zimbabwe National HIV and AIDS Strategic Plan 2006–2010. These include policy, prevention of infection, and treatment, support and mitigation programmes to attenuate the impact of the epidemic. Statistics for occurrences will not be given for obvious reasons. This chapter is essentially focused on examining ZAWWA women, as well as male and female health service providers. The participating males, as a special sub-set, were involved only as professionals and were not necessarily representing male voices in general. The male spouses of the ZDF women were also not covered by this study; however, it was agreed that the impact of the ZDF activities on this latter group should be the focus of further studies.

ZDF HIV/AIDS policy

The women interviewed were not aware of the fact that both the Zimbabwe National Army and Air Force of Zimbabwe had developed their HIV/AIDS policies in line with the national policy. The ZNA policy that was available at the time of writing demonstrates gender sensitivity. Within the internal policy of the ZDF, all HIV, AIDS and other development programmes, projects and activities in the ZNA are to be based in and around an analysis of and sensitivity to gender issues, that is to mainstream gender issues far more effectively than often seen to date. As a disciplined and gender-sensitive force, all gender stereotypes and damaging attitudes, behaviours and policies should be avoided, and there should be support for a gender-sensitive environment. The ZDF response activities are tailored to meet the national goal of reducing the spread of HIV, improving the quality of life of those infected and affected, and mitigating the socioeconomic impact of the epidemic.

Prevention of new infections

In this study, the ZDF's behavioural change approaches and programmes were scrutinized for their effectiveness in increasing knowledge of HIV/AIDS among women.

Information, education and communication

Of the scores of ZDF response activities to date, only one HIV/AIDS event was held in 2004, and it was for a limited number of ZDF women. Participants felt that their husbands were more informed about the HIV/AIDS epidemic than they were; in most cases, the men had not shared their new-found knowledge with their wives. The women concluded that, for the men, sharing any information that demanded sexual behavioural change was being intentionally avoided. Hence, the women remained less informed, save for the information they obtained from the media and clinics, as one participant lamented. Those who received information from the organization were fortunate to have had senior medical officers who ensured that their health promotion officers conducted IEC sessions at their respective bases. It was felt that a policy-directed and funded programme for the women would cover a larger number of the targeted group with organization-specific messages. This state of affairs confirmed the observation that it is often the case that those who are in need of IEC materials have limited access to them.

Participants hailed the ZAWWA HIV/AIDS Gala event that was sponsored by the AIDS Trust Fund in 2004 as a success. They reported learning a lot from the songs, drama and poetry competitions that were staged by the women. Participants stated that they learned about the challenges that the epidemic has placed on men, women, children, the community and the state. Participants regretted that no other gala event had been held for the women before. The voluntary membership of ZAWWA was also seen as a limitation, because there are more women who are not members of the Association than there are members. For the 2004 gala, a solution was to include non-ZAWWA members as participants. On the whole, it was felt that a very small proportion of the target population benefited from the event.

Unfortunately, women who lack health information may not recognize early symptoms of infection. They may also not make informed and appropriate decisions regarding pregnancy, nutrition, knowledge of their own status, and other treatment-seeking behaviours. On a positive note, participants applauded the formation of ZAWWA as a forum through which ZDF women could unite and officially lobby for some of their concerns, including HIV/AIDS.

Promotion of abstinence and mutual fidelity

There are some inherent challenges that stand in the way of promoting abstinence or mutual fidelity in marriage within the ZDF. The first is the long posting or deployment periods away from home that lead to protracted spousal separation. This situation is deemed to be a serious occupational hazard. The Zimbabwe National HIV and AIDS Strategic Plan 2006–2010 supports this observation, stating that spousal separation has significant implications for marital faithfulness and family life overall, and constitutes a major cause of vulnerability. Women admitted that they want to see their husbands as much as the husbands want to see them. They observed, however, that whereas the majority of men can find a surrogate partner, most women wait for their husband to return from deployment. The current monthly bussing of ZDF members on pay-weekends to towns where their spouses and families live (dubbed "Inter-city") was applauded. Facilitating regular visits has gone a long way in keeping the soldiers in touch with their families.

The second challenge relates to the involvement of husbands with sex workers within the theatres of operation. The participants felt that it should be possible to keep their husbands away from sex workers, who they believed could infect them. Although it could be argued that the men use condoms, the participants noted that, with the influence of alcohol as well as the sense of trust arising from prolonged relationships, the condom is usually abandoned. The economic power that is derived from field allowances was thought to encourage soldiers into promiscuity and also attract the sex workers looking for survival and financial gain. Leisure time was also blamed for exposing men to extramarital temptations. It was felt that it could also be the task of the chaplains to promote an ethical change in behavioural patterns. Input from the peer review workshop suggested that leisure time should be filled with sport, exercises and other interesting entertainment, in order to engage the mind and the body in mental and physical activities.

The third challenge to abstinence and fidelity in the ZDF was the lack of adequate accommodation within the military quarters to promote spousal cohabitation. This forces a large number of wives to live in civilian communities away from their husband. Participants acknowledged with appreciation the current efforts to build accommodation for ZDF members but felt that it may be "too little too late" for those already infected. For now, without the desired accommodation, the ideal of cohabitation of married couples as a preventive measure remains elusive.

Condom use

Ideally, all sexually active persons need access to male and female condoms. This was, however, not the case with the participants. The women reported constraints on negotiating safe sex in marriage. Participants stated that condom negotiation was taboo between married couples and, as one participant lamented,

> [W]e find condoms in the men's pockets. But when you suggest its use in marriage, the men refuse or conflicts arise. You are labelled a prostitute if you suggest using it. Prostitutes and "small houses"[34] are more protected from HIV infection than married women.[35]

This comment is in line with the observation that condom use in regular and married relationships remains low, and that long-term relationships do not necessarily protect against the spread of the virus.[36] In fact, when introducing condom use, health workers should note that women may not be empowered to insist that their male partner uses a condom.[37] Condoms introduced at the beginning of the campaign had a number of disadvantages. Women found male condoms disempowering because this gives men the power to choose whether or not to use them. Some others stated that women have often negative attitudes towards condoms.

In contrast, participants reported that female condoms arrived as a late solution for those who were already infected, and reached only a small percentage of users owing to their high cost and low availability. The ZDF has not been able to source female condoms to the same extent as the male condoms. A number of limitations to their usefulness were noted. Some women despise the female condom and men say it is too noisy and they do not like the external ring. Its thickness reduces the transmission of body temperature and the feeling of intimacy that men desire. Others noted that it is bulky, restricts foreplay and is not popular with either gender. It has not received as much official or media publicity as the male condom continues to enjoy, and most men refuse it outright.

Addressing underlying factors of HIV vulnerability

In Zimbabwe, HIV/AIDS programmes and interventions were intended to go beyond awareness-raising and the "abstain, be faithful, use condoms" (ABC) approach. They were meant to address underlying factors of vulnerability and the reasons people engage in risky behaviour. These factors include poverty, gender inequality and cultural and religious values and norms that permit men, in particular, to have multiple sexual relationships. Since the commencement of the HIV/AIDS response activities in the late 1980s, women have either lived or witnessed experiences that have rendered them vulnerable to HIV infection. Gender and culture have emerged as strong hindrances to the prevention of sexual transmission. Indeed, local value systems allow for a number of practices that make Zimbabwean men and women vulnerable to HIV infection. The participants' experiences are corroborated by earlier studies that analyse how men's patriarchal authority and sense of superiority are embedded in prevailing customs and traditional practices.[38] Gender inequality is a critical factor in the spread of HIV in Zimbabwe and most of Africa, because it determines how people are cared for when they are sick, what happens when they die, and the beneficiaries of inheritance.

Participants regrettably reported that society finds promiscuity by married men permissible and easy to condone. It has been noted elsewhere that there tends to be less social stigma for men who have sexual liaisons prior to and during marriage, whereas the same behaviour is frowned upon and dubbed prostitution when practised by women.[39]

There was a preponderance of social myths and stereotypes about women among male colleagues. This exposes women to the risk of infection and, in some cases, to the risk of sexual abuse. The stereotyping of women according to these myths is not confined to the military but is equally common within the broader society. Examples of such myths and stereotypes include: women are beautiful maidens who are to be pursued by men, to be teased and not taken seriously no matter what rank they hold, or "as sleeping beauties to be kissed awake". Other common stereotypes include: when a woman says "no" to sex, in fact she means "yes"; and "all that a woman needs is to be lured to a secluded place and when assured of privacy and no disclosure, she will agree to illicit sex".

The "low social status of women" that often makes it difficult for them either to challenge retrogressive cultural norms or to catalyse change in their favour at individual, organizational and societal levels makes them vulnerable to HIV infection. This low social status is reflected in the ZDF, given the mainly low ranks held by women. Despite the increase in the numbers of women in the ZDF, there has not been a corresponding increase in their numbers in the policy-making echelons. To date, the highest rank held by women (four of them) in the ZNA is Colonel (ranked above Lt. Colonel and below Brigadier), with the first two having been promoted in 2005. In the Air Force of Zimbabwe, there is only one woman holding the rank of Group Captain, following the death of a female doctor of the same rank. The Group Captain and Colonel ranks are, in effect, at the action or implementation level. Thus, despite the necessity to address women's needs in policy-making forums, most such needs tend to be overlooked and ignored because they are unknown to men in the policy formulation ranks. Some interview participants felt it was not feasible for men to think about or champion the needs of women, which they neither know nor experience. The women in high ranks were also accused of failing to address the plight of other women.

Participants noted the gender-related complexities that arise from the disparity in the status between men and women in the ZDF. For example, serving women found that there is hardly any assured procedure for recourse in the event of sexual abuse. Owing to the stunted rank structure that places almost all women at subordinate levels, they find themselves helpless to redress wrongdoings. "It's risky to try and report a superior because he has all the instruments and other elements in his favour and you may end up worse than you started", commented one serving female soldier.[40] Wives, on the other hand, disclosed that some husbands tend to apply military-style command at home, thereby instilling fear and submission even regarding sexual issues. That leaves out any possibility of negotiating the practice of safe sex.

Although Christian teaching accepts sex only during – and not before – a monogamous marriage, people usually flout that requirement. Many men and women are facing a dilemma because of religious opposition to condom use. The woman who sought a private audience with the author was experiencing a spiritually based internal struggle:

> I am confused and I do not know what to do. I am a Christian and want to live according to the Scriptures. We are told not to withhold conjugal rights from each other in marriage (according to 1 Corinthians 7:5). My problem is that my husband has a "Small House" and is also involved with other women. He has other children out there. My problem is that when he comes to me he demands unprotected sex. I am at serious risk of infection because I have not been able to stop him. What can I do?[41]

Access to VCT and PMTCT centres and related services

VCT services have been established within the ZDF, and these are located inside the military quarters. Although the establishment of the PMTCT services by the government was welcomed by participants, the women reported that they find travelling from the suburbs in search of those services costly, and access to the military quarters can be cumbersome owing to rigorous security checks. Accordingly, it may be easier for some women to access VCT and PMTCT services that are mainly available in civilian institutions. Unfortunately, the ZDF patients may not easily access ARV treatment at civilian institutions, and are therefore compelled to attend ZDF centres.

Service women also experienced a lack of "female-user-friendly" structures in operational areas. For both internal and external operations, the infrastructure that is made available does not address women's sanitary needs. Except for some new buildings, facilities remain essentially male oriented. Consequently, in much the same way as is done for the disabled population, the lobbying process performed by women's groups entails all the stages of development from architectural design to the actual construction and furnishing of the building. In addition, other preventive services essential to women's health were found to be lacking in the ZDF. These include the "well woman clinic" concept where women can undergo pap smear tests for cervical cancer, breast examinations for breast cancer, and related conditions. These treatments appear essential to provide adequate health conditions that would promote the operational capacity of female officers in the ZDF.

Confidentiality and human rights challenges

Observance of the confidentiality principle by health providers is extremely important. In fact, it was regarded as so important that some female participants revealed that they chose not to visit certain health units where they knew breaches of confidentiality had taken place. It became a double bind for the women when it came to disclosure of HIV/AIDS. Some participants loathed the fact that some husbands are put on ARV treatment by doctors without the need to disclose the husband's status and treatment programme to spouses. Yet it is problematic for health professionals and counsellors to breach the confidentiality of their patient and inform the spouse without the patient's consent. Some women discovered their husband's ARV drugs stored in containers such as aspirin bottles, and such discoveries led to conflicts. Women found themselves at risk as they "clean the mess, blood and other fluids" from their husbands with unprotected hands. Furthermore, to worsen the protective capacity of women and increase the risk to exposure of the virus, the sick husband and his family considered it unfaithful if the wife wears protective clothing, especially gloves, when providing treatment to her partner.

There was a challenge related to the counselling of high-ranking officers by very junior counsellors. To a certain extent, they often were unable to convince their superiors of the prudence of disclosing their HIV-positive status to their spouse. Sadly, very few senior health services personnel are prepared to undertake counselling training. Yet this would aid peer counselling of senior officers.

Guiding Principle 23 in the 1999 National Policy on HIV/AIDS for Zimbabwe specifies that "partner notification of HIV status is an important issue for both men and women and should be encouraged and supported". Participants felt that the term "encourage" leaves the ignorant spouse at the mercy and will of the tested and informed spouse, and their experience was that the latter did not disclose their status. Respecting the spouse's choice to remain silent was seen as acquiescence and tantamount to putting a hedge of protection around the infected spouse, providing him or her with ARV treatment while exposing the wife or husband or the caring relatives (mainly women) to the risk of infection. Participants proposed that disclosure to a spouse be made a mandatory step before any patient can be put on ARV drugs. On the other hand, disclosure was considered to constitute a human rights challenge that demanded further urgent debate in order to arrive at a balanced decision that would be of mutual benefit to both parties.

In respect of ZAWWA's proposed mandatory disclosure of HIV status to spouses, the input from the peer review workshop was that such a rule may constitute a breach of human rights. There is a valid concern by ZDF health service professionals that, if not handled sensitively and appropriately, the issue of disclosure of status may destroy a patient's confidence in the health adviser and may reduce the effectiveness of care. Granted that this raises complex human rights and confidentiality issues for an

HIV-positive person, the participants felt that upholding the rights of the HIV-positive spouse leaves them at risk of infection. Human rights, according to participants, are like a coin whose two sides demand equal attention if justice is to be attained.

In most cases, there was consensus in the views expressed by the participants and by the healthcare providers. The healthcare providers, including the male providers, felt guilty and thought a measure of balance was lacking, in that rules of confidentiality catered only for the partner who presents him/herself as a patient. All the healthcare providers who participated in the discussion felt conflicted by treating a person on the ARV programme without the knowledge of their spouse. Their struggle, they said, was made worse when the other partner presented with problems whose resolution depended on their knowledge of their HIV status. Participants admitted that, at this point, provider-initiated testing becomes ideal but the patient does not always agree to it. Yet, if they knew their spouse was already receiving ARV treatment, it would be easier to convince them to establish their own status. There was general agreement that the guideline on disclosure should be reconsidered, notwithstanding the likely complication that making disclosure mandatory might drive some patients underground. It was felt that the greater good for the majority should be considered, together with the experience that mandatory disclosure has worked for other STIs.

Treatment, care, support and impact mitigation

Although the participants applauded the launch of standard ART in the ZDF, they observed that women were again left behind, as in the prevention programmes. Health services personnel raised the dilemma of watching a man receive ART when he had refused to disclose his HIV status to his wife. Most women knew little about, and lacked access to, OI services. One concern – particularly for dependent women – is the rule that states that, on retirement, dependants of military personnel cease to be beneficiaries of ART. This is problematic in cases where dependent spouses need to remain on ART treatment but can no longer afford it, particularly without a steady, substantial income to rely on. Some women cited the lack of a marriage certificate as a hindrance for female spouses attempting to access treatment. Although some women would like to formalize their marriage, some husbands are inclined to postpone the formalities to a later date, unfortunately sometimes until death overtakes them.

A few women were briefly involved in activities that were meant to lessen the impact of HIV on the infected and affected. These included mushroom farming and poultry projects. Proceeds from these activities were invested back into the project and some of the produce was used to supplement the diet of the sick. These activities have since waned and women wish they could be revived. ZAWWA's promotion of talent-driven projects was hailed as viable, in that it involves its members in the areas they know best. Training programmes by ZAWWA such as "How to start your business", "How to improve your business", "Poultry and mushroom farming", "Cutting and designing", "Learning for transformation", "Marriage enrichment" and others were hailed as steps in the right direction.

Bereavement, widows and orphans

Women invariably support each other in times of sickness and bereavement, reporting that they sometimes experience "grief fatigue". Others noted with regret that they have had to take care of child-headed families or orphaned children to whom they are not related, when the children's relatives did not claim them. Some women felt that a home for such orphans would be helpful, because they cannot keep the unclaimed orphans forever. Participants raised the plight of widows who are now in civilian life without their husband. Some widows have to fend for themselves and their children on their own, sometimes without a home of their own. ZAWWA was applauded for coming to the rescue of homeless widows who were due to vacate their military homes in the camps to make way for new officers. This rescue plan was achieved under the Chigumba Housing Initiative.[42] Women commended the efforts by the Commander of the ZNA who stages the Army Commander's Charity Horse Race annually to raise funds for vulnerable groups, including widows and orphans. Participants also applauded the scholarships that have been disbursed to orphans by the Education Directorate.

HIV/AIDS and spirituality

ZAWWA women regard HIV/AIDS as a spiritual issue and have set themselves to pray for the nation in this regard. They feel that the emphasis should no longer be on information, because this does not seem to yield the desired behaviour change. Instead, it is time to reach people's hearts. Moreover, a divine intervention is needed in the area of a vaccine and a cure. ZAWWA felt that those who are infected, affected and bereaved by HIV/AIDS not only should be assisted materially and morally but also should be prayed for. According to the World Council of Churches:

> Just as Christ identifies with our suffering and enters into it, we are called to enter into the suffering of those living with HIV/AIDS. Prayer goes beyond compassion, as it calls upon the highest interventions possible.[43]

To this end, ZAWWA set up Chapter-based weekly and national days of prayer to intercede for the nation in this and other needy areas of the Zimbabwean HIV/AIDS challenge. Apart from praying for the nation and the organization, ZAWWA members felt that chaplains should play a major preventive role by engaging deployed people in worship and related spiritual activities. Delivering the HIV/AIDS message in a spiritual milieu was meant to appeal to more than simply cognitive thought processes.

A review of the participants' narratives

How has the ZDF fared in addressing the needs of women in their HIV/AIDS response activities? This study seeks to draw conclusions on five key issues that would make ZDF women HIV/AIDS competent: the provision of gender-sensitive policies; effective response activities to prevent infection; creating awareness on the availability of – and ensuring access to or participation in – VCT, PMTCT, ART, OI centres; imparting knowledge, developing skills, providing resources, and designing and implementing programmes for safe participation in home-based care and support of the infected and affected; and enabling women to negotiate effectively for safe sex.

Policy

The Zimbabwean government has adopted a gender-sensitive approach at legislative and policy formulation levels in its response to HIV/AIDS. The ZDF has also been gender sensitive, in keeping with national trends. Both the government and the ZDF have masterminded comprehensive programmes to tackle HIV/AIDS. The decline in the prevalence and incidence rates is testimony to the effectiveness of the policies and programmes. The government acknowledges the vulnerability of women and underscores the need to address this in HIV/AIDS response activities. It seems, however, from this study that implementing these gender-sensitive legal instruments and policy guidelines has raised complex challenges. Hence women's needs are apparently overlooked or undermined and the subordinate role of women remains. The underlying factors that militate against the empowerment of women remain endemic, putting them at risk of HIV infection.

Prevention

From the focus group discussions, the ZDF women felt that they have been at the margins of HIV/AIDS prevention programmes. There are six main reasons for this assertion.

First, ZDF women have not received as much information and know-ledge to equip them for prevention against infection as their husbands have. This is despite the existence of Guiding Principle 35 of the National Policy, which stipulates that men and women "should be accorded equal status with equal opportunity for education and advancement in all spheres of life". Some ZDF women admit that they gained some infor-mation from media campaigns and health education sessions at clinics but that it is inadequate, and that not all women are equally privy to such information. In order to achieve sustainable behavioural change, an enabling environment should be created to disseminate relevant information.

Second, the ideal of abstention and mutual fidelity is not achievable. Deployments and postings away from home persist with the ZDF's in-volvement in peacekeeping and observer missions. Spousal separation also continues because of the lack of married accommodation within the cantonments. As well as freeing the soldiers from traditional social con-trols, this removes them from contact with their spouse or regular partner and encourages them to get involved in the sex market.

Third, condom use is not easy for women to implement, which may constitute a major risk on the part of women. The majority of inter-viewed women were not able to talk about condoms with their spouse or to negotiate their use in marriage, owing to cultural and related constraints.

Fourth, the underlying customary and traditional norms that militate against women attaining HIV/AIDS competence in preventing infection remain strongly embedded in society, including cultural beliefs and atti-tudes that condone men having sexual liaisons prior to and during mar-riage. The culturally assigned superiority of men disempowers women because negotiating safe sex or condom use is difficult, even when they know that the man is engaging in multiple relationships.[44] Cultural prac-tices such as widow inheritance and girl-pledging still have to be fought, though to a lesser extent in modern-day Zimbabwe. The comparatively lower status of women in the ZDF can have a disempowering effect in cases of sexual abuse, and after the fact in terms of accessing justice. The low status of women in the ZDF and non-involvement at the policy for-mulation level remain a serious impediment.

Fifth, the question of human rights and confidentiality poses problems for ZDF health professionals. They experience a dilemma when provid-ing ART to a man while simultaneously refusing to disclose his HIV/AIDS status to his spouse. Their experiences confirmed the women's complaint that some husbands take ART medications secretly without disclosing their HIV status their spouse.

Sixth, considering the meagre resources available to fund gender-sensitive HIV/AIDS programmes in Zimbabwe, the government-allocated funding for gender-sensitive activities is very minimal. It was also concluded that the international sanctions imposed on Zimbabwe have hurt women and children more than the government. In other words, the imposition of punitive measures on the Zimbabwean government was seen as a direct assault on women and children. More fund-raising activities, such as the ZNA Commander's Charity Horse Race, were suggested as necessary means to achieve adequate funding for HIV/AIDS programmes.

Treatment, care, support and impact mitigation

Some women were unaware of the availability of VCT, PMTCT, ART and OI services. Those who knew about these services experienced difficulties trying to access them because they are scarce and located in cantonments with restricted entry. Some women are not able to access treatment because they do not have a marriage certificate as proof of marriage. Scarcity of other female-friendly services such as maternity facilities and "well woman" clinics was also found to be counterproductive in the fight against HIV/AIDS.

On a positive note, the formation of ZAWWA and its focus on the economic advancement of its members have assisted, to some extent, in mitigating the impact of HIV. ZAWWA's focus on economic advancement is a direct strategy to tackle poverty – one of the underlying factors that exacerbate the HIV/AIDS crisis. ZAWWA provides an organized platform for IEC and the promotion of HIV/AIDS-specific nutritional information, which helps to involve women meaningfully in the fight against the epidemic. Although some of the ZAWWA members were trained in peer education and home-based care, there have not been viable programmes for them to utilize their learned skills. Support groups and impact mitigation projects that were initiated ran for short periods and died out owing to serious financial constraints. The women felt that these groups and projects should be revived.

Women care for and support each other in times of bereavement. They also, in some cases, care for orphaned children who are not claimed by relatives when both parents die. But because this is individually driven and not organizationally supported, this social support may be short-lived because the caring families may not be able to care for the orphans indefinitely. Given that HIV/AIDS-orphaned children face a highly insecure future, there exists a need for institutional involvement and support for this initiative.

Recommendations

The participants recommended the following:

Policy

The ZDF should regard the female population as defined in this study as deserving of equitable treatment at all times in the struggle against HIV. Bearing in mind that women constitute more than half of the population of sub-Saharan Africa – the hardest-hit region in the world in terms of AIDS – it is important to tackle questions of gender in the control of the epidemic. Women bear the heavy burden of the HIV/AIDS crisis, and those in the armed forces have an additional burden and responsibility, taking into consideration the nature of their job or that of their spouse. In addition, HIV/AIDS policies of the ZDF should remain gender sensitive. To sustain the spirit of the stated policy, male and female health professionals and some non-health members in relevant posts should attend gender-related courses, possibly at the Zimbabwe Institute of Public Administration and Management, on such topics as: gender in the workplace; gender awareness; gender mainstreaming in the workplace; gender training of trainers; and women in leadership.[45]

Prevention

To promote the prevention of infections, ZDF women should attend IEC programmes at least twice a year. This is because prevention of transmission requires first and foremost that people are properly informed about how the virus can and cannot be transmitted. Cost-free IEC activities could be carried out in military cantonments. ZAWWA should have the services of gender-competent and gender-sensitive health services officers who can address women's health-related needs.

Second, sexual transmission of HIV can be prevented by sexual abstinence or mutual fidelity. Promotion of such behaviour could be enhanced through the provision of accommodation for married ZDF members. Periods of separation should be reduced, possibly to six months. Members on deployment or posting should return home or be visited by their spouse regularly. For deployments longer than six months, spouses should move together and be near each other to cohabit or to allow regular visits unless constrained by the type of mission. Strict regulatory measures should be put in place to reduce potential interactions between sex workers and deployed members. Part of the allowance for operations should be paid at home, while a small amount is paid in the field.[46] The current "Intercity" monthly bussing of members to their families on pay-weekends should continue. Resources permitting, fortnightly "Intercity" payments would contribute significantly to promoting regular contact between spouses and, with this, mutual fidelity.

Condom use

Research should be carried out to design a more user-friendly and acceptable female condom. Both male and female condoms should be made readily available and more campaigns carried out to enhance spousal consensus on their use. Additionally, the male and female condoms should receive equal publicity and advertising.

Addressing underlying factors

In line with ZAWWA's objectives, women should be empowered by creating enabling environments for their personal, intellectual, social and economic advancement. More women should be promoted to policy- and decision-making ranks in order to ensure relevant or appropriate representation. Effective procedures and mechanisms for redressing sexual abuse should be put in place and vigorously implemented.

Education against the stereotyping of women and the use of language that criticizes them as inferior, and consequently exposes them to abuse, should form part of standard military training. Similarly, education to address oppressive cultural practices should be included in IEC messages.

Efforts to address the impact of HIV/AIDS on ZDF women should not be antagonistic to men. As in most gender discourses, men should be seen as part of the solution rather than treated as the problem. Laying gender-based guilt on men may in fact be counterproductive.

Regarding the dilemma over Christian teachings on conjugal rights, the Church should evolve a theological perspective that does not offer women as sacrificial victims in this era of the complex HIV/AIDS crisis. Women should not be made to surrender their life in order to be deemed a "good wife" to an unfaithful spouse. Stressing the inseparable divine injunctions of absolute mutual fidelity on the one hand, and assured conjugal rights on the other, is critical to achieving justice for all concerned. Padre's Hours[47] could be used to publicize the HIV/AIDS issues related to Christianity and convince members to use condoms when there are incompatible sexual practices between spouses, thereby avoiding the risk of infection.

Vigorous campaigns should be carried out to create awareness of the importance of having a marriage certificate for members and their spouse and children. That way, there would be no need to forfeit the benefits of free treatment, which should rightly be enjoyed with ZDF spouses.

Access to VCT, PMTCT, ART and OI services

Awareness campaigns should be carried out to make women aware of the available VCT, PMTCT, ART, OI and "well woman" services in an environment that is supportive and non-judgemental. Alternatively, courses on maternal and child health as well as family planning should be organized regularly to enable health personnel to carry out pap smears and breast surveillance for cancer and other health conditions. VCT centres provided by the ZDF should be sited in easily accessible locations in the cities. These centres should dispense ARV treatments and other related services.

There is a need to re-evaluate the human rights debate so as to retain high levels of confidentiality between patients and doctors, while making disclosure of HIV/AIDS status to spouses obligatory. It should be regulated that a person can start ARV treatment only after disclosing his/her status to his/her spouse. Counselling courses should be held for senior officers to serve as peer counsellors for senior-ranking officers. It is hoped that peer counselling might yield better results in convincing high-ranking officers to disclose their status to their peers. Adequate knowledge, attitudes, skills and resources should be made available to make care and support of infected persons less risky for the carers and more comfortable for the cared. IEC messages should promote the use of protective clothing as a rule. There is need for information on an essential diet to ensure appropriate nutrition for the infected.

Bereavement, widows and orphans

More fund-raising activities should be carried out to source additional funds to assist widows and orphans. As proposed by ZAWWA, a home for orphans who are unable to be cared for by relatives should be seriously considered. ZAWWA should be financially assisted with this initiative.

Cautionary notes on the general applicability of the study results

Because the focus groups for this study are rather small, the results may not be significant enough to extrapolate from and apply to the general population of ZDF women. Qualitatively, however, the narratives are good indicators of the challenges facing ZDF women in the fight against HIV/AIDS.

Notes

1. National AIDS Council Zimbabwe, *National Policy on HIV/AIDS for Zimbabwe 1999*, ⟨http://www.youth-policy.com/Policies/Zimbabwe_National_Policy_on_HIV_AIDS. cfm?ignore&r=A1714223881⟩ (accessed 19 September 2011).

2. S. S. Kimaryo, J. O. Okpaku, A. Githuku-Shongwe and J. Feeney, eds, *Turning a Crisis into an Opportunity: Strategies for Scaling up the National Response to the HIV/AIDS Epidemic in Lesotho* (New Rochelle, NY: Third Press Publishers, 2004).
3. Ibid., p. 2.
4. Getrude P. S. Mutasa, "HIV/AIDS and Women in the Military in Zimbabwe: A Review of Response Activities Hitherto", unpublished paper presented to a Policy Advisory Group Meeting in Windhoek, Namibia, 9–10 February 2006 (on file with the author).
5. For an articulation of some of these practices, see the Centre for Conflict Resolution, University of Cape Town, "HIV/AIDS and Militaries in Southern Africa", Report on the Policy Seminar, Windhoek, Namibia, 9–10 February 2006.
6. Helen Jackson, *AIDS Africa: Continent in Crisis* (Harare: SAFAIDS Africa, 2002), p. 134.
7. Ibid.
8. National AIDS Council Zimbabwe, *Zimbabwe National Behavioural Change Strategy 2006–2010*, ⟨http://www.nac.org.zw/program-areas/behaviour-change⟩ (accessed 19 September 2011).
9. Jackson, *AIDS Africa*, p. 134.
10. E. Kotzé and D. J. Kotzé, eds, *Telling Narratives* (Pretoria: Ethics Alive, 2001), p. 18.
11. L. Isherwood and D. McEwan, *Introducing Feminist Theology* (Sheffield: South End Press, 1993).
12. On narrative discourse, see Michael White and David Epston, *Narrative Means to Therapeutic Ends* (New York: Norton, 1990).
13. Alice Morgan, *What Is Narrative Therapy? An Easy-to-Read Introduction* (Adelaide: Dulwich Centre Publications, 2000).
14. Dirk J. Kotzé, "Doing Participatory Ethics", in Dirk J. Kotzé, Johan Myburg, Johann Roux, and associates, eds, *Ethical Ways of Being* (Pretoria: Ethics Alive, 2002), p. 1.
15. K. Weingarten, *Common Shock Witnessing Violence Every Day: How We Are Harmed, How We Can Heal* (New York: Dutton, 2003).
16. Mutasa, "HIV/AIDS and Women in the Military in Zimbabwe".
17. Centre for Conflict Resolution, "HIV/AIDS and Militaries in Southern Africa".
18. Kotzé and Kotzé, *Telling Narratives*.
19. On participatory action research, see R. McTaggart, ed., *Participatory Action Research: International Context and Consequences* (Albany: SUNY Press, 1997).
20. Morgan, *What Is Narrative Therapy?*
21. National AIDS Council Zimbabwe, *National Policy on HIV/AIDS*.
22. Joint United Nations Programme on HIV/AIDS (UNAIDS), *Zimbabwe National HIV and AIDS Strategic Plan 2006–2010* (National AIDS Council Zimbabwe, 2006).
23. Paidamoyo Chibunza, "Zimbabwe: HIV Rate Down to 15.6 Percent", *The Herald* (Zimbabwe daily newspaper), 1 November 2007, ⟨http://allafrica.com/stories/200711010001.html⟩ (accessed 19 September 2011).
24. UNAIDS, *Global Report: UNAIDS Report on the Global AIDS Epidemic 2010* (Geneva: Joint United Nations Programme on HIV/AIDS, 2010), p. 25.
25. Ibid., p. 19.
26. National AIDS Council Zimbabwe, *National Policy on HIV/AIDS*.
27. Ibid.
28. Section 7 Guiding Principle (GP) 35 states that "men and women should be accorded equal status with equal opportunity for education and advancement in all spheres". Section 7.1 GP 36 states that "men and women need to understand and respect their own and each others' sexuality". Section 7.1 GP 37 states that "all HIV/AIDS/STI programmes should be gender sensitive and include gender-related issues". Section 7.2 acknowledges that different power relations between the men and women of Zimbabwe have a bearing on the transmission of HIV and should be dealt with effectively. GP 9

advocates the supply of both male and female condoms. GP 10 calls for "access to accurate information about HIV infection and pregnancy and Voluntary Counselling and Testing", and GP 11 advocates the promotion of breastfeeding.

29. National AIDS Council Zimbabwe, *National Policy on HIV/AIDS*.
30. Section 3.3 provides a framework for integrating gender into the overall HIV and AIDS responses to ensure that all prevention and advocacy strategies and programmes are gender sensitive in order to reduce vulnerability and risk. Section 3.5 acknowledges the vulnerability of married women, citing "low status" as an obstacle to changing their position in a way that would reduce their vulnerability. Section 3.6 advocates universal access to treatment, noting that only 7 per cent of the people in need are receiving treatment.
31. Zimbabwe Ministry of Health and Child Welfare, "National Psychosocial Support Guidelines for the Prevention of Mother to Child HIV Transmission in Zimbabwe", December 2006.
32. Reginald Matchaba-Hove, "HIV/AIDS in the Zimbabwean Defence Force: A Civil Society Perspective", in M. Rupiya, ed., *The Enemy Within: Southern African Militaries' Quarter-Century Battle with HIV/AIDS* (Pretoria: ISS, 2006), pp. 157–188.
33. Zimbabwe Ministry of Health and Child Welfare, "Zimbabwe HIV And AIDS Care 2004: Plan for the Nationwide Provision of Antiretroviral Therapy 2005–2007".
34. "Small house" is a term used in Zimbabwe to refer to women who are in illicit love relationships with legally married men, sometimes even establishing private families outside the official ones. This term is also mentioned in the *Zimbabwe National Behavioural Change Strategy 2006–2010*, p. 13.
35. Narrative of ZAWWA women, interview with author.
36. National AIDS Council Zimbabwe, *National Policy on HIV/AIDS*.
37. R. Bor, "The Family and HIV", in *Old Ways – New Theories: Traditional and Contemporary Family Therapy Connect in Africa*, Vol. 1 (Harare: Connect [Zimbabwe Institute of Systemic Therapy], 1995), pp. 49–59.
38. See, for example, Kimaryo et al., *Turning a Crisis into an Opportunity*.
39. Ibid.
40. Narrative of ZAWWA women, interview with author.
41. Narrative of ZAWWA women, interview with author.
42. This is a housing cooperative to which ZAWWA members subscribed, and, in times of desperate need such as becoming a near-homeless widow, ZAWWA managed to persuade the cooperative authorities to disregard the waiting list in favour of the women.
43. World Council of Churches, *Facing AIDS: The Challenge, the Churches' Response* (Geneva: World Council of Churches Publications, 2000).
44. Rupiya, ed., *The Enemy Within*.
45. Zimbabwe Institute of Public Administration and Management, "Training Calendar: Facilitating Organisational Learning and Development", Norton, 2006.
46. Centre for Conflict Resolution, "HIV/AIDS and Militaries in Southern Africa".
47. In the ZDF, Padre's Hour is the time when the padre or chaplain gathers members of his unit for worship and preaching the Word of God. This is the time that is proposed to link Christianity and HIV and to clarify the misconceptions that put believers at risk of infection.

17

Rape and HIV/AIDS as weapons of war: Human rights and health issues in post-conflict societies

Obijiofor Aginam

In the one hundred days of genocide that ravaged the small Central African nation of Rwanda ..., an estimated 250,000 to 500,000 women and girls were raped ... [R]ape was the rule, its absence the exception. Sexual violence occurred everywhere, and no one was spared. (Anne-Marie de Brouwer and Sandra Ka Hon Chu[1])

For 60 days, my body was used as a thoroughfare for all the hoodlums, militia men and soldiers in the district.... Those men completely destroyed me; they caused me so much pain. They raped me in front of my six children.... Three years ago, I discovered I had HIV/AIDS. There is no doubt in my mind that I was infected during these rapes. (Testimony of a rape victim during the genocide in Rwanda[2])

Introduction: Making the point

Although the history of wars and conflicts is replete with incidents of systematic sexual violence against vulnerable women, modern-day wars have witnessed large-scale indiscriminate deployment of rape as a "weapon" of war by combatants. Focusing on the linkages between wars, conflicts and HIV/AIDS, this chapter argues for effective and adequate reparation for victims of rape. This will be analysed with a particular focus on the reconstruction of post-conflict societies in the process of Disarmament, Demobilization and Reintegration (DDR). It is undeniable that the AIDS crisis is exacerbated in complex ways by violent conflicts and civil wars and that is manifested in the indiscriminate deployment of rape by

HIV/AIDS and the security sector in Africa, Aginam and Rupiya (eds),
United Nations University Press, 2012, ISBN 978-92-808-1209-1

combatants, the breakdown of public health infrastructure in war/conflict zones and sexual relations between peacekeepers/combatants and either commercial sex workers or vulnerable women/girls who are desperate to survive.

One conspicuous phenomenon of recent armed conflicts in Africa and elsewhere is the widespread deployment of rape as a systematic tool of warfare, for example in former Yugoslavia, Liberia, the Democratic Republic of the Congo (DRC), Sudan, the Central African Republic, Sierra Leone and Rwanda. One striking difference in the use of rape as a weapon of war between pre-1990 conflicts and latter-day wars is the emergence of HIV and its "wilful" transmission to the victims – an incurable virus that destroys the immune system of the human body. Serious questions have been raised in the social science literature about the actual time of transmission and infection, and whether the "intent" of the perpetrators could conclusively be to infect the victim with HIV. Nonetheless, there is evidence from the victims' accounts confirming the deliberate nature of these acts. In the context of Rwanda, the quotes at the beginning of this chapter offer some persuasive proof that rape was widespread during the conflict and that there was clear intent by the perpetrators to infect the victims with HIV.

This chapter argues that women who have been the victim of rape during conflicts have an inalienable right to reparation, psychological and physical rehabilitation, and access to social measures and health security. Since cash payments are often made to ex-combatants to demobilize and lay down their arms, there appears no reason why cash payments should not be made to HIV-infected victims of rape. This policy would enable victims to survive while undergoing anti-retroviral therapies. In efforts to reconstruct post-conflict societies, DDR processes should include sustainable policies and programmes aimed at holistic reparation for victims of rape during wars and conflicts.

Conflict, war and disease in history

For most millennia of recorded history, diseases have posed enormous challenges during situations of war and conflict. Eminent historians have recorded how the destruction of human lives by epidemics during conflicts led to the collapse of states, cities and empires. In one of the earliest historical accounts of wars, Thucydides demonstrated how the plague devastated the city of Athens during the Peloponnesian War in 430 BC.[3] Historians postulated that the plague of Justinian led to the collapse of the Roman Empire.[4] Smallpox and other "exotic" diseases devastated the native populations of North America and led to the collapse of the Aztec and Incan civilizations during the conquest campaign by European societies.[5] In the American War of Independence in 1776, smallpox prevented the US troops from overcoming Canada.[6] As Brundtland stated:

> Cholera and other diseases killed at least three times more soldiers in the Crimean war than did the actual conflict. Malaria, measles, mumps, smallpox, and typhoid felled more combatants than did bullets in the American Civil War.[7]

Paraphrasing Hans Zinsser,[8] it has been argued that in the course of history soldiers have rarely won wars; microbes have. The epidemics get the blame for defeat, the military generals the credit for victory.[9] Although the linkage between wars and disease is almost as old as human history, modern-day wars and conflicts, as the quotes above illustrate, have witnessed an increased and indiscriminate use of rape and the wilful transmission of HIV/AIDS as weapons of war by combatants. The emergence of HIV/AIDS in the past two decades, and the complex interaction between the virus and conflicts, has reinforced both the human security and the state security dimensions of disease. Whereas the state security dimension focuses on the collapse of the apparatus of governance, the human security dimension focuses on threats to vulnerable groups, especially women and girls, during conflicts. As Brundtland observed:

> [W]e should broaden debate to accept that health is an underlying determinant of development, security, and global stability. We must consider the impact of armed conflict and, perhaps more importantly, the silent march of diseases that devastate populations over time.... The explosion of conflict immediately brings to light the links between health and security.[10]

Although the history of wars and conflicts is replete with massive and systematic sexual violence against vulnerable women, modern-day wars in African nations and elsewhere are increasingly characterized by the use of rape as a weapon of war, the intentional or wilful transmission of HIV to innocent victims and the neglect of these victims in post-conflict reconstruction programmes.

HIV/AIDS and rape in recent African conflicts

The "securitization" of HIV/AIDS has led to intense academic and policy debates since the popularization of the notion of human security by the United Nations Development Programme (UNDP) in 1994.[11] In the post-1994 human security discourse,[12] the link between disease, especially HIV/

AIDS, and conflicts has elicited a voluminous literature.[13] Human security recognizes the emergence of new threats to the security of peoples: chronic threats such as hunger, environmental degradation and natural disasters, disease and repression.[14] The International Crisis Group, in its 2001 report entitled *HIV/AIDS as a Security Issue*, categorized HIV/AIDS as a personal security issue, an economic security issue, a communal security issue, a national security issue and an international security issue.[15] Influenced by the UNDP report, the Commission on Global Governance argued that "the security of people recognizes that global security extends beyond the protection of borders, ruling elites, and exclusive state interests to include the protection of the people".[16]

The Commission on Human Security noted that human security embraces far more than the absence of violent conflict. It encompasses human rights, good governance, access to education and healthcare, and ensuring that each individual has opportunities and choices to fulfil his or her potential.[17] One of the core policy conclusions advanced by the Commission on Human Security focuses on the health challenges for human security in three key areas: global infectious disease, poverty-related threats, and violence and crisis.[18] HIV/AIDS neatly fits into these three categories because it is a global pandemic, it is poverty related, at least in most poor countries, and the pandemic is exacerbated in complex ways by violent conflicts and civil wars that are marked by the rape of women by combatants, a breakdown of health infrastructure and sexual relations between peacekeepers/combatants and commercial sex workers.

Although one school of thought led by some prominent African and Africanist scholars, especially Whiteside, de Waal and Gebre-Tensae, has strongly contested the common assertion that wartime rape is a significant factor in the spread of HIV either by design or as a by-product of systematic sexual violence, it nonetheless concedes that there is strong evidence to support and prove this assertion at least in the case of the Rwandan genocide.[19] Whiteside, de Waal and Gebre-Tensae argued that the case of Rwanda "was a concerted and systematic attempt to completely eradicate a population and is an exceptional case by any standards".[20] However, the structural problem with the scholarship and school of thought of Whiteside, de Waal and Gebre-Tensae is the fact that, as Brouwer and Ka Hon Chu stated, "the magnitude of sexual violence in conflict situations will never be fully known, since the stigma associated with being a victim discourages women and girls from reporting the crime".[21] This is particularly true of most African conflict situations where cultural and traditional practices, beliefs and norms shape societal values and ethics. Although rape is systematically deployed in past, recent and ongoing conflicts in Sudan, the DRC, the Central African Republic, Sierra Leone, Liberia and elsewhere, we may not be able to empirically determine the linkages between these acts and the transmission of HIV. As persuasively argued by Elbe:

> One of the most striking aspects of recent armed conflicts in Africa is the deliberate targeting of civilians and the widespread use of rape, which has been deployed as a systematic tool of warfare in conflicts in Liberia, Mozambique, Rwanda, and Sierra Leone.[22]

Relying on unofficial statistics and data, Elbe observed that human rights workers in Sierra Leone reported that "during the country's eight-year civil war, armed rebels and insurgent forces raped thousands of women".[23] It is estimated that between 200,000 and 500,000 women were raped during the genocide in Rwanda, which lasted 100 days.[24]

In the eastern region of the DRC, various civil society groups and United Nations agencies have reported widespread systematic rape involving thousands of women and young girls. These rapes and other acts of sexual violence are being performed with impunity and brutality and in flagrant violation of age-old laws, customs and norms of war by virtually all sides in the conflict – civilians, militiamen, armed groups and members of the Congolese Armed Forces. During the Liberian civil war, between 1999 and 2003, about 49 per cent of women between the ages of 15 and 70 experienced at least one act of sexual violence from a soldier or armed militia member.[25] In Sierra Leone, about 64,000 internally displaced women experienced war-related sexual violence between 1991 and 2001.[26] When compared with the atrocities and gross violations of the dignity and basic rights of vulnerable women in the conflicts in the Balkans, which often involved mass rape and cleansing of ethnic minorities, it is fair to state that this is not therefore an African phenomenon. Going as far back as World War I (1914–1918), Brouwer and Ka Hon Chu stated that rape, forced prostitution and other forms of sexual violence were prevalent in Europe during World War I (largely by the German army and the armies of other Axis powers); in Asia during World War II (involving the Japanese Imperial Army); in Europe during World War II (involving the German army); and in Bosnia-Herzegovina and Kosovo during the Balkan conflicts in the 1990s.[27]

Going by the evidence from the Rwandan genocide and the ongoing conflict in the DRC, it is obvious that armed militias and combatants may have started using HIV as a weapon of war. As already stated, one striking phenomenon of modern-day wars is the "wilful" transmission of HIV to innocent women. Notwithstanding the seriousness of the questions that have been raised concerning whether the actual intent of the perpetrators of rape could have been to infect the victim with the virus, Elbe cites the account of one rape victim in Rwanda whom the rapists taunted:

"We are not killing you. We are giving you something worse. You will die a slow death."[28] There is also another account that captured women in Rwanda were taken to HIV-positive soldiers specifically to be raped.[29]

These types of incident, driven by the "weaponization" of HIV, raise serious human security issues in post-conflict societies. The complementary nature of human and state security therefore makes HIV less recondite in security discourses because the virus strikes soldiers and civilians in war situations because of the breakdown of infrastructure and the indiscriminate deployment of rape as a weapon of war by combatants.[30] In international humanitarian law – the set of norms that generally criminalize genocide, war crimes and crimes against humanity – precedents now abound on the criminal conviction of individuals who systematically deployed rape as a weapon of war in Rwanda and former Yugoslavia.[31] In the trial of Jean-Paul Akayesu for genocide before the International Criminal Tribunal for Rwanda, the Tribunal found the accused guilty of aiding and abetting acts of sexual violence involving the systematic rape of Tutsi women. These acts of systematic rape, carried out in areas under the authority of Akayesu, were accompanied with the intent to kill these women on the grounds of their ethnicity. Despite the legal precedents of cases such as that of Akayesu, do international legal mechanisms offer a holistic paradigm for the reconstruction of post-war societies? Has the link between HIV, victims of rape and psychological and other reparation been taken into account in post-conflict reconstruction and peacebuilding processes?

Postscript: DDR and victims of rape in post-conflict societies

DDR programmes have now been recognized by the United Nations and other important actors as an integral component of post-conflict peacebuilding and reconstruction processes. Nonetheless, DDR programmes remain complex. This is simply because of their multidimensional nature, which involves military, humanitarian and other socioeconomic components. The DDR process raises a lot of challenges for its non-military components. In the context of victims of rape during conflicts, Françoise Nduwimana, in her study of the victims of rape during the Rwandan genocide, *The Right to Survive: Sexual Violence, Women and HIV/AIDS,*[32] interviewed 30 women who were among the thousands of victims of rape infected with HIV. Writing in 2004, more than a decade after the Rwandan genocide, Nduwimana queried whether we can accurately refer to these women as survivors of the genocide when, every day, "these women, linked by the miserable three-pronged destiny of genocide, rape and HIV/AIDS, witness their friends, acquaintances, neighbors, and family members dying in anonymity, with the world utterly indifferent to their fate".[33] Can these women be considered survivors of genocide when, in the absence of medical treatments for HIV/AIDS, they can see only death on the horizon? What is the point of surviving when they will die slowly a few years later completely dehumanized?[34] In the absence of health and social measures, Nduwimana argues that,

> [W]omen who have been raped and who are living with HIV/AIDS are condemned to death.... As it is blatantly clear that the high incidence of HIV/AIDS, estimated at between 66.7% and 80% among surviving women, is closely linked to rape and the other physical violence suffered by these women during the genocide, the justice system must include HIV/AIDS as one of the consequences of these crimes and adopt the appropriate legal and reparation measures.[35]

Rwanda is not an isolated event. Similar calls and proposals have been canvassed for victims of rape during the civil wars in Liberia and Sierra Leone. DDR processes in the case of Rwanda and other post-conflict societies – though mostly in Africa – have overly emphasized disarmament and demobilization (the two "Ds") to the detriment of reintegration (the "R"). Even where reintegration receives attention and resources, it often neglects the victims of rape by focusing more on the reintegration of child soldiers and ex-combatants into their communities. Victims of rape intended as a weapon of war, I argue, have an inalienable right to financial reparation, psychological and physical rehabilitation, and access to social measures and health security. If, as in most DDR programmes, cash payments are often made to ex-combatants for demobilization, there is no reason why equal payments should not be made to rape victims infected with HIV. The "right to survive", as Nduwimana, calls it, should take centre stage in contemporary AIDS diplomacy. The DDR process in most post-conflict African societies must strive to integrate this very important social problem – the psycho-medical rehabilitation of HIV-infected victims of rape during conflicts.

Notes

1. Anne-Marie de Brouwer and Sandra Ka Hon Chu, *The Men Who Killed Me: Rwandan Survivors of Sexual Violence* (Vancouver: Douglas & McIntyre, 2009), p. 11.
2. Reported in F. Nduwimana, *The Right to Survive: Sexual Violence, Women and HIV/AIDS* (Montreal: Rights & Democracy, 2004), pp. 75–76.
3. Thucydides, *History of the Peloponnesian War*, transl. R. Warner (Harmondsworth: Penguin Books, 1954).
4. W. H. McNeill, *Plagues and Peoples* (New York: Doubleday, 1976).

5. A. W. Crosby, *The Columbian Exchange: Biological and Cultural Consequences of 1492* (Westport, CT: Greenwood Press, 1972).
6. Andrew T. Price-Smith, *The Health of Nations: Infectious Disease, Environmental Change, and Their Effects on National Security and Development* (Massachusetts: MIT Press, 2002).
7. Gro Harlem Brundtland, "Global Health and International Security", *Global Governance*, 9 (2003), p. 417.
8. Han Zinsser, *Rats, Lice and History* (London: George Routledge, 1937).
9. C. Coker, "War and Disease", unpublished Senior Fellow's Report, Disease and Security Conference, 21st Century Trust, Varenna, Lake Como, Italy, 23 April – 1 May 2004. See also Stefan Elbe, *Strategic Implications of HIV/AIDS*, Adelphi Paper 357 (New York: Oxford University Press, 2003), p. 13, stating that "American microbiologist Hans Zinsser advanced the provocative thesis that soldiers have only rarely won wars; rather they mop up after a barrage of epidemics. And typhus, with its brothers and sisters, – plague, cholera, typhoid, dysentery – has decided more campaigns than Caesar, Hannibal, Napoleon, and all the inspector generals of history. The epidemics get the blame for defeat, the generals the credit for victory."
10. Brundtland, "Global Health and International Security", p. 417.
11. United Nations Development Programme (UNDP), *Human Development Report 1994: New Dimensions of Human Security* (New York: Oxford University Press, 1994).
12. For a discussion of human security, see Commission on Human Security, *Human Security Now: Protecting and Empowering People* (New York: Commission on Human Security, 2003); Fen Osler Hampson, *Madness in the Multitude: Human Security and World Disorder* (Toronto: Oxford University Press, 2001); R. McRae and D. Hubert, eds, *Human Security and the New Diplomacy: Protecting People, Promoting Peace* (Montreal: McGill-Queen's University Press, 2001); B. Ramcharan, *Human Rights and Human Security* (The Hague: Martinus Nijhoff, 2002); Lloyd Axworthy, "Human Security and Global Governance: Putting People First", *Global Governance*, 7, 2001, pp. 19–23. For a critique of human security, see R. Paris, "Human Security: Paradigm Shift or Hot Air", *International Security*, 26, 2001, p. 67.
13. Price-Smith, *The Health of Nations*; Jennifer Brower and Peter Chalk, *The Global Threat of New and Reemerging Infectious Diseases: Reconciling U.S. National Security and Public Health Policy* (Santa Monica: RAND, 2003); Stefan Elbe, "HIV/AIDS and the Changing Landscape of War in Africa", *International Security*, 27(2), 2002, pp. 159–177; Stefan Elbe, "HIV/AIDS: A Human Security Challenge for the 21st Century", *Whitehead Journal of Diplomacy and International Relations*, 7, 2006, pp. 101–113; Stefan Elbe, "Should HIV/AIDS Be Securitized? The Ethical Dilemmas of Linking HIV/AIDS and Security", *International Studies Quarterly*, 50(1), 2006, pp. 119–144; Laurie Garrett, *HIV and National Security: Where Are the Links?* (New York: Council on Foreign Relations, 2005); Obijiofor Aginam, "Bio-terrorism, Human Security and Public Health: Can International Law Bring Them Together in an Age of Globalization?", *Medicine and Law*, 24(3), 2005, pp. 455–462.
14. UNDP, *Human Development Report 1994*, pp. 24–25.
15. International Crisis Group, *HIV/AIDS as a Security Issue* (Washington/Brussels: ICG, 2001).
16. Commission on Global Governance, *Our Global Neighborhood: The Report of the Commission on Global Governance* (New York: Oxford University Press, 1995), pp. 78, 81.
17. Commission on Human Security, *Human Security Now*, p. 4.
18. Ibid.

19. Alan Whiteside, Alex de Waal and Tsadkan Gebre-Tensae, "AIDS, Security and the Military in Africa: A Sober Appraisal", *African Affairs*, 105, 2006, pp. 201–218.
20. Ibid., p. 214.
21. Brouwer and Ka Hon Chu, eds, *The Men Who Killed Me*, p. 23.
22. Elbe, "HIV/AIDS and the Changing Landscape of War in Africa", p. 167.
23. Ibid., citing Douglas Farah, "A War Against Women", *Washington Post*, 11 April 2001, p. 1.
24. Lisa Sharlach, "Rape as Genocide: Bangladesh, the Former Yugoslavia and Rwanda", *New Political Science*, 22(1), 2000, p. 28; Brouwer and Ka Hon Chu, eds, *The Men Who Killed Me*; Nduwimana, *The Right to Survive*.
25. Shana Swiss et al., "Violence Against Women During the Liberian Civil Conflict", cited in Brouwer and Ka Hon Chu, eds, *The Men Who Killed Me*, p. 25.
26. Marie Vlachova and Lea Biason, eds, *Women in an Insecure World* (Geneva: Geneva Centre for the Democratic Control of Armed Forces, 2005).
27. Brouwer and Ka Hon Chu, eds, *The Men Who Killed Me*, pp. 23–26.
28. Elbe, "HIV/AIDS and the Changing Landscape of War in Africa", p. 168, citing Margaret Owen, "Widows Expose HIV War Threat", *Worldwoman News*, 12 June 2001, p. 1.
29. Elbe, "HIV/AIDS and the Changing Landscape of War in Africa", p. 169. For an insightful discussion of the wilful transmission of HIV to rape victims during the Rwandan genocide, see V. Randell, "Sexual Violence and Genocide against Tutsi Women. Propaganda and Sexual Violence in the Rwandan Genocide: An Argument for Intersectionality in International Law", *Columbia Human Rights Law Review*, 33(3), 2002, pp. 733–776.
30. Virginia van der Vliet, *The Politics of AIDS* (London: Bowerdean, 1996), stating that "wars and anarchy create ideal conditions for the transmission of HIV. Soldiers and civilians, many moving without partners or families for extended periods, live outside of conventional morality, many resort to prostitution to satisfy their needs. War brutalises human relationships ... and ... brings sexual violence in its wake."
31. See the judgment of the International Criminal Tribunal for Rwanda (ICTR-11996-4), October 1998, in which the Tribunal convicted Jean-Paul Akayesu, former Prefect of Taba, Rwanda, for the crime of genocide involving acts of rape and sexual violence.
32. Nduwimana, *The Right to Survive*.
33. Ibid., p. 9.
34. Ibid.
35. Ibid., p. 10.

Index